Manual for the
Total
Consecration
to Mary

Manual for the
Total
Consecration
to Mary

According to

Saint Louis De Montfort's

Preparation for

Total Consecration

as a

Slave of Mary

Saint Benedict Center
The Slaves of the Immaculate Heart of Mary
Still River, Massachusetts 01467

Saint Benedict Center
The Slaves of the Immaculate Heart of Mary

True Devotion to Mary
by St. Louis Marie Grignion De Montfort
*Translated from the Original French by
Father Frederick William Faber, D.D.*

The Secret of Mary
by St. Louis Marie Grignion De Montfort

The Holy Bible
Douay Version
Translated from the Latin Vulgate
(Douay, A.D. 1609: Rheims, A.D. 1582)

The Imitation of Christ
by Thomas à Kempis
*Translated from the Original Latin
by the Right Rev.
Richard Challoner, D.D.*

ISBN 0-9716822-1-6

PREFACE

To become skillful in any field of endeavor, we go to an expert in that field and ask for advice or, better still, we place ourselves under the tutelage of that expert. We see this done in the realm of sports all the time, whether it be neighborhood competition, professional sports, or the Olympic Games. Behind every "superstar" there is a coach. So, also, must it be in the spiritual realm.

In the great competitive struggle to overcome the enemies of our salvation—the world, the flesh, and the Devil—and to become a true disciple of Jesus Christ, we must look for advice from the Church and the writings of the saints—those spiritual giants who have gone before us. Best of all, however, is to place ourselves under the guardianship and guidance of the greatest and holiest creature that God ever made, the Blessed Virgin Mary.

Saint Louis Marie de Montfort put his whole heart and soul into the task of finding the best way to place oneself under the patronage of the Mother of God. After extensive research in to the writings of the great saints, he found the best method: Slavery to Mary. This approach was not new but, at that time, little known and not thoroughly formulated. He developed and expounded this Slavery—and defended it, too—in his popular book, "True Devotion to the Blessed Virgin."

The essence of this true devotion is the total offering of one's self and all one's goods both temporal and spiritual to Our Lady—in as much as the duties of one's state in life will allow—and then living as dependent upon her as a slave to a Queen. The practice of this humble relationship is the source of many unique graces and privileges. This Queen will undoubtedly use us and all that we give her to the furthering of the glory of God and His kingdom on earth.

This book sets forth under one cover the texts and prayers that Saint Louis Marie recommended to be used daily in preparing to make a solemn consecration of oneself. The period recommended lasts thirty-three days. What the novitiate is to religious life and basic training is to athletics, this preparation is to slavery to Mary. If you spend it well, you will begin to be taken up with the thought of Mary in all you do. Out of love for her you will learn to sacrifice whatever is displeasing to her and her Divine Son. From there you will have a singleness of purpose and earnestly do all through her, with her, in her, and for her. This is True Devotion.

> Mancipia Immaculati Cordis Mariae
> The Slaves of the Immaculate Heart of Mary

May 13, 1998
Our Lady of Fatima

CONTENTS

Second Period
Second Week
Knowledge of The Blessed Virgin

Second Period
Third Week
Knowledge of Jesus Christ

Prayers, Acts, and Practices

"Put thy feet into her fetters, and thy neck into her chains."

Ecclesiasticus 6:25

"You must make the sacrifice of yourself to the Blessed Mother, you must disappear in her, so that you may find God alone."

Saint Louis Marie De Montfort

INTRODUCTION

Total Consecration to Mary is not a one time commitment. It is a way of life.

Each year those who have made their consecration renew it with prayerful preparation lasting thirty-three days. This manual has been compiled for that purpose. Herein are contained all the prayers, readings, and meditations, conveniently arranged for each day.

It is no longer necessary to carry your Holy Scripture, True Devotion, Secret of Mary and Imitation of Christ, for they are all in this one volume. We felt it necessary at times to repeat some of the readings in order to keep uniformity. Each reading begins with specific prayers which are essential to the consecration. Why are the prayers first? Well, "Prayer," we are taught from the catechism, "is the lifting of the mind and heart to God." Saint Augustine also states that, "Prayer is conversation with God. When you read, God speaks to you; but when you pray, you speak to God." So prepare yourself properly to hear God's voice in what you read. Please also note that during the Second Period of the Third Week there are two Scripture readings for each day. You may choose whichever of the two you prefer, you do not have to read both.

It is our fondest hope that this manual will increase the number of those who have chosen to join the ranks of Our Lady's Slaves and thereby bring about the triumphant reign of Christ the King.

If, after completing this consecration, you wish to be enrolled as a Consecrated Soul with the Slaves of the Immaculate Heart of Mary, simply send your full name, date of consecration and an offering and you will receive a beautiful Consecration Certificate from Saint Benedict Center.

Ave Maria!

True Devotion Preparation

Consecration to Jesus Through Mary

Saint Louis De Montfort advises you to prepare for the consecration by exercises which certainly are not compulsory, but which assure its great efficacy because of the purity and other dispositions which they tend to develop in your soul.

Two different periods are assigned for these exercises: a preliminary period of twelve days during which you endeavor "to free yourself from the spirit of the world;" and a second period of three weeks: the first devoted to the knowledge of yourself, the second to that of the Blessed Virgin and the third to that of Jesus Christ.

These periods mentioned by Saint Louis De Montfort do not constitute a rigorous and unchangeable division. According to circumstances, they may be lengthened or shortened. The faithful often take but three days to prepare for the annual renewal of their consecration.

The object of this consecration is to cast off the spirit of the world, which is contrary to that of Jesus Christ, in order to acquire fully the spirit of Jesus Christ through the Blessed Virgin. Hence the practices suggested by Saint Louis Marie: renouncement of the world, knowledge of self, and knowledge of the Blessed Virgin and of Jesus Christ.

Renouncement of the World

Twelve Preliminary Days

"The first part of the preparation should be employed in casting off the spirit of the world, which is contrary to that of Jesus Christ."

The spirit of the world consists essentially in the denial of the supreme dominion of God, a denial which is manifested in practice by sin and disobedience; thus it is principally opposed to the spirit of Christ, which is also that of Mary.

It manifests itself by the concupiscence of the flesh, by the concupiscence of the eyes and by the pride of life; by disobedience to God's laws and the abuse of created things. Its works are, first, sin in all its forms; and then all else by which the devil leads to sin; works which bring error and darkness to the mind, and seduction and corruption to the will. Its pomps are the splendor and the charms employed by the devil to render sin alluring in persons, places and things.

Daily Prayers during the Twelve Preliminary Days:Veni Creator, and the *Ave Maris Stella.*

Spiritual Exercises during the Twelve Preliminary Days: Examine your conscience, pray, practice renouncement, mortification, purity of heart; this purity is the indispensable condition for contemplating God in Heaven, seeing Him on earth and knowing Him by the light of Faith.

First Day _____

Daily Prayers: Veni Creator page 155, *Ave Maris Stella* page 156.

Gospel according to Saint Matthew 5:1-12

And seeing the multitudes, He went up onto a mountain, and when He was set down, His disciples came unto Him.

2. And opening His mouth, He taught them, saying:

3. Blessed are the poor in spirit; for theirs is the kingdom of Heaven.

4. Blessed are the meek; for they shall possess the land.

5. Blessed are they that mourn; for they shall be comforted.

6. Blessed are they that hunger and thirst after justice; for they shall have their fill.

7. Blessed are the merciful; for they shall obtain mercy.

8. Blessed are the clean of heart; for they shall see God.

9. Blessed are the peacemakers; for they shall be called the children of God.

10. Blessed are they that suffer persecution for justice' sake; for theirs is the kingdom of Heaven.

11. Blessed are you when they shall revile you, and persecute you, and speak all that is evil against you, untruly, for My sake;

12. Be glad and rejoice, for your reward is very great in Heaven. For so they persecuted the prophets that were before you.

Imitation of Christ, Book I, Chapter 13, 1-4
Of Resisting Temptation

As long as we live in this world we cannot be without tribulation and temptation.

Hence it is written in Job: "The life of man upon earth is a warfare."

Therefore ought everyone to be solicitous about his temptations, and to watch in prayer, lest the devil, who never sleeps, but "goeth about seeking whom he may devour," find room to deceive him.

No man is so perfect and holy as not to have sometimes temptations, and we cannot be wholly without them.

2. Yet temptations are often very profitable to a man, although they be troublesome and grievous, for in them a man is humbled, purified, and instructed.

All the saints have passed through many tribulations and temptations, and have profited by them; and they who could not support temptations, have become reprobates, and fallen away.

There is no order so holy, nor place so retired, where there are not temptations and adversities.

3. A man is never entirely secure from temptations as long as he lives, because we have within us the source of temptation, having been born in concupiscence.

When one temptation or tribulation is over, another comes on; and we shall have always something to suffer, because we have lost the good of our original happiness.

Many seek to fly temptations, and fall more grievously into them.

By flight alone we cannot overcome; but by patience and true humility we are made stronger than our enemies.

He who only declines them outwardly, and does not pluck out the root, will profit little; nay, temptations will sooner return to him, and he will find himself in a worse condition.

By degrees, and by patience, with longanimity, thou shalt by God's grace better overcome them than by harshness and thine own importunity.

Mancipia Publications

In temptations often take counsel, and deal not roughly with one that is tempted; but comfort him as thou wouldst wish to be done to thyself.

4. Inconstancy of mind, and small confidence in God, is the beginning of all evil temptations.

For as a ship without a rudder is tossed to and fro by the waves, so the man who is remiss, and who quits his resolution, is many ways tempted.

Fire tries iron, and temptation tries a just man.

We often know not what we can do; but temptation discovers what we are.

However, we must be watchful, especially in the beginning of temptation, because then the enemy is easier overcome, if he is not suffered to come in at all at the door of the soul, but is kept out and resisted at his first knock.

Whence a certain man said; "Withstand the beginning, after—remedies come too late."

For first a bare thought comes to the mind; then a strong imagination; afterwards delight, and evil motion and consent.

And thus, by little and little, the wicked enemy gets full entrance, when he is not resisted in the beginning.

And the longer a man is negligent in resisting, so much the weaker does he daily become in himself, and the enemy becomes stronger against him.

Second Day

Daily Prayers: Veni Creator page 155, *Ave Maris Stella* page 156.

Continuation of the holy Gospel according to Saint Matthew 5:13-20

You are the salt of the earth. But if the salt lose its savour, wherewith shall it be salted? It is good for nothing any more but to be cast out, and to be trodden on by men.

14. You are the light of the world. A city seated on a mountain cannot be hid.

15. Neither do men light a candle and put it under a bushel, but upon a candlestick, that it may shine to all that are in the house.

16. So let your light shine before men, that they may see your good works, and glorify your Father Who is in Heaven.

17. Do not think that I am come to destroy the law, or the prophets. I am not come to destroy, but to fulfill.

18. For, amen I say unto you, till heaven and earth pass, one jot, or one tittle shall not pass of the law, till all be fulfilled.

19. He therefore that shall break one of these least commandments, and shall so teach men, shall be called the least in the kingdom of Heaven. But he that shall do and teach, he shall be called great in the kingdom of Heaven.

20. For I tell you, that unless your justice abound more than that of the Scribes and Pharisees, you shall not enter into the kingdom of Heaven.

Continuation of Imitation of Christ, Book 1, Chapter 13:5-7

5. Some suffer grievous temptations in the beginning of their conversion, others in the end; and some are much troubled nearly their whole life.

Some are very lightly tempted, according to the wisdom and equity of the ordinance of God, Who weighs man's condition and merits, and preordains all things for the salvation of His elect.

6. We must not, therefore, despair when we are tempted, but the more fervently pray God to vouchsafe to help us in every tribulation: Who of a truth, according to the saying of Saint Paul, will make such issue with the temptation, that we may be able to sustain it.

Let us, then, humble our souls under the hand of God in every temptation and tribulation; for the humble in spirit He will save and exalt.

7. In temptations and tribulations is it proved what progress a man has made; and there also is there greater merit, and virtue is made more manifest.

Neither is it a great thing for a man to be devout and fervent while he feels no weight of adversity in time of trouble; but if he suffers patiently there will be hope of great profit.

Some are preserved from great temptations, and are often overcome in daily little ones; that, thus humbled, they may never presume upon themselves in great trials, when they are so weak in such trifling occurrences.

Third Day _____

Daily Prayers: Veni Creator page 155, *Ave Maris Stella* page 156.

Continuation of the holy Gospel according to Saint Matthew 5:21-30

You have heard that it was said to them of old: Thou shalt not kill. And whosoever shall kill shall be in danger of the judgment.

22. But I say to you, that whosoever is angry with his brother, shall be in danger of the judgment. And whosoever shall say to his brother, Raca, shall be in danger of the council. And whosoever shall say, You fool, shall be in danger of hell fire.

23. If therefore you offer your gift at the altar, and there you remember that your brother has anything against you;

24. Leave there your offering before the altar, and go first to be reconciled to your brother; and then coming offer your gift.

25. Be at agreement with your adversary betimes, while you are in the way with him: lest perhaps the adversary deliver you to the judge, and the judge deliver you to the officer, and you be cast into prison.

26. Amen I say to you, you shall not go out from thence till you repay the last farthing.

27. You have heard that it was said to them of old: You shall not commit adultery.

28. But I say to you, that whosoever shall look on a woman to lust after

Mancipia Publications

her, has already committed adultery with her in his heart.

29. And if your right eye scandalizes you, pluck it out and cast it from you. For it is expedient for you that one of your members should perish, rather than that your whole body be cast into Hell.

30. And if your right hand scandalizes you, cut it off, and cast it from you: for it is expedient for you that one of your members should perish, rather than that your whole body go into Hell.

Imitation of Christ, Book 1, Chapter 18:1-3
Of the Examples of the Holy Fathers

Look upon the lively examples of the holy Fathers, in whom true perfection and religion were most shining, and thou wilt see how little, and almost nothing, that is which we do.

Alas! what is our life, if compared to theirs?

The saints and friends of Christ served the Lord in hunger and thirst, in cold and nakedness, in labor and weariness, in watchings and fastings, in prayers and holy meditations, in persecutions and many reproaches. (Heb. 11:37)

2. Ah! how many and how grievous tribulations have the Apostles, martyrs, confessors, virgins, and all the rest undergone, who have been willing to follow Christ's footsteps!

For they hated their lives in this world, that they might possess them for eternity. (John 12:25)

Oh, how strict and mortified a life did the holy Fathers lead in the desert! What long and grievous temptations did they endure! How often were they molested by the enemy! What frequent and fervent prayers did they offer to God! What rigorous abstinence did they go through! What great zeal and fervor had they for their spiritual progress! How strong a war did they wage for overcoming vice! How pure and upright was their intention to God!

They labored all the day, and in the night they gave themselves to prayer: though even while they were at work they ceased not from mental prayer.

3. They spent all their time profitably: every hour seemed short which they spent with God, and through the great sweetness of divine contemplation they forgot even the necessity of their bodily refreshment.

They renounced all riches, dignities, honors, friends, and kindred; they desired to have nothing of this world; they scarcely allowed themselves the necessaries of life; the serving the body, even in necessity, was irksome to them.

They were poor, therefore, as to earthly things, but very rich in grace and virtue.

Outwardly they were in want, but inwardly they were refreshed with divine graces and consolations.

Fourth Day _____

Daily Prayers: Veni Creator page 155, *Ave Maris Stella* page 156.

Continuation of the holy Gospel according to Saint Matthew 5:31-42

And it has been said, Whosoever shall put away his wife, let him give her a bill of divorce.

32. But I say to you, that whosoever shall put away his wife, excepting for the cause of fornication, makes her to commit adultery: and he that shall marry her that is put away, commits adultery.

33. Again you have heard that it was said to them of old, you shall not forswear thyself: but thou shalt perform thy oaths to the Lord.

34. But I say to you not to swear at all, neither by Heaven, for it is the throne of God:

35. Nor by the earth, for it is His footstool: nor by Jerusalem, for it is the city of the great king:

36. Neither shall you swear by your head, because you cannot make one hair white or black.

37. But let your speech be yes, yes: no, no: and that which is over and above these, is of evil.

38. You have heard that it has been said, An eye for an eye, and a tooth for a tooth.

39. But I say to you not to resist evil: but if one strike you on your right cheek, turn to him also the other:

40. And if a man will contend with you in judgment, and take away your coat, let go your cloak also unto him.

41. And whosoever will force you one mile, go with him another two.

42. Give to him that asks of you and from him that would borrow of you turn not away.

Continuation of Imitation of Christ, Book 1, Chapter 18:4-6

They were strangers to the world, but they were very near and familiar friends to God.

They seemed to themselves as nothing, and were despised by this world; but in the eyes of God they were very precious and beloved.

They stood in true humility, they lived in simple obedience, they walked in charity and patience; and therefore they daily advanced in spirit, and obtained great favor with God.

They were given as an example for all religious, and ought more to excite us to make good progress, than the number of the lukewarm to grow slack.

5. Oh, how great was the fervor of all religious in the beginning of their holy institution!

Oh, how great was their devotion in prayer! How great their zeal for virtue! What great discipline was in force among them! What great reverence and obedience in all, flourished under the rule of a superior!

Mancipia Publications

The footsteps remaining, still bear witness that they were truly perfect and holy men, who, waging war so stoutly, trod the world under their feet.

Now he is thought great who is not a transgressor, and who can with patience endure what he has undertaken.

6. Ah, the lukewarmness and negligence of our state, that we so quickly fall away from our former fervor, and are now even weary of living through sloth and tepidity.

Would to God that advancement in virtues was not wholly asleep in thee who has so often seen many examples of the devout!

Fifth Day ⸻⸻⸻

Daily Prayers: Veni Creator page 155, Ave Maris Stella page 156.

Continuation of the holy Gospel according to Saint Matthew 5:43-48
You have heard that it has been said, You shall love your neighbor, and hate your enemy.

44. But I say to you: Love your enemies: do good to them that hate you: and pray for them that persecute and calumniate you:

45. That you may be the children of your Father Who is in Heaven, Who makes His sun to rise upon the good, and bad, and rain upon the just and the unjust.

46. For if you love them that love you, what reward shall you have? do not even the publicans this?

47. And if you salute your brethren only, what do you more? do not also the heathens this?

48. Be you therefore perfect, as also your heavenly Father is perfect.

Imitation of Christ, Book 1, Chapter 25:1-2
Of the Fervent Amendment of Our Whole Life
Be vigilant and diligent in God's service, and often think with thyself to what end thou came hither, and why thou did leave the world: Was it not that thou might live in God and become a spiritual man?

Be fervent, therefore, in thy spiritual progress, for thou shall shortly receive the reward of thy labors; and then grief and fear shall no more come near thee.

Thou shall labor now a little and thou shall find great rest; yea, everlasting joy.

If thou continue faithful and fervent in working, God will doubtless be faithful and liberal in rewarding.

Thou must preserve a good and firm hope of winning the victory; but must not think thyself secure, lest thou grow negligent or proud.

2. When a certain person in anxiety of mind was often wavering between hope and fear, and, on a time, being overwhelmed with grief, had prostrated himself in prayer in the church before a certain altar, he revolved these things within himself saying: "If I did but know that I should still persevere"; and presently he heard within himself this answer from God: "And if thou did know this what would thou do? do now what you would then do, and thou shall be very secure."

And immediately, being comforted and strengthened, he committed himself to the divine will, and his anxious wavering ceased.

Neither had he a mind anymore to search curiously, to know what should befall him hereafter; but rather studied to inquire what was the will of God, "well pleasing and perfect" (Rom. 12:2), for the beginning and accomplishment of every good work.

Sixth Day _____

Daily Prayers: *Veni Creator* page 155, *Ave Maris Stella* page 156.

Gospel according to Saint Matthew 6:1-13

Take heed that you do not your justice before men, to be seen by them; otherwise you shall not have a reward of your Father Who is in Heaven.

2. Therefore, when you do an alms deed, sound not a trumpet before you, as the hypocrites do in the synagogues and in the streets, that they may be honored by men. Amen, I say to you, they have received their reward.

3. But when you do alms, let not your left hand know what your right hand does,

4. That your alms may be in secret, and your Father Who sees in secret will repay you.

5. And when you pray, you shall not be as the hypocrites that love to stand and pray in the synagogues and corners of the streets, that they may be seen by men: Amen, I say to you, they have received their reward.

6. But you when you shall pray, enter into your chamber and having shut the door, pray to your Father in secret; and your Father Who sees in secret will repay you.

7. And when you are praying, speak not much, as the heathens. For they think that in their much speaking they may be heard.

8. Be not you therefore like to them, for our Father knows what is needful for you, before you ask Him.

9. Thus therefore shall you pray: Our Father Who art in Heaven, hallowed be Thy name.

10. Thy kingdom come. Thy will be done on earth as it is in Heaven.

 Mancipia Publications

11. Give us this day our supersubstantial bread.

12. And forgive us our debts, as we also forgive our debtors.

13. And lead us not into temptation. But deliver us from evil. Amen.

Continuation of Imitation of Christ, Book 1, Chapter 25:3-4

Hope in the Lord, and do good," said the Prophet: "and inhabit the land, and you shall be fed with the riches thereof."

There is one thing that keeps many back from spiritual progress, and from fervor in amendment; namely, a dread of the difficulty or of the labor of the struggle.

And assuredly they especially advance beyond others in virtue, who strive the most manfully to overcome the very things which are the hardest and most contrary to them.

For there a man improves most and merits more abundant grace, when he overcomes himself and mortifies his spirit.

4. All have not, indeed, equal difficulties to overcome and mortify; but a diligent and zealous person will make greater progress, though he has more passions than another, who is well-regulated, but less fervent in the pursuit of virtues.

Two things especially conduce us to great improvement; namely, to forcibly withdraw one's self from what our nature is viciously inclined to, and to labor fervently for that good which we need most.

Be careful also to guard against those things in yourself, for such things often displease you in others. Study, likewise, especially to guard against and to get the better of such things as oftenest displease thee in others.

Seventh Day ─────────────

Daily Prayers: Veni Creator page 155, *Ave Maris Stella* page 156.

Continuation of the holy Gospel according to Saint Matthew 6: 14-23

For if you will forgive men their offenses, your heavenly Father will forgive you also your offenses.

15. But, if you will not forgive men, neither will your Father forgive you your offenses.

16. And when you fast, be not as the hypocrites, sad. For they disfigure their faces, that they may appear unto men to fast. Amen I say to you, they have received their reward.

17. But you, when you fast, anoint your head and wash your face;

18. That you appear not to men to fast, but to your Father Who is in secret; and your Father Who sees in secret, will repay you.

19. Lay not up to yourselves treasures on earth; where the rust and moth

consume, and where thieves break through and steal.

20. But lay up to yourselves treasures in Heaven; where neither rust nor moth consume, and where thieves do not break through, nor steal.

21. For where your treasure is, there is your heart also.

22. The light of your body is your eye. If your eye be single, your whole body shall be lightsome.

23. But if your eye be evil, your whole body shall be darksome. If then the light that is in you, be darkness: the darkness itself how great shall it be!

Continuation of Imitation of Christ, Book 1, Chapter 25:5-7

Turn all occasions to thy spiritual profit: so that if thou see or hear any good examples thou may be spurred on to imitate them.

But if thou observe anything that is reprehensible take heed thou commit not the same; or if thou at any time has done it, labor to amend it quickly.

As thine eye observes others so are thou also observed by others.

Oh, how sweet and comfortable is it to see brethren fervent and devout, regular and well disciplined! (Ps. 132:1)

How sad a thing and how afflicting to see them walk disorderly, and practice nothing of what they are called to!

How hurtful it is to neglect the intent of our vocation and turn our minds to things that are not our business.

6. Be mindful of the resolution thou has taken, and set before thee the image of the crucifix.

Well may thou be ashamed if thou has looked upon the life of Jesus Christ, that thou has not yet studied to conform thyself more to His pattern, although thou has been long in the way of God.

A religious man, who exercises himself seriously and devoutly in the most holy life and Passion of Our Lord, shall find there abundantly all things profitable and necessary for him; nor need he seek any better model than that of Jesus.

Oh, if our crucified Jesus did but come into our heart, how quickly and sufficiently learned should we be!

7. A fervent religious man bears and takes all things well that are commanded him.

A negligent and lukewarm religious man has trouble upon trouble, and on every side suffers anguish, because he has no comfort within and is hindered from seeking any without.

A religious man that lives not in discipline lies open to dreadful ruin.

He that seeks to be more loose and remiss will always be uneasy, for one thing or other will always displease him.

Mancipia Publications

Eighth Day ──────────

Daily Prayers: Veni Creator page 155, *Ave Maris Stella* page 156.

Continuation of the holy Gospel according to Saint Matthew 6: 24-34

No man can serve two masters. For either he will hate the one and love the other; or he will sustain the one and despise the other. You cannot serve God and mammon.

25. Therefore I say to you, be not solicitous for your life, what you shall eat, nor for your body, what you shall put on. Is not the life more than the meat and the body more than the raiment?

26. Behold the birds of the air, for they neither sow, nor do they reap, nor gather into barns; and your heavenly Father feeds them. Are not you of much more value than they?

27. And which of you by taking thought, can add to his stature one cubit?

28. And for raiment why are you solicitous? Consider the lilies of the field, how they grow; they labor not, neither do they spin.

29. But I say to you, that not even Solomon in all his glory was arrayed as one of these.

30. And if the grass of the field, which is today and tomorrow is cast into the oven, God does so clothe: how much more you, of ye of little faith?

31. Be not solicitous therefore, saying: What shall we eat; or, what shall we drink; or, wherewith shall we be clothed?

32. For after all these things do the heathens seek. For your Father knows that you have need of all these things.

33. Seek therefore first the kingdom of God, and His justice, and all these things shall be added unto you.

34. Be not therefore solicitous for tomorrow; for the morrow will be solicitous for itself. Sufficient for the day is the evil thereof.

Continuation of Imitation of Christ, Book 1, Chapter 25:8-11

How do so many other religious do who live under strict monastic discipline?

They seldom go abroad, they live very retired, their diet is very poor, their habit coarse, they labor much, they speak little, they watch long, they rise early, they spend much time in prayer, they read often and keep themselves in all discipline.

Consider the Carthusians, the Cistercians, and the monks and nuns of divers Orders, how every night they rise to sing psalms to the Lord.

It would, therefore, be a shame for thee to be sluggish at so holy a time, when such multitudes of religious begin with joy to give praise to God.

9. Oh, that we had nothing else to do but to praise the Lord our God with our whole heart and mouth!

Oh, that thou did never want to eat, nor drink, nor sleep, but could always

Manual for the Total Consecration to Mary 13

praise God and be employed solely in spiritual exercises!

Thou would then be much more happy than now while thou are under the necessity of serving the flesh.

Would there were no such necessities, but only the spiritual refreshments of the soul, which, alas, we taste too seldom.

10. When a man is come to this, that he seeks comfort from nothing created, then he begins perfectly to relish God; then likewise will he be well content, however matters happen to him.

Then will he neither rejoice for much, nor be sorrowful for little, but will commit himself wholly and confidently to God, Who is to him all in all; to whom nothing perishes or dies, but all things live to Him and serve Him at a nod without delay.

11. Always remember thine end and that time once lost never returns. Without care and diligence thou shall never acquire virtues.

If thou begin to grow lukewarm thou will begin to be uneasy.

But if thou give thyself to fervor thou shall find great peace, and the grace of God and love of virtue will make thee feel less labor.

A fervent and diligent man is ready for all things.

It is a greater task to resist vices and passions than to toil at bodily labors.

He that does not shun small defects by little and little falls into greater.

Thou shall always rejoice in the evening if thou spend the day profitably.

Watch over thyself, stir up thyself, admonish thyself, and whatever becomes of others neglect not thyself.

The greater violence thou offer to thyself the greater progress thou shall make.

Ninth Day ⸻⸻⸻

Daily Prayers: Veni Creator page 155, *Ave Maris Stella* page 156.

Gospel according to Saint Matthew 7:1-12

Judge not, that you may not be judged.

2. For with what judgment you judge, you shall be judged; and with what measure you mete, it shall be measured to you again.

3. And why see you the mote that is in your brother's eye; and see not the beam that is in your own eye?

4. Or how say you to your brother: Let me cast the mote out of your eye; and behold a beam is in your own eye?

5. You hypocrite, cast out first the beam out of your own eye; and then shall you see to cast out the mote out of your brother's eye.

6. Give not that which is holy to dogs; neither cast your pearls before swine, lest perhaps they trample them under their feet, and turning upon you,

they tear you.

7. Ask, and it shall be given you; seek, and you shall find; knock, and it shall be opened to you.

8. For every one that asks, receives; and he that seeks finds; and to him that knocks, it shall be opened.

9. Or what man is there among you, of whom if his son shall ask bread, will he reach him a stone?

10. Or if he shall ask him a fish, will he reach him a serpent?

11. If you then being evil, know how to give good gifts to your children; how much more will your Father Who is in Heaven give good things to them that ask Him?

12. All things therefore whatsoever you would that men should do to you, do you also to them. For this is the law and the prophets.

Imitation of Christ, Book 3, Chapter 10:1-3
It Is Sweet to Serve God, Despising This World
DISCIPLE

Now will I speak, O Lord, and will not be silent; I will say in the hearing of my God, my Lord and my King that is on high.

Oh, how great is the multitude of Thy sweetness, O Lord, which Thou has hidden from them that fear Thee. But what art Thou to those that love Thee? What to those that serve Thee with their whole heart?

Unspeakable indeed is the sweetness of Thy contemplation, which Thou bestow on those that love Thee.

In this most of all has Thou shown me the sweetness of Thy love, that when I had no being Thou has made me, and when I strayed far from Thee Thou has brought me back again, that I might serve Thee, and Thou has commanded me to love Thee.

2. O Fountain of everlasting love, what shall I say of Thee?

How can I ever forget Thee who has vouchsafed to remember me, even after I was corrupted and lost.

Thou has, beyond all hope, showed mercy to Thy servant, and beyond all my desert bestowed Thy grace and friendship upon me.

What returns shall I make to Thee for this favor? For it is a favor not granted to all to forsake all things and renounce the world and choose a monastic life.

Can it be much to serve Thee whom the whole creation is bound to serve?

It ought not to seem much to serve Thee, but this seems rather great and wonderful to me, that Thou vouchsafe to receive one so wretched and unworthy into Thy service and to associate him to Thy beloved servants.

3. Behold all things are Thine which I have and with which I serve Thee.

Although, on the contrary, Thou dost rather serve me than I Thee.

Lo! Heaven and earth, which Thou has created for the service of man, are ready at Thy beck and daily do whatever Thou has commanded them.

And this is yet but little, for Thou has also appointed the angels for the service of man.

But what is above all this is that Thou Thyself has vouchsafed to serve man and has promised that Thou will give him Thyself.

Tenth Day _____

Daily Prayers: Veni Creator page 155, *Ave Maris Stella* page 156.

Continuation of the holy Gospel according to Saint Matthew 7:12-20

All things therefore whatsoever you would that men should do to you, do you also to them. For this is the law and the prophets.

13. Enter in at the narrow gate; for wide is the gate, and broad is the way that leads to destruction, and many there are who go in there.

14. How narrow is the gate, and strait is the way that leads to life; and few there are that find it!

15. Beware of false prophets, who come to you in the clothing of sheep, but inwardly they are ravening wolves.

16. By their fruits you shall know them. Do men gather grapes of thorns, or figs of thistles?

17. Even so, every good tree brings forth good fruit, and the evil tree brings forth evil fruit.

18. A good tree cannot bring forth evil fruit, neither can an evil tree bring forth good fruit.

19. Every tree that brings not forth good fruit shall be cut down, and shall be cast into the fire.

20. Wherefore by their fruits you shall know them.

Continuation of Imitation of Christ, Book 3, Chapter 10:4-6

What shall I give Thee for so many thousands of favors? Oh, that I could serve Thee all the days of my life!

Oh, that I were able, if it were but for one day, to serve Thee worthily!

Indeed Thou are worthy of all service, of all honor, and of eternal praise!

Thou art truly my Lord and I am Thy poor servant, who am bound with all my strength to serve Thee and ought never to grow weary of praising Thee.

This is my will, this is my desire, and whatever is wanting to me do Thou vouchsafe to supply.

5. It is a great honor, a great glory to serve Thee and to despise all things for Thee.

For they who willingly subject themselves to Thy most holy service shall have great grace.

They shall find the most sweet consolations of the Holy Ghost who, for

Mancipia Publications

the love of Thee, have cast away all carnal delights.

They shall gain great freedom of mind who, for Thy name, enter upon the narrow way and neglect all worldly care.

6. O pleasant and delightful service of God, which makes a man truly free and holy!

O sacred state of religious bondage, which makes men equal to angels, pleasing to God, terrible to the devils and commendable to all the faithful.

O service worthy to be embraced and always wished for, which leads to the supreme good and procures a joy that will never end.

Eleventh Day ─────────────

Daily Prayers: Veni Creator page 155, *Ave Maris Stella* page 156.

Continuation of the holy Gospel according to Saint Matthew 7: 21-29

Not every one that says to me, Lord, Lord, shall enter into the kingdom of Heaven; but he that does the will of My Father Who is in Heaven, he shall enter into the kingdom of Heaven.

22. Many will say to Me in that day: Lord, Lord, have not we prophesied in Thy name and cast out devils in Thy name and done many miracles in Thy name?

23. And then will I profess unto them: I never knew you; depart from Me, you that work iniquity.

24. Every one therefore that hears these my words, and does them, shall be likened to a wise man that built his house upon a rock.

25. And the rain fell and the floods came and the winds blew, and they beat upon that house, and it fell not, for it was founded on a rock.

26. And every one that hears these My words, and does them not, shall be like a foolish man that built his house upon the sand,

27. And the rain fell, and the floods came, and the winds blew, and they beat upon that house, and it fell, and great was the fall thereof.

28. And it came to pass when Jesus had fully ended these words, the people were in admiration at His doctrine.

29. For He was teaching them as one having power and not as the Scribes and Pharisees.

Imitation of Christ, Book 3, Chapter 40:1-3
Man Has No Good of Himself, and Cannot Glory in Anything

Lord, what is man, that Thou are mindful of him; or the son of man, that Thou visit him?

What has man deserved, that Thou should give him Thy grace?

Lord, what cause have I to complain, if Thou forsake me? Or what can I justly allege if Thou refuse to grant my petition?

This, indeed, I may truly think and say, Lord, I am nothing, I can do nothing, I have nothing of myself that is good; but I fail and am defective in all things, and ever tend to nothing.

And unless I am supported and interiorly instructed by You, I become wholly tepid and dissolute.

2. But Thou, O Lord, are always the same, and endure forever; always good, just, and holy; doing all things well, justly, and holily, and disposing them in wisdom.

But I, who am more inclined to go back than to go forward, continue not always in one state; for seven different seasons are changed over me.

Yet it quickly becomes better when it pleases Thee, and Thou stretch out Thy helping hand; for Thou alone without man's aid can assist and so strengthen me, that my countenance shall be no more diversely changed; but my heart be converted, and find its rest in Thee alone.

3. Wherefore, if I did but well know how to cast from me all human comfort, either for the sake of devotion, or through the necessity of seeking Thee, because there is no man that can comfort me, then might I justly depend on Thy grace, and rejoice in the gift of new consolation.

Twelfth Day _____

Daily Prayers: *Veni Creator* page 155, *Ave Maris Stella* page 156.

Continuation of the holy Gospel according to Saint Matthew 7: 21-29 *(repeated from 11th day)*

Not every one that says to me, Lord, Lord, shall enter into the kingdom of Heaven; but he that does the will of My Father Who is in Heaven, he shall enter into the kingdom of Heaven.

22. Many will say to Me in that day: Lord, Lord, have not we prophesied in Thy name and cast out devils in Thy name and done many miracles in Thy name?

23. And then will I profess unto them: I never knew you; depart from Me, you that work iniquity.

24. Every one therefore that hears these My words, and does them, shall be likened to a wise man that built his house upon a rock.

25. And the rain fell and the floods came, and the winds blew, and they beat upon that house, and it fell not, for it was founded on a rock.

26. And every one that hears these My words, and does them not, shall be like a foolish man that built his house upon the sand,

27. And the rain fell, and the floods came, and the winds blew, and they

Mancipia Publications

beat upon that house, and it fell, and great was the fall thereof.

28. And it came to pass when Jesus had fully ended these words, the people were in admiration at His doctrine.

29. For He was teaching them as one having power, and not as the Scribes and Pharisees.

Continuation of Imitation of Christ, Book 3, Chapter 40:4-6

Thanks be to Thee, from Whom all proceeds, as often as it goes well with me.

But, for my part, I am but mere vanity, and nothing in Thy sight; an inconstant and weak man.

What have I then to glory in? or why do I desire to be esteemed?

Is it not for nothing? and this is most vain.

Truly vainglory is an evil plague, a very great vanity, because it draws us away from true glory, and robs us of heavenly grace.

For while a man takes complacency in himself, he displeases Thee; while he seeks after the praises of men, he is deprived of true virtues.

5. But true glory and holy exultation is to glory in Thee, and not in one's self; to rejoice in Thy Name, not in one's self; to rejoice in Thy name, and not to be delighted in one's own virtue, nor in any creature, save only for Thy sake.

Let Thy Name be praised, not mine; let Thy work by extolled, not mine; let Thy holy Name be blessed, but to me let nothing be attributed of the praises of men.

Thou are my glory, Thou are the joy of my heart.

In Thee will I glory and rejoice all the day; but for myself I will glory in nothing but in my infirmities.

6. Let the Jews seek the glory which one man receives from another; I will seek that which is from God alone.

All human glory, all temporal honor, all worldly grandeur, compared to Thine eternal glory is but vanity and foolishness.

O my truth and my mercy, O my God, O blessed Trinity! To Thee alone be all praise, honor, power, and glory, for endless ages of ages.

Her eyes were the first to gaze on the face of God,
her hands the first to touch His sacred body.
Only purity itself would win this privilege.
That is why we say to Mary:
Mary Most Pure, pray for us!

Knowledge of Self

Second Period — First Week

During the first week you should offer up all your prayers and pious actions to ask for a knowledge of yourself and contrition for your sins; and you should do this in a spirit of humility. You can look upon yourself during the six days of this week as a snail, crawling things, a toad, a swine, a serpent and unclean animals; or you can reflect on these three considerations of Saint Bernard: the vileness of your origin, the dishonor of your present state, and your ending as the food of worms. You should pray that Our Lord and the Holy Ghost enlighten you; and for that end you might use the ejaculations, "Lord, that I may see!;" or "May I know myself!;" or "Come, Holy Ghost," together with the Litany of the Holy Ghost. You should have recourse to the Blessed Virgin and ask her to grant you this immense grace, which must be the foundation of all others.

During this week, consider not so much the opposition that exists between the spirit of Jesus and you, as the miserable and humiliating state to which your sins have reduced you. Moreover, the True Devotion being an easy, short, sure and perfect way to arrive at that union with Our Lord which is Christian perfection, you should enter seriously upon this way, strongly convinced of your misery and helplessness. But how can you attain this without a knowledge of yourself?

Daily Prayers during the First Week: Litany of the Holy Ghost, the *Ave Maris Stella*, and the *Litany of the Blessed Virgin*.

Spiritual Exercises during the First Week: Prayers, examens, reflection, acts of renouncement of your will, of contrition for your sins, of contempt of self—all performed at the feet of Mary, for it is from her you hope for light to know yourself, and it is near her that you shall be able to measure the abyss of your miseries without despairing.

First Day _____

Daily Prayers during the First Week: Litany of the Holy Ghost on page 160, the *Ave Maris Stella* on page 156, and the *Litany of the Blessed Virgin* on page 161.

Gospel according to Saint Matthew 24

And Jesus being come out of the temple, went away. And His disciples came to show Him the buildings of the temple.

2. And He answering, said to them: Do you see all these things? Amen I say to you there shall not be left here a stone upon a stone that shall not be destroyed.

3. And when He was sitting on Mount Olivet, the disciples came to Him privately, saying: Tell us when shall these things be? And what shall be the sign of Thy coming, and of the consummation of the world?

4. And Jesus answering, said to them: Take heed that no man seduce you:

5. For many will come in My Name saying, I am Christ: and they will seduce many.

6. And you shall hear of wars and rumors of wars. See that you be not troubled. For these things must come to pass, but the end is not yet.

7. For nation shall rise against nation, and kingdom against kingdom; and there shall be pestilences, and famines, and earthquakes in places:

8. Now all these are the beginnings of sorrows.

9. Then shall they deliver you up to be afflicted, and shall put you to death: and you shall be hated by all nations for My Name's sake.

10. And then shall many be scandalized: and shall betray one another: and shall hate one another.

11. And many false prophets shall rise, and shall seduce many.

12. And because iniquity hath abounded, the charity of many shall grow cold.

13. But he that shall perservere to the end, he shall be saved.

14. And this Gospel of the kingdom, shall be preached in the whole world, for a testimony to all nations, and then shall the consummation come.

15. When therefore you shall see the abomination of desolation, which was spoken of by Daniel the prophet, standing in the holy place: he that readeth let him understand.

16. Then they that are in Judea, let them flee to the mountains:

17. And he that is on the housetop, let him not come down to take anything out of his house:

18. And he that is in the field, let him not go back to take his coat.

19. And woe to them that are with child, and that give suck in those days.

20. But pray that your flight be not in the winter, or on the sabbath.

21. For there shall be then great tribulation, such as has not been from the beginning of the world until now, neither shall be.

22. And unless those days had been shortened, no flesh should be saved: but for the sake of the elect those days shall be shortened.

Mancipia Publications

23. Then if any man shall say to you: Lo here is Christ, or there, do not believe him.

24. For there shall arise false Christs and false prophets, and shall show great signs and wonders, insomuch as to deceive (if possible) even the elect.

25. Behold I have told it to you, beforehand.

26. If therefore they shall say to you: Behold he is in the desert, go not out: Behold he is in the closets, believe it not.

27. For as lightning comes out of the east, and appears even into the west: so shall the coming of the Son of Man be.

28. Wheresoever the body shall be, there shall the eagles also be gathered together.

29. And immediately after the tribulation of those days, the sun shall be darkened and the moon shall not give her light, and the stars shall fall from heaven, and the powers of heaven shall be moved:

30. And then shall appear the sign of the Son of Man in Heaven: and then shall all tribes of the earth mourn: and they shall see the Son of Man coming in the clouds of Heaven with much power and majesty.

31. And He shall send His angels with a trumpet, and a great voice: and they shall gather together His elect from the four winds, from the farthest parts of the Heavens to the utmost bounds of them.

32. And from the fig tree learn a parable: When the branch thereof is now tender, and the leaves come forth, you know that summer is nigh.

33. So you also, when you shall see all these things, know that it is nigh, even at the doors.

34. Amen I say to you, that this generation shall not pass, till all these things be done.

35. Heaven and earth shall pass, but my words shall not pass.

36. But of that day and hour no one knoweth, no not the angels of Heaven, but the Father alone.

37. And as in the days of Noe, so shall also the coming of the Son of Man be.

38. For as in the days before the flood, they were eating and drinking, marrying and giving in marriage, even till that day in which Noe entered into the ark,

39. And they knew not till the flood came, and took them all away; so also shall the coming of the Son of Man be.

40. Then two shall be in the field: one shall be taken, and one shall be left.

41. Two women shall be grinding at the mill: one shall be taken, and one shall be left.

42. Watch ye therefore, because you know not what hour your Lord will come.

43. But this know ye, that if the good man of the house knew at what hour the thief would come, he would certainly watch, and would not suffer his house to be broken open.

44. Wherefore be you also ready, because at what hour you know not the Son of Man will come.

45. Who, thinkest thou, is a faithful and wise servant, whom his lord has

appointed over his family, to give them meat in season?

46. Blessed is that servant, whom when his lord shall come he shall find so doing.

47. Amen I say to you, he shall place him over all his goods.

48. But if the evil servant shall say in his heart: My lord is long a coming:

49. And shall begin to strike his fellow servants, and shall eat and drink with drunkards:

50. The lord of that servant shall come in a day that he hopeth not, and at an hour that he knoweth not:

51. And shall separate him, and appoint his portion with the hypocrites. There shall be weeping and gnashing of teeth.

Imitation of Christ, Book 1 Chapter 24
Of Judgment, and the Punishment of Our Sins

In all things look to thine end, and how thou shall be able to stand before a severe Judge, from whom nothing is hidden, who takes no bribes, nor receives excuses, but will judge that which is just.

O most wretched and foolish sinner, what answer will thou make to God, who knows all thine evils? Thou who are sometimes afraid of the looks of an angry man.

Why do thou not provide for thyself against the Day of Judgment, when no man can be excused or defended by another, but every one shall have enough to do to answer for himself?

At present thy labor is profitable; thy tears are acceptable, thy sighs will be heard, thy sorrow is satisfactory, and may purge away thy sins.

2. A patient man has a great and wholesome purgatory, who, receiving injuries, is more concerned at the person's sin than his own wrong; who willingly prays for his adversaries, and from his heart forgives offenses; who delays not to ask forgiveness of others; who is easier moved to compassion than to anger; who frequently uses violence to himself, and labors to bring the flesh wholly under subjection to the spirit.

It is better now to purge away our sins and to cut up our vices than to reserve them to be purged hereafter.

Truly we deceive ourselves through the inordinate love we bear to our flesh.

3. What other things shall the fire feed on but thy sins?

The more thou spare thyself now and follow the flesh the more grievously shall thou suffer hereafter and the more fuel do thou lay up for that fire.

In those things which a man has more sinned shall he be more heavily punished.

There the slothful shall be pricked forward with burning goads, and the glutton will be tormented with extreme hunger and thirst.

There the luxurious and the lovers of pleasure shall be covered all over with burning pitch and stinking brimstone, and the envious like mad dogs shall howl for grief.

Mancipia Publications

4. There is no vice which will not there have its proper torment.

There the proud shall be filled with all confusion, and the covetous be straitened with most miserable want.

There one hour of suffering will be more sharp than a hundred years here spent in the most rigid penance.

There is no rest, no comfort for the damned; but here there is sometimes intermission of labor, and we receive comfort from our friends.

Be careful at present and sorrowful for thy sins, that in the Day of Judgment thou may be secure with the blessed.

"For then shall the just stand with great constancy against those that have afflicted and oppressed them."

Then will he stand to judge who now humbly submits himself to the judgment of men.

Then the poor and the humble shall have great confidence and the proud shall fear on every side.

5. Then will it appear that he was wise in this world who learned for Christ's sake to be a fool and despised.

Then all tribulation suffered with patience will be pleasing "and all iniquity shall stop her mouth."

Then every devout person shall rejoice and the irreligious shall be sad.

Then the flesh that has been mortified shall triumph more than if it had always been pampered in delights.

Then shall the mean habit shine and fine clothing appear contemptible.

Then shall the poor cottage be more commended than the gilded palace.

Then constant patience shall more avail than all the power of the world.

Then simple obedience shall be more prized than all worldly craftiness.

6. Then a pure and good conscience shall be a greater subject of joy than learned philosophy.

Then the contempt of riches shall weigh more than all the treasures of worldlings.

Then will thou be more comforted that thou has prayed devoutly than that thou has fared daintily.

Then will thou rejoice more that thou has kept silence than that thou has made long discourses or talked much.

Then will holy works be of greater value than many fair words.

Then will a strict life and hard penance be more pleasing than all the delights of the earth.

Learn, at present, to suffer in little things, that then thou may be delivered from more grievous sufferings.

Try first here what thou can suffer hereafter.

If thou can now endure so little how will thou be able to bear everlasting torments?

If a little suffering now makes thee so impatient what will hellfire do hereafter?

Surely thou can not have both joys—take thy pleasure in this world and afterwards reign with Christ.

7. If to this day thou had always lived in honors and pleasures what would it avail thee if thou were now in a moment to die?

All then is vanity but to love God and to serve Him alone.

For he that loves God with his whole heart neither fears death, nor punishment, nor judgment, nor Hell; because perfect love gives secure access to God.

But he that is yet delighted with sin no wonder if he be afraid of death and judgment.

It is good, however, that if love, as yet, reclaim thee not from evil, at least the fear of Hell restrain thee.

But he that lays aside the fear of God will not be able to continue long in good, but will quickly fall into the snares of the devil.

True Devotion #228

During the first week they should offer up all their prayers and pious actions to ask for a knowledge of themselves and contrition for their sins; and they should do this in a spirit of humility. For that end they can, if they choose, meditate on what I have said before of our inward corruption. They can look upon themselves during the six days of this week as snails, crawling things, toads, swine, serpents and unclean animals; or they can reflect on these three considerations of Saint Bernard: the vileness of our origin, the dishonors of our present state, and our ending as the food of worms. They should pray Our Lord and the Holy Ghost to enlighten them; and for that end they might use the ejaculations, "Lord, that I may see!" or "May I know myself!" or "Come, Holy Ghost," together with the *Litany of the Holy Ghost* and the prayer which follows, as indicated in the first part of this work. They should have recourse to the Blessed Virgin and ask her to grant them this immense grace, which must be the foundation of all the others; for this end, they should say daily the *Ave Maris Stella* and the *Litany of the Blessed Virgin.*

The more you spare yourself now and follow the flesh the more grievously will you suffer hereafter and more fuel you lay up for that fire.

Second Day _____

Daily Prayers during the First Week: Litany of the Holy Ghost on page 160, the *Ave Maris Stella* on page 156, and the *Litany of the Blessed Virgin* on page 161.

Gospel according to Saint Matthew 25

Then shall the kingdom of Heaven be like to ten virgins, who taking their lamps went out to meet the bridegroom and the bride.

2. And five of them were foolish, and five wise.

3. But the five foolish, having taken their lamps, did not take oil with them:

4. But the wise took oil in their vessels with the lamps.

5. And the bridegroom tarrying, they all slumbered and slept.

6. And at midnight there was a cry made: Behold the bridegroom comes, go forth to meet him.

7. Then all those virgins arose and trimmed their lamps.

8. And the foolish said to the wise: Give us of your oil, for our lamps are gone out.

9. The wise answered, saying: Lest perhaps there be not enough for us and for you, go rather to them that sell, and buy for yourselves.

10. Now while they went to buy, the bridegroom came: and they that were ready, went in with him to the marriage, and the door was shut.

11. But at last came also the other virgins, saying: Lord, Lord, open to us.

12. But he answering said: Amen I say to you, I know you not.

13. Watch ye therefore, because you know not the day nor the hour.

14. For even as a man going into a far country, called his servants, and delivered to them his goods;

15. And to one he gave five talents, and to another two, and to another one, to every one according to his proper ability: and immediately he took his journey.

16. And he that had received the five talents, went his way, and traded with the same, and gained other five.

17. And in like manner he that had received the two, gained other two.

18. But he that had received the one, going his way dug into the earth, and hid his lord's money.

19. But after a long time the lord of those servants came, and reckoned with them.

20. And he that had received the five talents coming, brought other five talents, saying: Lord, you delivered to me five talents, behold I have gained other five over and above.

21. His lord said to him: Well done, good and faithful servant, because you have been faithful over a few things, I will place you over many things: enter into the joy of the lord.

22. And he also that had received the two talents came and said: Lord, you gave me two talents: behold I have gained other two.

23. His lord said to him: Well done, good and faithful servant: because you

have been faithful over a few things, I will place you over many things: enter into the joy of the lord.

24. But he that had received the one talent, came and said: Lord, I know that you are a hard man; you reap where you have not sown, and gather where you have not strewn.

25. And being afraid I went and hid the talent in the earth: behold here you have back what is yours.

26. And his lord answering, said to him: Wicked and slothful servant, you knew that I reap where I have not sowed, and gather where I have not strewn:

27. Thou oughtest therefore to have committed my money to the bankers, and at my coming I should have received my own with usury.

28. Take ye away therefore the talent from him, and give it to him that hath ten talents.

29. For to every one that hath shall be given, and he shall abound: but from him that has not, that also which he seemeth to have shall be taken away.

30. And the unprofitable servant was cast out into the exterior darkness. There shall be weeping and gnashing of teeth.

31. And when the Son of Man shall come in His majesty, and all the angels with Him, then shall He sit upon the seat of His majesty:

32. And all nations shall be gathered together before Him, and He shall separate them one from another, as the shepherd separates the sheep from the goats:

33. And He shall set the sheep on His right hand, but the goats on His left.

34. Then shall the king say to them that shall be on His right hand: Come, ye blessed of my Father, possess you the kingdom prepared for you from the foundation of the world.

35. For I was hungry, and you gave Me to eat; I was thirsty, and you gave Me to drink; I was a stranger, and you took Me in:

36. Naked, and you covered Me: sick, and you visited Me: I was in prison, and you came to Me.

37. Then shall the just answer Him, saying: Lord, when did we see You hungry, and fed You; thirsty, and gave You drink?

38. And when did we see You a stranger, and took You in? or naked, and covered You?

39. Or when did we see You sick or in prison and came to You?

40. And the king answering, shall say to them: Amen I say to you, as long as you did it to one of these My least brethren, you did it to Me.

41. Then He shall say to them also that shall be on His left hand: Depart from Me, you cursed, into everlasting fire which was prepared for the Devil and his angels.

42. For I was hungry, and you gave Me not to eat: I was thirsty, and you gave Me not to drink.

43. I was a stranger, and you took Me not in: naked, and you covered Me not: sick and in prison, and you did not visit Me.

44. Then they also shall answer Him, saying: Lord, when did we see You

Mancipia Publications

hungry, or thirsty, or a stranger, or naked, or sick, or in prison, and did not minister to You?

45. Then He shall answer them, saying: Amen I say to you, as long as you did it not to one of these least, neither did you do it to Me.

46. And these shall go into everlasting punishment: but the just, into life everlasting.

Imitation of Christ, Book 2 Chapter 5
Of the Consideration of One's Self

We cannot trust much to ourselves, because we often want grace and understanding.

There is but little light in us and this we quickly lose through negligence.

Many times also we perceive not that we are so blind interiorly.

We often do ill and do worse in excusing it.

We are sometimes moved with passion, and we mistake it for zeal.

We blame little things in others and pass over great things in ourselves.

We are quick enough at perceiving and weighing what we suffer from others, but we mind not what others suffer from us.

He that would well and duly weigh his own deeds would have no room to judge harshly of others.

2. An internal man prefers the care of himself before all other cares, and he that diligently attends to himself is easily silent with regard to others.

You will never be internal and devout unless you pass over in silence other men's concerns and particularly look to yourself.

If you attend wholly to yourself and to God, you will be little moved with what you perceive around you.

Where are you when you are not present to yourself?

If you desire to have peace and true union you must set all the rest aside and turn your eyes upon yourself alone.

3. You will then make great progress if you keep yourself free from all temporal care.

But if you set a value upon anything temporal you will fail exceedingly.

Let nothing be great in your eyes, nothing high, nothing pleasant, nothing agreeable to you, except it be purely God or of God.

Look upon all the comfort which you meet with from any creature as vain.

A soul that loves God despises all things that are less than God.

None but God, eternal and incomprehensible, Who fills all things, can afford true comfort to the soul and true joy to the heart.

True Devotion # 78

Our best actions are ordinarily stained and corrupted by our corrupt nature. When we put clean, clear water into a vessel which has a foul and evil smell, or wine into a cask the inside of which has been tainted by another wine which has been in it, the clear water and the good wine are spoilt, and readily take on the bad odor. In like manner, when God puts into the vessel of our soul, spoilt by original and actual sin, His graces and heavenly dews, or the delicious wine of His love, His gifts are ordinarily spoilt and corrupted by the bad leaven and the evil which sin has left within us. Our actions, even the most sublime and virtuous, feel the effects of it. It is therefore of great importance in the acquiring of perfection—which, it must be remembered, is only acquired by union with Jesus Christ—to rid ourselves of everything that is bad within us; otherwise Our Lord, Who is infinitely pure and hates infinitely the least stain upon our souls, will not unite Himself to us, and will cast us out from His presence.

Third Day _____

Daily Prayers during the First Week: Litany of the Holy Ghost on page 160, the *Ave Maris Stella* on page 156, and the *Litany of the Blessed Virgin* on page 161.

Gospel according to Saint Luke 11

And it came to pass, that as He was in a certain place praying, when He ceased, one of His disciples said to Him: Lord, teach us to pray, as John also taught his disciples.

2. And He said to them: When you pray, say: Father, hallowed be Thy Name. Thy kingdom come.

3. Give us this day our daily bread.

4. And forgive us our sins, for we also forgive every one that is indebted to us. And lead us not into temptation.

5. And He said to them: Which of you shall have a friend, and shall go to him at midnight, and shall say to him: Friend, lend me three loaves,

6. Because a friend of mine is come off his journey to me, and I have not what to set before him.

7. And he from within should answer, and say: Trouble me not, the door is now shut, and my children are with me in bed; I cannot rise and give thee.

8. Yet if he shall continue knocking, I say to you, although he will not rise and give him, because he is his friend: yet, because of his importunity, he will rise, and give him as many as he needs.

9. And I say to you, Ask, and it shall be given you: seek, and you shall find: knock, and it shall be opened to you.

10. For every one that asketh, receiveth; and he that seeketh, findeth; and to him that knocketh, it shall be opened.

11. And which of you, if he ask his father bread, will he give him a stone? or a fish, will he for a fish give him a serpent?

12. Or if he shall ask an egg, will he reach him a scorpion?

13. If you then, being evil, know how to give good gifts to your children, how much more will your Father from Heaven give the good Spirit to them that ask Him?

14. And He was casting out a devil, and the same was dumb: and when He had cast out the devil, the dumb spoke: and the multitudes were in admiration at it:

15. But some of them said: He casts out devils by Beelzebub, the prince of devils.

16. And others tempting, asked of Him a sign from Heaven.

17. But He seeing their thoughts, said to them: Every kingdom divided against itself, shall be brought to desolation, and house upon house shall fall.

18. And if Satan also be divided against himself, how shall his kingdom stand? Because you say, that through Beelzebub I cast out devils.

19. Now if I cast out devils by Beelzebub, by whom do your children cast them out? Therefore they shall be your judges.

20. But if I by the finger of God cast out devils; doubtless the kingdom of God is come upon you.

21. When a strong man armed keeps his court, those things are in peace which he possesses.

22. But if a stronger than he come upon him, and overcome him; he will take away all his armor wherein he trusted, and will distribute his spoils.

23. He that is not with Me, is against Me: and he that gathereth not with Me, scattereth.

24. When the unclean spirit is gone out of a man, he walketh through places without water, seeking rest: and not finding, he saith: I will return into my house whence I came out.

25. And when he is come, he findeth it swept and garnished.

26. Then he goes and takes with him seven other spirits more wicked than himself, and entering in they dwell there. And the last state of that man becomes worse than the first.

27. And it came to pass, as He spoke these things, a certain woman from the crowd, lifting up her voice, said to Him: Blessed is the womb that bore Thee, and the paps that gave Thee suck.

28. But He said: Yea rather, blessed are they who hear the word of God, and keep it.

29. And the multitudes were gathered together, He began to say: This generation is a wicked generation: it asketh a sign, and a sign shall not be given it, but the sign of Jonas the prophet.

30. For as Jonas was a sign to the Ninivites; so shall the Son of Man also be to this generation.

31. The queen of the south shall rise in the judgment with the men of this generation, and shall condemn them: because she came from the ends of the earth to hear the wisdom of Solomon; and behold more than Solomon here.

32. The men of Ninive shall rise in the judgment with this generation, and shall condemn it; because they did penance at the preaching of Jonas; and behold more than Jonas here.

33. No man lighteth a candle, and putteth it in a hidden place, nor under a

bushel; but upon a candlestick, that they that come in, may see the light.

34. The light of thy body is thy eye. If thy eye be single, thy whole body will be lightsome: but if it be evil, thy body also will be darksome.

35. Take heed therefore, that the light which is in thee, be not darkness.

36. If then thy whole body be lightsome, having no part of darkness; the whole shall be lightsome; and as a bright lamp, shall enlighten thee.

37. And as He was speaking, a certain Pharisee prayed Him, that He would dine with him. And He going in, sat down to eat.

38. And the Pharisee began to say, thinking within himself, why He was not washed before dinner.

39. And the Lord said to him: Now you Pharisees make clean the outside of the cup and of the platter; but your inside is full of rapine and iniquity.

40. Ye fools, did not He that made that which is without, make also that which is within?

41. But yet that which remaineth, give alms: and behold, all things are clean unto you.

42. But woe to you, Pharisees, because you tithe mint and rue and every herb; and pass over judgment, and the charity of God. Now these things you ought to have done, and not to leave the other undone.

43. Woe to you, Pharisees, because you love the uppermost seats in the synagogues, and salutations in the market place.

44. Woe to you, because you are as sepulchres that appear not, and men that walk over are not aware.

45. And one of the lawyers answering, saith to Him: Master, in saying these things, Thou reproachest us also.

46. But He said: Woe to you lawyers also, because you load men with burdens which they cannot bear, and you yourselves touch not the packs with one of your fingers.

47. Woe to you who build the monuments of the prophets: and your fathers killed them.

48. Truly you bear witness that you consent to the doings of your fathers: for they indeed killed them, and you build their sepulchres.

49. For this cause also the wisdom of God said: I will send to them prophets and apostles; and some of them they will kill and persecute.

50. That the blood of all the prophets which was shed from the foundation of the world, may be required of this generation,

51. From the blood of Abel unto the blood of Zacharias, who was slain between the altar and the temple: Yea I say to you, it shall be required of this generation.

52. Woe to you lawyers, for you have taken away the key of knowledge: you yourselves have not entered in, and those that were entering in, you have hindered.

53. And as He was saying these things to them, the Pharisees and the lawyers began violently to urge Him, and to oppress His mouth about many

Mancipia Publications

54. Lying in wait for Him, and seeking to catch something from His mouth, that they might accuse Him.

Imitation of Christ, Book 3, Chapter 7
Grace Is to be Hid under the Guardianship of Humility

My son, it is more profitable and more safe for thee to hide the grace of devotion and not to be elevated with it, not to speak much of it, not to consider it much, but rather to despise thyself the more and to be afraid of it, as given to one unworthy.

Thou must not depend too much on this affection which may be quickly changed into the contrary.

When thou has grace think within thyself how miserable and poor thou are wont to be when thou are without it.

Nor does the progress of a spiritual life consist so much in having the grace of consolation, as in bearing the want of it with humility, resignation, and patience, so as not to grow remiss in your exercise of prayer at that time, nor to suffer thyself to omit any of your accustomed good works.

But that thou willingly do what lies in thee, according to the best of thy ability and understanding, and take care not wholly to neglect thyself through the dryness or anxiety of mind which thou feel.

2. For there are many who when things succeed not well with them presently grow impatient or slothful.

Now the way of man is not always in his own power, but it belongs to God to give and to comfort when He will, and as much as He will, and to whom He will, and as it shall please Him and no more.

Some, wanting discretion, have ruined themselves upon occasion of the grace of devotion, because they were desirous of doing more than they could, not weighing well the measure of their own weakness, but following rather the inclinations of the heart than the dictates of reason.

And because they presumptuously undertook greater things than were pleasing to God, therefore they quickly lost His grace.

They became needy and were left in a wretched condition, who had built themselves a nest in Heaven to the end, that being thus humbled and impoverished they might learn not to trust to their own wings, but to hide themselves under Mine.

Those who are yet but novices and unexperienced in the way of the Lord, if they will not govern themselves by the counsel of discreet persons, will be easily deceived and overthrown.

3. And if they will rather follow their own judgment than believe others who have more experience, their future is full of danger if they continue to refuse to lay down their own conceits.

They that are wise in their own eyes seldom humbly suffer themselves to be ruled by others.

It is better to have little knowledge with humility and a weak understanding, than greater treasures of learning with self-conceit.

It is better for thee to have less than much, which may puff thee up with pride.

He is not so discreet as he ought to be who gives himself up wholly to joy, forgetting his former poverty and the chaste fear of God, which apprehends the loss of that grace which is offered.

Neither is he so virtuously wise who, in the time of adversity or any tribulation whatsoever, carries himself in a desponding way and conceives and reposes less confidence in Me than he ought.

4. He who is too secure in time of peace will often be found too much dejected and fearful in time of war.

If thou could but always continue humble and little in thine own eyes and keep thy spirit in due order and subjection, thou would not fall so easily into dangers and offenses.

It is a good counsel that when thou has conceived the spirit of fervor, thou should meditate how it will be with thee when that light shall leave thee.

Which, when it shall happen, remember that the light may return again, which, for thine instruction and My glory I have withdrawn from thee for a time.

5. Such a trial is oftentimes more profitable than if thou were always to have prosperity according to thy will.

For a man's merits are not to be estimated by his having many visions or consolations, nor by his knowledge in scriptures, nor by his being placed in a more elevated station.

But by his being grounded in true humility and replenished with divine charity; by his seeking always purely and entirely the honor of God; by his esteeming himself as nothing and sincerely despising himself, and being better pleased to be despised and humbled by others than to be the object of their esteem.

True Devotion #79

To rid ourselves of self we must: thoroughly recognize, by the light of the Holy Ghost, our inward corruption, our incapacity for every good thing useful for salvation, our weakness in all things, our inconstancy at all times, our unworthiness of every grace, and our iniquity in every position. The sin of our first father has spoilt us all, soured us, puffed us up and corrupted us, as the leaven sours, puffs up and corrupts the dough into which it is put. The actual sins which we have committed, whether mortal or venial, pardoned though they may be, have nevertheless increased our concupiscence, our weakness, our inconstancy and our corruption, and have left evil remains in our souls.

Our bodies are so corrupted that they are called by the Holy Ghost bodies of sin, conceived in sin, nourished in sin, and capable of all sin—bodies subject to thousands of maladies, which go on corrupting from day to day, and which engender nothing but disease, vermin and corruption.

Our soul, united to our body, has become so carnal that it is called flesh: "All flesh having corrupted its way." We have nothing for our portion but pride and blindness of spirit, hardness of heart, weakness and inconstancy of soul, concupiscence, revolted passions, and sicknesses in the body. We are naturally prouder than peacocks, more groveling than toads, more vile than unclean animals, more envious than serpents, more gluttonous than hogs, more furious than tigers, lazier than tortoises, weaker than reeds, and more capricious than weathercocks. We have within ourselves nothing but nothingness and sin, and we deserve nothing but the anger of God and everlasting Hell.

Fourth Day ———————

Daily Prayers during the First Week: Litany of the Holy Ghost on page 160, the *Ave Maris Stella* on page 156, and the *Litany of the Blessed Virgin* on page 161.

Gospel according to Saint Luke 13

And there were present, at that very time, some that told Him of the Galileans whose blood Pilate had mingled with their sacrifices.

2. And He answering, said to them: Think you that these Galileans were sinners above all the men of Galilee, because they suffered such things?

3. No, I say to you: but unless you shall do penance, you shall all likewise perish.

4. Or those eighteen upon whom the tower fell in Siloe, and slew them: think you, that they also were debtors above all the men that dwelt in Jerusalem?

5. No, I say to you; but except you do penance, you shall all likewise perish.

6. He spoke also this parable: A certain man had a fig tree planted in his vineyard, and he came seeking fruit on it, and found none.

7. And he said to the dresser of the vineyard: behold, for these three years I come seeking fruit on this fig tree, and I find none. Cut it down therefore: why let it cumber the ground?

8. But he answering, said to him: Lord, let it alone this year also, until I dig about it, and dung it.

9. And if happily it bear fruit: but if not, then after that you shall cut it down.

10. And He was teaching in their synagogue on their Sabbath.

11. And behold there was a woman, who had a spirit of infirmity eighteen years: and she was bowed together, neither could she look upwards at all.

12. Whom when Jesus saw, He called her to Him and said to her: Woman, you are delivered from your infirmity.

13. And He laid His hands upon her, and immediately she was made straight, and glorified God.

14. And the ruler of the synagogue (being angry that Jesus had healed on the Sabbath) answering, said to the multitude: Six days there are wherein you ought to work. In them therefore come, and be healed; and not on the Sabbath day.

15. And the Lord answering him, said: You hypocrites, do not every one of

you, on the Sabbath day, loose his ox or his ass from the manger, and lead them to water?

16. And ought not this daughter of Abraham, whom Satan has bound these eighteen years, be loosed from this bond on the Sabbath day?

17. And when He said these things, all His adversaries were ashamed: and all the people rejoiced for all the things that were gloriously done by Him.

18. He said therefore: To what is the Kingdom of God like and whereunto shall I resemble it?

19. It is like to a grain of mustard seed, which a man took and cast into his garden, and it grew and became a great tree, and the birds of the air lodged in the branches thereof.

20. And again He said: Whereunto shall I esteem the Kingdom of God to be like?

21. It is like to leaven, which a woman took and hid in three measures of meal, till the whole was leavened.

22. And He went through the cities and towns teaching, and making His journey to Jerusalem.

23. And a certain man said to Him: Lord, are they few that are saved? But He said to them:

24. Strive to enter by the narrow gate; for many, I say to you, shall seek to enter, and shall not be able.

25. But when the master of the house shall be gone in, and shall shut the door, and you shall begin to stand without, and knock at the door, saying: Lord, open to us. And he answering, shall say to you: I know you not, from whence you are.

26. Then you shall begin to say: We have eaten and drunk in your presence, and you have taught in our streets.

27. And he shall say to you: I know you not, from whence are you: depart from me, all you workers of iniquity.

28. There shall be weeping and gnashing of teeth, when you shall see Abraham and Isaac and Jacob, and all the prophets, in the Kingdom of God, and you yourselves thrust out.

29. And they shall come from the east and the west, and the north and the south; and shall sit down in the Kingdom of God.

30. And behold, they are last that shall be first, and they are first that shall be last.

31. The same day, there came some of the Pharisees, saying to Him: Depart, and get thee hence, for Herod has a mind to kill thee.

32. And He said to them: Go and tell that fox, Behold, I cast out devils, and do cures today and tomorrow, and the third day I am consummated.

33. Nevertheless I must walk today and tomorrow, and the day following, because it cannot be that a prophet perish, out of Jerusalem.

34. Jerusalem, Jerusalem, that kills the prophets, and stones them that are sent to you, how often would I have gathered your children as the bird does her brood under her wings, and you would not?

Mancipia Publications

35. Behold your house shall be left to you desolate. And I say to you that you shall not see Me till the time come when you shall say: Blessed is He that comes in the name of the Lord.

Imitation of Christ, Book 3, Chapter 8
Of Acknowledging Our Unworthiness in the Sight of God
DISCIPLE

I will speak to my Lord, I who am but dust and ashes. If I think anything better of myself, behold Thou stand against me and my sins bear witness to the truth, and I cannot contradict it.

But if I humble myself and acknowledge my own nothingness, and cast away all manner of esteem of myself and (as I really am) account myself to be mere dust, Thy grace will be favorable to me and Thy light will draw near to my heart; and all self-esteem, how ever small, will be sunk in the depth of my own nothingness and there lose itself forever.

It is there Thou show me to myself, what I am, what I have been and what I am to come to; for I am nothing and I knew it not.

If I am left to myself, behold I am nothing and all weakness; but if Thou should graciously look upon me, I presently become strong and am filled with a new joy.

And it is very wonderful that I am so quickly raised up and so graciously embraced by Thee; I, who by my own weight, am always sinking to the bottom.

2. It is Thy love that effects this, freely preventing me and assisting me in so many necessities, reserving me also from grievous dangers, and as I may truly say, delivering me from innumerable evils.

For by an evil loving of myself, I lost myself, and by seeking Thee alone and purely loving Thee, I found both myself and Thee, and by this love have more profoundly annihilated myself.

Because Thou, O most sweet Lord, art bountiful to me above all desert and above all I dare hope or ask for.

3. Blessed be Thou, O my God, for though I am unworthy of all good, yet Thy generosity and infinite goodness never ceases to do good, even to those who are ungrateful and that are turned away from Thee.

Oh, convert us unto Thee, that we may be thankful, humble, and devout; for Thou art our salvation, our power, and our strength.

Imitation of Christ, Book 3, Chapter 13
The Obedience of a Humble Subject after the Example of Jesus Christ
CHRIST

Son, he who strives to withdraw himself from obedience withdraws himself from grace, and he that seeks to have things for his own particular use loses such as are common.

If a man does not freely and willingly submit himself to his superior, it is a sign that his flesh is not, as yet, perfectly obedient to him, but often times rebels and murmurs.

Learn then to submit thyself readily to thy superior if thou desire to subdue thine own flesh.

For the outward enemy is sooner overcome if the inward man be not laid waste.

There is no more troublesome or worse enemy to the soul than thyself, when not agreeing well with the Spirit.

You must, in good earnest, conceive a true contempt of yourself if you will prevail over flesh and blood.

Because you have yet a too inordinate love for yourself, therefore are you afraid to resign yourself wholly to the will of others.

2. But what great matter is it if you, who are but dust and a mere nothing, submit yourself for God's sake to man, when I, the Most High, Who created all things out of nothing, have for your sake humbly subjected Myself to man?

I became the most humble and most abject of all, that you might learn to overcome your pride by My humility.

Learn, O dust, to obey; learn to humble yourself, you that are but dirt and mire, and to cast yourself down under the feet of all men.

Learn to break your own will and to yield yourself up to all subjection.

3. Conceive an indignation against yourself; suffer not the swelling of pride to live in you, but make yourself so submissive and little, that all may trample on you and tread you underfoot as the dirt of the streets.

What have you, vain man, to complain of?

What answer can you make, O wretched sinner, to those that reproach you, you that have often offended God and many times deserved Hell?

But Mine eye has spared you, because your soul was precious in My sight, that you might know My love and might be always thankful for My favor and that you might give yourself continually to true subjection and humility, and bear with patience to be despised by all.

True Devotion #80

After this, ought we to be astonished if Our Lord has said that whoever wishes to follow Him must renounce himself and hate his own life, and that whosoever shall love his own life shall lose it, and whosoever shall hate it, shall save it?

He who is infinite Wisdom does not give commandments without reason, and He has commanded us to hate ourselves only because we so richly deserve to be hated. Nothing is worthier of love than God, and nothing is worthier of hatred than ourselves.

 "Lord, that I may see!"

Fifth Day ────────────

Daily Prayers during the First Week: *Litany of the Holy Ghost* on page 160, the *Ave Maris Stella* on page 156, and the *Litany of the Blessed Virgin* on page 161.

Gospel according to Saint Luke 16

And He said also to His disciples: there was a certain rich man who had a steward: and the same was accused to him, that he had wasted his goods.

2. And he called him, and said to him: How is it that I hear this of you? Give an account of your stewardship: for now you can be steward no longer.

3. And the steward said within himself: What shall I do, because my lord takes away from me the stewardship? To dig I am not able; to beg I am ashamed.

4. I know what I will do, that when I shall be removed from the stewardship, they may receive me into their houses.

5. Therefore calling together every one of his lord's debtors, he said to the first: How much do you owe my lord?

6. But he said: A hundred barrels of oil. And he said to him: Take your bill and sit down quickly, and write fifty.

7. Then he said to another: And how much do you owe? Who said: a hundred quarters of wheat. He said to him: Take your bill, and write eighty.

8. And the lord commended the unjust steward, forasmuch as he had done wisely: for the children of this world are wiser in their generation than the children of light.

9. And I say to you: Make to you friends of the mammon of iniquity; that when you shall fail, they may receive you into everlasting dwellings.

10. He that is faithful in that which is least, is faithful also in that which is greater: and he that is unjust in that which is little, is unjust also in that which is greater.

11. If then you have not been faithful in the unjust mammon; who will trust you with that which is true?

12. And if you have not been faithful in that which is another's; who will give you that which is your own?

13. No servant can serve two masters: for either he will hate the one, and love the other; or he will hold to the one, and despise the other. You cannot serve God and mammon.

14. Now the Pharisees, who were covetous, heard all these things: and they derided Him.

15. And He said to them: You are they who justify yourselves before men, but God knows your hearts; for that which is high to men, is an abomination before God.

16. The law and the prophets were until John; from that time the Kingdom of God is preached, and every one uses violence towards it.

17. And it is easier for Heaven and earth to pass, than one tittle of the law to fall.

18. Every one that puts away his wife, and marries another commits

Manual for the Total Consecration to Mary   39

adultery: and he that marries her that is put away from her husband, commits adultery.

19. There was a certain rich man, who was clothed in purple and fine linen; and feasted sumptuously every day.

20. And there was a certain beggar, named Lazarus, who lay at his gate, full of sores.

21. Desiring to be filled with the crumbs that fell from the rich man's table, and no one did give him; moreover the dogs came, and licked his sores.

22. And it came to pass, that the beggar died, and was carried by the angels into Abraham's bosom. And the rich man also died: and he was buried in Hell.

23. And lifting up his eyes when he was in torments, he saw Abraham afar off, and Lazarus in his bosom:

24. And he cried, and said: Father Abraham, have mercy on me and send Lazarus, that he may dip the tip of his finger in water, to cool my tongue: for I am tormented in this flame.

25. And Abraham said to him: Son, remember that you did receive good things in your lifetime and likewise Lazarus evil things, but now he is comforted; and you are tormented.

26. And besides all this, between us and you, there is fixed a great chaos; so that they who would pass from here to you cannot, nor from there come here.

27. And he said: Then, father, I beseech you, that you would send him to my father's house, for I have five brethren.

28. That he may testify to them, lest they also come into this place of torments.

29. And Abraham said to him: They have Moses and the prophets; let them hear them.

30. But he said: No, Father Abraham: but if one went to them from the dead, they will do penance.

31. And he said to him: If they hear not Moses and the prophets neither will they believe, if one rise again from the dead.

Imitation of Christ, Book 3, Chapter 20
The Confession of Our Own Infirmity and the Miseries of This Life
DISCIPLE

I will confess against myself my injustice. I will confess to Thee, O Lord, my infirmity.

It is oftentimes a small thing which casts me down and troubles me.

I make a resolution to behave myself valiantly; but when a small temptation comes I am brought into great straits.

It is sometimes a very trifling thing from which proceeds a grievous temptation.

And when I think myself somewhat safe, I find myself sometimes, when I least apprehend it, almost overcome with a small blast.

2. Behold, then, O Lord, my abjection and frailty, every way known to Thee.

Have pity on me and draw me out of the mire, that I stick not fast therein, that I may not be utterly cast down forever.

This it is which often drives me back and confounds me in Thy sight, to find that I am so subject to fall and have so little strength to resist my passions.

And although I do not altogether consent, yet their assaults are troublesome and grievous to me, and it is exceedingly irksome to live thus always in a conflict.

Hence my infirmity is made known to me, because wicked thoughts do always much more easily rush in upon me than they can be cast out again.

3. Oh, that Thou, the most mighty God of Israel, the zealous lover of faithful souls, wouldst behold the labor and sorrow of Thy servant, and stand by me in all my undertakings.

Strengthen me with heavenly fortitude, lest the old man, the miserable flesh, not fully subject to the spirit, prevail and get the upper hand, against which we must fight as long as we breathe in this most wretched life.

Alas! what kind of life is this, where afflictions and miseries are never wanting; where all things are full of snares and enemies.

For when one tribulation or temptation is gone another comes: yes, and while the first still lasts, many others come on and these unexpected.

4. How can a life be loved that has such great bitterness, that is subject to so many calamities and miseries.

How can it be called life since it begets so many deaths and plagues?

And yet it is loved and many seek their delight in it.

Many blame the world that it is deceitful and vain, yet they are not willing to quit it, because the concupiscence of the flesh overmuch prevails.

But there are some things that draw them to love the world—others to despise it.

The concupiscence of the flesh, the concupiscence of the eyes, and the pride of life (John 2:16), draw to the love of the world; but the pains and miseries, which justly follow these things, breed a hatred and loathing of the world.

5. But alas! the pleasure of sin prevails over the worldly soul and under these briers she imagines there are delights; because she has neither seen nor tasted the sweetness of God, nor the internal pleasures of virtue.

But they that perfectly despise the world and study to live to God under holy discipline, experience the divine sweetness that is promised for those who forsake all; and such clearly see how grievously the world is mistaken and how many ways it is imposed upon.

True Devotion #81

In order to rid ourselves of self, we must die to ourselves daily. That is to say, we must renounce the operations of the powers of our soul and of the senses of our body. We must see as if we saw not, understand as if we understood not, and make use of the things of this world as if we made no use of them at all. This is what Saint Paul calls dying daily. "Unless the grain of wheat falling into the ground die, itself remains alone," and brings forth no good fruit. If we do not die to ourselves, and if our holiest devotions do not incline us to this necessary and useful death, we shall bring forth no fruit worth anything, and our devotions will become useless. All our good works will be stained by self-love and our own will; and this will cause God to hold in abomination the greatest sacrifices we can make and the best actions we can do; so that at our death we shall find our hands empty of virtues and of merits and we shall not have one spark of pure love, which is only communicated to souls dead to themselves, souls whose life is hidden with Jesus Christ in God.

Sixth Day _____

Daily Prayers during the First Week: Litany of the Holy Ghost on page 160, the *Ave Maris Stella* on page 156, and the *Litany of the Blessed Virgin* on page 161.

Gospel according to Saint Luke 17

And He said to His disciples: It is impossible that scandals should not come: but woe to him through whom they come.

2. It were better for him, that a millstone were hanged about his neck, and he cast into the sea, than that he should scandalize one of these little ones.

3. Take heed to yourselves. If your brother sins against you, reprove him: and if he does penance, forgive him.

4. And if he sins against you seven times in a day, and seven times in a day be converted to you, saying: I repent; forgive him.

5. And the Apostles said to the Lord: Increase our faith.

6. And the Lord said: If you had faith like to a grain of mustard seed, you might say to this mulberry tree, Be ye rooted up, and be ye transplanted into the sea: and it would obey you.

7. But which of you having a servant ploughing, or feeding cattle, will say to him, when he is come from the field: immediately go, sit down to meat:

8. And will not rather say to him: Make ready my supper, and gird yourself and serve me, while I eat and drink, and afterwards you shall eat and drink?

9. Does he thank that servant, for doing the things which he commanded him?

10. I think not. So you also, when you shall have done all these things that are commanded you, say: We are unprofitable servants; we have done that which we ought to do.

11. And it came to pass, as He was going to Jerusalem, He passed through the midst of Samaria and Galilee.

12. And as He entered into a certain town, there met Him ten men that were lepers, who stood afar off:

13. And lifted up their voice saying: Jesus, Master, have mercy on us.

14. Whom when He saw, He said: Go, show yourselves to the priests. And it came to pass, as they went, they were made clean.

Mancipia Publications

15. And one of them, when he saw that he was made clean, went back, with a loud voice glorifying God.

16. And he fell on his face before His feet giving thanks: and this was a Samaritan.

17. And Jesus answering, said: Were not ten made clean? and where are the nine?

18. There is no one found to return and give glory to God, but this stranger.

19. And He said to him: Arise, go your way; for your faith has made you whole.

20. And being asked by the Pharisees, when the Kingdom of God should come, He answered them, and said: The Kingdom of God comes not with observation:

21. Neither shall they say: Behold here, or behold there. For lo, the Kingdom of God is within you.

22. And He said to His disciples: The days will come, when you shall desire to see one day of the Son of Man; and you shall not see it.

23. And they will say to you: See here, and see there. Go you not after, nor follow them:

24. For as the lightning that lightens from under Heaven, shines to the parts that are under Heaven, so shall the Son of Man be in His day.

25. But first He must suffer many things, and be rejected by this generation.

26. And as it came to pass in the days of Noe, so shall it be also in the days of the Son of Man.

27. They did eat and drink, they married wives, and were given in marriage, until the day that Noe entered into the ark: and the flood came and destroyed them all.

28. Likewise as it came to pass, in the days of Lot: they did eat and drink, they bought and sold, they planted and built.

29. And in the day that Lot went out of Sodom, it rained fire and brimstone from Heaven, and destroyed them all.

30. Even thus shall it be in the day when the Son of Man shall be revealed.

31. In that hour, he that shall be on the housetop, and his goods in the house, let him not go down to take them away: and he that shall be in the field, in like manner, let him not return back.

32. Remember Lot's wife.

33. Whosoever shall seek to save his life, shall lose it: and whosoever shall lose it, shall preserve it.

34. I say to you: in that night there shall be two men in one bed; the one shall be taken, and the other shall be left.

35. Two women shall be grinding together; the one shall be taken, and the other shall be left: two men shall be in the field; the one shall be taken, and the other shall be left.

36. They answering, say to Him: Where, Lord?

37. Who said to them: Wheresoever the body shall be, there will the eagles also be gathered together.

Imitation of Christ, Book 3, Chapter 30
Of Asking the Divine Assistance, and of Confidence of Recovering Grace
CHRIST

Son, I am the Lord, Who gives strength in the day of trouble.

Come to Me when it is not well with thee.

This is that which most of all hinders heavenly comfort, that thou art slow in turning thyself to prayer.

For before you earnestly pray to Me you seek in the meantime many comforts and delight thyself in outward things.

And hence it comes to pass that all things avail thee little till thou take notice that I am He that delivers those that trust in Me. Nor is there out of Me any powerful help, or profitable counsel, or lasting remedy.

But now having recovered spirit after the storm, grow thou strong again in the light of My tender mercies; for I am at hand to repair all, not only to the full, but even with abundance and above measure.

2. Is anything difficult to Me? or shall I be like one that promises and does not perform?

Where is thy faith? Stand firmly and with perseverance.

Have patience and be of good courage, comfort will come to thee in its proper season.

Wait for Me, wait, I will come and cure thee.

It is a temptation that troubles thee, and a vain fear that frightens thee.

What does that solicitude about future accidents bring thee but only sorrow upon sorrow? "Sufficient for the day is the evil thereof."

It is a vain and unprofitable thing to conceive either grief or joy for future things, which perhaps will never happen.

3. But it is incident to man to be deluded with such imaginations; and a sign of a soul that is yet weak and to be easily drawn away by the suggestions of the enemy.

For he cares not whether it be with things true or false that he abuses and deceives thee, whether he overthrows thee with the love of things present or the fear of things to come.

"Let not, therefore thy heart be troubled and let it not be afraid."

Believe in Me and trust in My mercy.

When you think I am far from thee, I am often nearest to thee.

When you judge that all is lost, then oftentimes it is that thou are in the way of gaining the greatest merit.

All is not lost when anything falls out otherwise than thou would have it.

Thou must not judge according to thy present feeling, nor give thyself up in such manner to any trouble, from whencesoever it comes, nor take it so as if all hope were gone of being delivered out of it.

4. Think not thyself wholly forsaken, although for a time I have sent thee some tribulation, or withdrawn from thee the comfort which thou desire; for this is the way to the Kingdom of Heaven.

And without doubt it is more expedient for thee, and for the rest of My

Mancipia Publications

servants, that thou be exercised by adversities than that thou should have all things according to thine inclination.

I know thy secret thoughts; I know that it is very expedient for thy soul that thou should sometimes be left without consolation, lest thou should be puffed up with much success and should take a complacence in thyself, imagining thyself to be what thou art not.

What I have given I can justly take away, and restore it again when I please.

5. When I give it, it is still Mine; when I take it away again I take not anything that is thine; for every good gift and every perfect gift is Mine.

If I send thee affliction or any adversity, repine not, neither let thy heart be cast down.

I can quickly raise thee up again and turn all thy burden into joy.

Nevertheless, I am just and greatly to be praised when I deal thus with thee.

6. If thou think rightly and consider things in truth thou ought never to be so much dejected and troubled for any adversity, but rather to rejoice and give thanks.

Yea, even to account this as a special subject of joy, that afflicting thee with sorrows I spare thee not.

"As My Father has loved me I also have loved you," said I to My beloved disciples, whom certainly I did not send temporal joys, but great conflicts; not honors, but contempt; not idleness, but labors; not rest, but to "bring forth much fruit in patience." Remember these words, O My son.

True Devotion #82

We must choose, therefore, among all the devotions to the Blessed Virgin, the one which draws us most toward this death to ourselves, inasmuch as it will be the best and the most sanctifying. For we must not think that all that shines is gold, that all that tastes sweet is honey, or that all that is easy to do and is done by the greatest number is the most sanctifying. As there are secrets of nature by which natural operations are performed more easily, in a short time and at little cost, so also are there secrets in the order of grace by which supernatural operations, such as ridding ourselves of self, filling ourselves with God, and becoming perfect, are performed more easily.

The practice which I am about to disclose is one of these secrets of grace, unknown to the greatest number of Christians, known even to few of the devout, and practiced and relished by a lesser number still.

Seventh Day _____

Daily Prayers during the First Week: Litany of the Holy Ghost on page 160,
the *Ave Maris Stella* on page 156, and the *Litany of the Blessed Virgin* on page 161.

Gospel according to Saint Luke 18

And He spoke also a parable to them, that we ought always to pray, and not to faint,

2. Saying: There was a judge in a certain city, who feared not God, nor regarded man.

3. And there was a certain widow in that city, and she came to him, saying: Avenge me of my adversary.

4. And he would not for a long time. But afterwards he said within himself: Although I fear not God, nor regard man.

5. Yet because this widow is troublesome to me, I will avenge her, lest continually coming she weary me.

6. And the Lord said: Hear what the unjust judge says.

7. And will not God revenge His elect who cry to Him day and night: and will He have patience in their regard?

8. I say to you, that He will quickly revenge them. But yet the Son of Man, when He comes, shall He find, think you, faith on earth?

9. And to some who trusted in themselves as just, and despised others, He spoke also this parable:

10. Two men went up into the temple to pray: the one a Pharisee, and the other a publican.

11. The Pharisee standing, prayed thus with himself: O God, I give you thanks that I am not as the rest of men, extortioners, unjust, adulterers, as also is this publican.

12. I fast twice in a week: I give tithes of all that I possess.

13. And the publican, standing afar off, would not so much as lift up his eyes towards Heaven; but struck his breast, saying: O God, be merciful to me a sinner.

14. I say to you, this man went down into his house justified rather than the other: because every one that exalts himself shall be humbled: and he that humbles himself shall be exalted.

15. And they brought to Him also infants, that He might touch them. Which when the disciples saw, they rebuked them.

16. But Jesus, calling them together, said: Suffer children to come to Me, and forbid them not: for of such is the Kingdom of God.

17. Amen, I say to you: Whosoever shall not receive the Kingdom of God as a child, shall not enter into it.

18. And a certain ruler asked Him, saying: Good Master, what shall I do to possess everlasting life?

19. And Jesus said to him: Why do you call Me good? None is good but God alone.

20. You know the commandments: You shall not kill: You shall not commit adultery: You shall not steal: You shall not bear false witness: Honor

Mancipia Publications

your father and mother.

21. Who said: All these things have I kept from my youth.

22. Which when Jesus had heard, He said to him: Yet one thing is wanting to you: sell all whatever you have, and give to the poor, and you shall have treasure in Heaven: and come, follow Me.

23. He having heard these things, became sorrowful; for he was very rich.

24. And Jesus seeing him become sorrowful, said: How hardly shall they that have riches enter into the Kingdom of God.

25. For it is easier for a camel to pass through the eye of a needle than for a rich man to enter into the Kingdom of God.

26. And they that heard it, said: Who then can be saved?

27. He said to them: The things that are impossible with men, are possible with God.

28. Then Peter said: Behold, we have left all things, and have followed You.

29. Who said to them: Amen, I say to you, there is no man that has left house, or parents, or brethren, or wife, or children, for the Kingdom of God's sake,

30. Who shall not receive much more in this present time, and in the world to come life everlasting.

31. Then Jesus took to Him the twelve, and said to them: Behold, we go up to Jerusalem, and all things shall be accomplished which were written by the prophets concerning the Son of Man.

32. For He shall be delivered to the Gentiles, and shall be mocked, and scourged, and spit upon:

33. And after they have scourged Him, they will put Him to death; and the third day He shall rise again.

34. And they understood none of these things, and this word was hid from them, and they understood not the things that were said.

35. Now it came to pass, when He drew near to Jericho, that a certain blind man sat by the wayside, begging.

36. And when he heard the multitude passing by, he asked what this meant.

37. And they told him, that Jesus of Nazareth was passing by.

38. And he cried out, saying: Jesus, Son of David, have mercy on me.

39. And they that went before, rebuked him, that he should hold his peace: but he cried out much more: Son of David, have mercy on me.

40. And Jesus standing, commanded him to be brought to Him. And when he was come near, He asked him,

41. Saying: What will you that I do to you? But he said: Lord, that I may see.

42. And Jesus said to him: Receive your sight: your faith has made you whole.

43. And immediately he saw, and followed Him glorifying God. And all the people, when they saw it gave praise to God.

Imitation of Christ, Book 3, Chapter 47
CHRIST

Son, be not dismayed with the labors which thou hast undertaken for Me; neither let the tribulations which befall thee cast thee down; but let My promise strengthen thee, and comfort thee in every event.

I am sufficient to reward thee beyond all measure.

Thou will not labor here long, nor will thou be always oppressed with sorrows.

Wait a little while and thou will see a speedy end of all thine evils.

The hour will come when labor and trouble will be no more.

All is little and short which passes away with time.

2. Do thy part well; mind what thou are about; labor faithfully in My vineyard, I will be thy reward.

Write, read, sing, sigh, keep silence, pray, bear thy crosses manfully; eternal life is worthy of all these, and greater combats.

Peace shall come in one day, which is known to the Lord; and it will not be a vicissitude of day and night, such as is at present; but everlasting light, infinite brightness, steadfast peace, and secure rest.

Thou will not then say: Who will deliver me from the body of this death? Nor will thou cry out: Woe is me, that my sojourning is prolonged. For death will be no more, but never-failing health; no anxiety, but blessed delight; and a society sweet and lovely.

Oh, if thou had seen the everlasting crown of the saints in Heaven, and in how great glory they now triumph who appeared contemptible heretofore to this world, and in a manner even unworthy of life, doubtless thou would immediately cast thyself down to the very earth, and would rather seek to be under the feet of all, than to have command over so much as one.

Neither would thou covet the pleasant days of this life, but would rather be glad to suffer tribulation for God's sake, and esteem it thy greatest gain to be reputed as nothing among men.

3. Ah! if thou did but relish these things, and suffer them to penetrate deeply into thy heart, how would thou dare so much as once to complain!

Are not all painful labors to be endured for everlasting life?

It is no small matter to lose or gain the Kingdom of God.

Lift up therefore thy face to Heaven. Behold, I, and all My saints with Me, who in this world have had a great conflict, do now rejoice, are now comforted, are now secure, are now at rest, and they will for all eternity abide with Me in the Kingdom of My Father.

Do thy part well; mind what thou are about;
labor faithfully in My vineyard, I will be thy reward.
Write, read, sing, sigh, keep silence, pray, bear thy
crosses manfully; eternal life is worthy
of all these, and greater combats.

Mancipia Publications

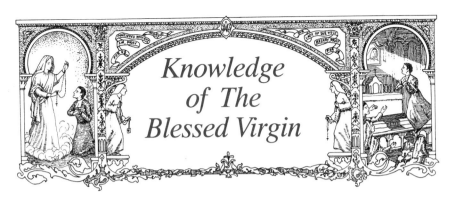

Second Period — Second Week

During the second week you should apply yourself, in all your prayers and works each day, to know the Blessed Virgin. You should ask this knowledge of the Holy Ghost. You must unite yourself to Jesus through Mary—this is the characteristic of the devotion; therefore, Saint Louis De Montfort asks that the second week be employed in acquiring a knowledge of the Blessed Virgin.

Mary is your sovereign and your mediatrix, your Mother and your Mistress. Endeavor then to know the effects of this loyalty, of this mediation, and of this maternity, as well as the grandeurs and prerogatives which are the foundation or consequences thereof. Our Mother is also a perfect mold wherein you are to be molded in order to make her intentions and dispositions yours. This you cannot achieve without studying the interior life of Mary; namely, her virtues, her sentiments, her actions, her participation in the mysteries of Christ and her union with Him.

Daily Prayers during the Second Week are the: *Litany of the Holy Ghost*, the *Ave Maris Stella*, Saint Louis De Montfort's *Prayer to Mary* and the Recitation of the *Rosary.*

Spiritual Exercises during the Second Week are: Acts of Love, pious affections for the Blessed Virgin, imitation of her virtues, especially her profound humility, her lively faith, her blind obedience, her continual mental prayer, her mortification in all things, her divine purity, her ardent charity, her heroic patience, her angelic sweetness and her divine wisdom; "these being," as Saint Louis De Montfort says, "the ten principal virtues of the Blessed Virgin."

First Day _____

Daily prayers during the Second Week: Litany of the Holy Ghost on page 160, the *Ave Maris Stella* on page 156, Saint Louis De Montfort's *Prayer to Mary* on page 157 and the Recitation of the *Rosary*.

Gospel according to Saint Luke 1:1-23

Forasmuch as many have taken in hand to set forth in order a narration of the things that have been accomplished among us;

2. According as they have delivered them unto us, who from the beginning were eyewitnesses and ministers of the word:

3. It seemed good to me also, having diligently attained to all things from the beginning, to write to thee in order, most excellent Theophilus,

4. That thou mayest know the verity of those words in which thou hast been instructed.

5. There was in the days of Herod, the king of Judea, a certain priest named Zachary, of the course of Abia; and his wife was of the daughters of Aaron, and her name Elizabeth.

6. And they were both just before God, walking in all the commandments and justifications of the Lord without blame.

7. And they had no son, for that Elizabeth was barren, and they both were well advanced in years.

8. And it came to pass, when he executed the priestly function in the order of his course before God,

9. According to the custom of the priestly office, it was his lot to offer incense, going into the temple of the Lord.

10. And all the multitude of the people was praying without, at the hour of incense.

11. And there appeared to him an angel of the Lord, standing at the right side of the altar of incense.

12. And Zachary seeing him, was troubled, and fear fell upon him.

13. But the angel said to him: Fear not, Zachary, for thy prayer is heard; and thy wife Elizabeth shall bear thee a son, and thou shalt call his name John:

14. And thou shalt have joy and gladness, and many shall rejoice in his nativity.

15. For he shall be great before the Lord: and shall drink no wine nor strong drink and he shall be filled with the Holy Ghost even from his mother's womb.

16. And he shall convert many of the children of Israel to the Lord their God.

17. And he shall go before Him in the spirit and power of Elias: that he may turn the hearts of the fathers unto the children, and the incredulous to the wisdom of the just, to prepare unto the Lord a perfect people.

18. And Zachary said to the angel: Whereby shall I know this? for I am an old man, and my wife is advanced in years.

19. And the angel answering, said to him: I am Gabriel, who stand before

Mancipia Publications

God; and am sent to speak to thee, and to bring thee these good tidings.

20. And behold, thou shalt be dumb, and shalt not be able to speak until the day wherein these things shall come to pass, because thou hast not believed my words, which shall be fulfilled in their time.

21. And the people were waiting for Zachary; and they wondered that he tarried so long in the temple.

22. And when he came out, he could not speak to them, and they understood that he had seen a vision in the temple. And he made signs to them, and remained dumb.

23. And it came to pass, after the days of his office were accomplished, he departed to his own house.

True Devotion #1-21

It is through the most holy Virgin Mary that Jesus Christ came into the world, and it is also through her, He has to reign in the world.

Mary was singularly hidden during her life. It is on this account that the Holy Ghost and the Church call her *Alma Mater*—Mother secret and hidden. Her humility was so profound that she had no inclination on earth more powerful or more constant than that of hiding herself, from herself as well as from every other creature, so as to be known to God only.

He heard her prayers when she begged to be hidden, to be humbled and to be treated as in all respects poor and of no account. He took pleasure in hiding her from all human creatures, in her conception, in her birth, in her life, in her mysteries, and in her resurrection and Assumption. Even her parents did not know her, and the angels often asked one another: Who is that? (Cant. 3:6, 8:5), because the Most High either had hidden her from them, or if He did reveal anything, it was nothing compared to what He kept undisclosed.

God the Father consented that she should work no miracle, at least no public one, during her life, although He had given her the power to do so. God the Son consented that she should hardly ever speak, though He had communicated His wisdom to her. God the Holy Ghost, though she was His faithful spouse, consented that His Apostles and Evangelists should speak very little of her, and no more than was necessary to make Jesus Christ known.

Mary is the excellent masterpiece of the Most High, the knowledge and possession of which He has reserved to Himself. Mary is the admirable Mother of the Son, who took pleasure in humbling and concealing her during her life in order to favor her humility calling her by the name of woman, (John 2:4, 19:26) as if she were a stranger, although in His heart He esteemed and loved her above all angels and all men. Mary is the sealed fountain, the faithful spouse of the Holy Ghost, to whom He alone has entrance. Mary is the sanctuary and the repose of the Holy Trinity, where God dwells more magnificently and more divinely than in any other place in the universe, not excepting His dwelling between the Cherubim and Seraphim. Nor is any creature, no matter how pure, allowed to enter into that sanctuary except by a great and special privilege.

I say with the saints, the divine Mary is the terrestrial paradise of the New Adam, where He was made flesh by the operation of the Holy Ghost, in order to work there incomprehensible marvels. She is the grand and divine world of God, where there are beauties and treasures unspeakable. She is the magnificence of the Most High, where He hid, as in her bosom, His only Son, and in Him all that is most excellent and most precious. Oh, what grand and hidden things that mighty God has wrought in this admirable creature, as she herself had to acknowledge, in spite of her profound humility: He that is mighty has done great things to me. (Luke 1:49) The world knows them not, because it is both incapable and unworthy of such knowledge.

The saints have said admirable things of this holy city of God; and, as they themselves avow, they were never more eloquent and more content than when they spoke of her. Yet, after all they have said, they cry out that the height of her merits, which she has raised up to the throne of the Divinity, cannot be fully seen; that the breadth of her charity, which is broader than the earth, is in truth immeasurable; that the length of her power, which she exercises even over God Himself, is incomprehensible; and finally, that the depth of her humility, and of all her virtues and graces, is an abyss which never can be sounded. O height incomprehensible! O breadth unspeakable! O length immeasurable! O abyss impenetrable!

Every day, from one end of the earth to the other, in the highest heights of the heavens and in the profoundest depths of the abysses, everything preaches, everything publishes, the admirable Mary! The nine choirs of angels, men of all ages, sexes, conditions and religions, the good and the bad, nay, even the devils themselves, willingly or unwillingly, are compelled by force of truth to call her Blessed. Saint Bonaventure tells us that all the angels in Heaven cry out incessantly to her: "Holy, holy, holy Mary, Mother of God and Virgin;" and that they offer to her millions and millions of times a day, the Angelical Salutation, *Ave Maria*, prostrating themselves before her, and begging of her in her graciousness to honor them with some of her commands. Even Saint Michael, as Saint Augustine says, although the prince of the heavenly court, is the most zealous in honoring her and causing her to be honored, and is always anxiously awaiting the honor of going at her bidding to render service to some one of her servants.

The whole earth is full of her glory, especially among Christians, by whom she is taken as the protectress of many kingdoms, provinces, dioceses and cities. Many cathedrals are consecrated to God under her name. There is not a church without an altar in her honor, not a country nor a canton where there are not some miraculous images where all sorts of evils are cured, and all sorts of good gifts obtained. Who can count the confraternities and congregations in her honor? How many religious orders have been founded in her name and under her protection? How many members in these confraternities, and how many religious men and women in all these orders, who publish her praises and confess her mercies! There is not a little child who,

Mancipia Publications

as it lisps the *Hail Mary*, does not praise her. There is scarcely a sinner who, even in his obduracy, has not some spark of confidence in her. Nay, the very devils in Hell respect her while they fear her.

After that, we must cry out with the saints: "Of Mary there is never enough." We have not yet praised, exalted, honored, loved and served Mary as we ought. She deserves still more praise, still more respect, still more love and still more service.

After that, we must say with the Holy Ghost: All the glory of the King's daughter is within. (Ps. 44:14) The outward glory which Heaven and earth rival each other in laying at her feet, is as nothing in comparison with that which she receives within from the Creator and which is not known by creatures, who in their littleness are unable to penetrate the secret of secrets of the King.

After that, we must cry out with the Apostle, Eye has not seen, nor ear heard, nor man's heart comprehended (I Cor. 2:9) the beauties, the grandeurs, the excellences of Mary—the miracle of the miracles of grace, of nature and of glory. "If you wish to comprehend the Mother," says Saint Eucherius, "comprehend the Son; for she is the worthy Mother of God." "Here let every tongue be mute."

It is with a particular joy that my heart has dictated what I have just written, in order to show that the divine Mary has been up to this time unknown, and that this is one of the reasons that Jesus Christ is not known as He ought to be. If then, as is certain, the knowledge and the Kingdom of Jesus Christ are to come into the world, they will be but a necessary consequence of the knowledge and the kingdom of the most holy Virgin Mary, who brought Him into the world for the first time, and will make His second advent full of splendor.

Necessity of the Blessed Virgin and of Devotion to Her

I avow, with all the Church, that Mary, being a mere creature that has come from the hands of the Most High, is in comparison with His infinite Majesty less than an atom; or rather, she is nothing at all, because He only is He Who Is. (Exod. 3:14) Consequently that grand Lord, always independent and sufficient to Himself, never had, and has not now, any absolute need of the holy Virgin for the accomplishment of His will and for the manifestation of His glory. He has but to will in order to do everything.

Nevertheless, I say that, things being as they are now, that is, God having willed to commence and to complete His greatest works by the most holy Virgin ever since He created her, we may well think He will not change His conduct in the eternal ages; for He is God, and He changes not, either in His sentiments or in His conduct.

Article I—Mary was necessary to God in the Incarnation of the Word

It was only through Mary that God the Father gave His Only-begotten to the world. Whatever sighs the patriarchs may have sent forth, whatever prayers the prophets and the saints of the Old Law may have offered up to obtain this treasure, for full four thousand years—it was only Mary who merited and found grace before God by the force of her prayers and the eminence of her virtues. The world was unworthy, says Saint Augustine, to receive the Son of God directly from the Father's hands. He gave Him to Mary in order that the world might receive Him through her.

The Son of God became man for our salvation; but it was in Mary and by Mary. God the Holy Ghost formed Jesus Christ in Mary; but it was only after having asked her consent by one of the first ministers of His court.

God the Father communicated to Mary His fruitfulness, inasmuch as a mere creature was capable of it, in order that He might give her that power to produce His Son and all the members of His Mystical Body.

God the Son descended into her virginal womb, as the New Adam into His terrestrial paradise, to take His pleasure there, and to work in secret marvels of grace.

God, made Man, found His liberty in seeing Himself imprisoned in her womb. He made His omnipotence shine forth in letting Himself be carried by that humble maiden. He found His glory and His Father's in hiding His splendors from all creatures here below, and revealing them to Mary only. He glorified His independence and His majesty in depending on that sweet Virgin, in His conception, in His birth, in His presentation in the temple, in His hidden life of thirty years, and even in His death, where she was to be present in order that He might make with her but one same sacrifice, and be immolated to the Eternal Father by her consent; just as Isaac of old was offered by Abraham's consent to the will of God. It is she who nourished Him, supported Him, brought Him up and then sacrificed Him for us.

Oh, admirable and incomprehensible dependence of God, which the Holy Ghost could not pass over in silence in the Gospel, although He has hidden from us nearly all the admirable things which the Incarnate Wisdom did in His hidden life—as if He would enable us, by His revelation of that at least, to understand something of its excellence and infinite glory! Jesus Christ gave more glory to God the Father by submission to His Mother during those thirty years than He would have given Him in converting the whole world by the working of the most stupendous miracles. Oh, how highly we glorify God when, to please Him, we submit ourselves to Mary, after the example of Jesus Christ, our sole Exemplar!

If we examine closely the rest of Our Blessed Lord's life, we shall see that it was His will to begin His miracles by Mary. He sanctified Saint John in the womb of his mother, Saint Elizabeth, but it was by Mary's word. No sooner had she spoken than John was sanctified; and this was His first miracle of grace.

At the marriage of Cana He changed the water into wine, but it was at Mary's humble prayer; and this was His first miracle of nature. He began and continued His miracles by Mary, and He will continue them to the end of ages by Mary.

God the Holy Ghost, being barren in God—that is to say, not producing

54

another Divine Person—is become fruitful by Mary whom He has espoused. It was with her, in her and of her that He produced His Masterpiece, which is God made Man, and that He goes on producing daily, to the end of the world, the predestinate and the members of the Body of the adorable Head. This is the reason why He, the Holy Ghost, the more He finds Mary, His dear and inseparable Spouse, in any soul, the more active and mighty He becomes in producing Jesus Christ in that soul, and that soul in Jesus Christ.

It is not that we mean that Our Blessed Lady gives the Holy Ghost His fruitfulness, as if He had it not Himself. For inasmuch as He is God, He has the same fruitfulness or capacity of producing as the Father and the Son; only He does not bring it into action, as He does not produce another Divine person. But what we mean is, that the Holy Ghost chose to make use of Our Blessed Lady, though He had no absolute need of her, to bring His fruitfulness into action, by producing in her and by her Jesus Christ and His members—a mystery of grace unknown to even the wisest and the most spiritual among Christians.

Secret of Mary #23
A True Devotion to the Blessed Virgin is Indispensable

The difficulty, then, is to find really and truly the Most Blessed Virgin Mary in order to find all abundant grace. God, being the absolute Master, can confer directly by Himself that which He usually grants only through Mary. It would even be rash to deny that sometimes He does so. Nevertheless, Saint Thomas teaches that in the order of grace, established by Divine Wisdom, God ordinarily communicates Himself to men only through Mary. Therefore, if we would go up to Him and be united with Him, we must use the same means He used to come down to us, to be made man and to impart His graces to us. That means is a true devotion to Our Blessed Lady.

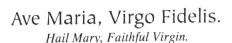

Ave Maria, Virgo Fidelis.
Hail Mary, Faithful Virgin.

Ave Maria, Mater Misericordiae.
Hail Mary, Mother of Mercy.

Second Day _____

Daily prayers during the Second Week: Litany of the Holy Ghost on page 160, the *Ave Maris Stella* on page 156, Saint Louis De Montfort's *Prayer to Mary* on page 157 and the Recitation of the *Rosary*.

Continuation of the holy Gospel according to Saint Luke 1:24-45

And after those days, Elizabeth his wife conceived, and hid herself five months, saying:

25. Thus hath the Lord dealt with me in the days wherein He hath had regard to take away my reproach among men.

26. And in the sixth month, the angel Gabriel was sent from God into a city of Galilee, called Nazareth,

27. To a virgin espoused to a man whose name was Joseph, of the house of David; and the virgin's name was Mary.

28. And the angel being come in, said unto her: Hail, full of grace, the Lord is with thee: Blessed art thou among women.

29. Who having heard, was troubled at his saying, and thought with herself what manner of salutation this should be.

30. And the angel said to her: Fear not, Mary, for thou hast found grace with God.

31. Behold thou shalt conceive in thy womb, and shalt bring forth a son; and thou shalt call His name JESUS.

32. He shall be great, and shall be called the Son of the most High; and the Lord God shall give unto Him the throne of David His father; and He shall reign in the house of Jacob forever.

33. And of His kingdom there shall be no end.

34. And Mary said to the angel: How shall this be done, because I know not man?

35. And the angel answering, said to her: The Holy Ghost shall come upon thee, and the power of the most High shall overshadow thee. And therefore also the Holy which shall be born of thee shall be called the Son of God.

36. And behold thy cousin Elizabeth, she also hath conceived a son in her old age; and this is the sixth month with her that is called barren:

37. Because no word shall be impossible with God.

38. And Mary said: Behold the handmaid of the Lord; be it done to me according to thy word. And the angel departed from her.

39. And Mary rising up in those days, went into the hill country with haste into a city of Juda.

40. And she entered into the house of Zachary, and saluted Elizabeth.

41. And it came to pass, that when Elizabeth heard the salutation of Mary, the infant leaped in her womb. And Elizabeth was filled with the Holy Ghost:

42. And she cried out with a loud voice, and said: Blessed art thou among women, and blessed is the Fruit of thy womb.

43. And whence is this to me, that the mother of my Lord should come to me?

44. For behold as soon as the voice of thy salutation sounded in my ears,

Mancipia Publications

the infant in my womb leaped for joy.

45. And blessed art thou that has believed, because those things shall be accomplished that were spoken to thee by the Lord.

True Devotion #22-48
Mary is Necessary to God in the Sanctification of Souls

The conduct which the Three Persons of the Most Holy Trinity have deigned to pursue in the Incarnation and the first coming of Jesus Christ, They still pursue daily, in an invisible manner, throughout the whole Church; and They will still pursue it even to the consummation of ages in the last coming of Jesus Christ.

God the Father made an assemblage of all the waters and He named it the *sea* (mare). He made an assemblage of all His graces and He called it *Mary* (Maria). This great God has a most rich treasury in which He has laid up all that He has of beauty and splendor, of rarity and preciousness, including even His own Son: and this immense treasury is none other than Mary, whom the saints have named the Treasure of the Lord, out of whose plenitude all men are made rich.

God the Son has communicated to His Mother all that He acquired by His life and His death, His infinite merits and His admirable virtues; and He has made her the treasurer of all that His Father gave Him for His inheritance. It is by her that He applies His merits to His members, and that He communicates His virtues, and distributes His graces. She is His mysterious canal; she is His aqueduct, through which He makes His mercies flow gently and abundantly.

To Mary, His faithful spouse, God the Holy Ghost has communicated His unspeakable gifts; and He has chosen her to be the dispenser of all He possesses, in such wise that she distributes to whom she wills, as much as she wills, as she wills and when she wills, all His gifts and graces. The Holy Ghost gives no heavenly gift to men which He does not have pass through her virginal hands. Such has been the will of God, Who has willed that we should have everything through Mary; so that she who, impoverished, humbled, and who hid herself even unto the abyss of nothingness by her profound humility her whole life long, should now be enriched and exalted and honored by the Most High. Such are the sentiments of the Church and the holy Fathers.

If I were speaking to the freethinkers of these times, I would prove what I have said so simply here, drawing it out more at length, and confirming it by the Holy Scriptures and the Fathers, quoting the original passages, and adducing various solid reasons, which may be seen at length in the book of Father Poiré, *La Triple Couronne de la Ste. Vierge.* But as I speak particularly to the poor and simple, who being of good will, and having more faith than the common run of scholars, believe more simply and more meritoriously, I content myself with stating the truth quite plainly, without stopping to quote the Latin passages, which they would not understand. Nevertheless, without making much research, I shall not fail to bring forward some of them from time to time. But now let us go on with our subject.

Inasmuch as grace perfects nature, and glory perfects grace, it is certain that Our Lord is still, in Heaven, as much the Son of Mary as He was on earth; and that, consequently, He has retained the obedience and submission of the most perfect Child toward the best of all mothers. But we must take great pains not to conceive this dependence as any abasement or imperfection in Jesus Christ. For Mary is infinitely below her Son, Who is God, and therefore she does not command Him as a mother here below would command her child who is below her. Mary, being altogether transformed into God by grace and by the glory which transforms all the saints into Him, asks nothing, wishes nothing, does nothing contrary to the eternal and immutable will of God. When we read then in the writings of Saints Bernard, Bernardine, Bonaventure and others that in Heaven and on earth everything, even God Himself, is subject to the Blessed Virgin, they mean that the authority which God has been well pleased to give her is so great that it seems as if she had the same power as God; and that her prayers and petitions are so powerful with God that they always pass for commandments with His Majesty, Who never resists the prayer of His dear Mother, because she is always humble and conformed to His will.

If Moses, by the force of his prayer, stayed the anger of God against the Israelites in a manner so powerful that the most high and infinitely merciful Lord, being unable to resist him, told him to let Him alone that He might be angry with and punish that rebellious people, what must we not, with much greater reason, think of the prayer of the humble Mary, that worthy Mother of God, which is more powerful with His Majesty than the prayers and intercessions of all the angels and saints both in Heaven and on earth?

In the heavens Mary commands the angels and the blessed. As a recompense for her profound humility, God has empowered her and commissioned her to fill with saints the empty thrones from which the apostate angels fell by pride. The will of the Most High, who exalts the humble, is that Heaven, earth and Hell bend, with good will or bad will, to the commandments of the humble Mary, whom He has made sovereign of Heaven and earth, general of His armies, treasurer of His treasures, dispenser of His graces, worker of His greatest marvels, restorer of the human race, Mediatrix of men, the exterminator of the enemies of God, and the faithful companion of His grandeurs and triumphs.

God the Father wishes to have children by Mary till the consummation of the world; and He speaks to her these words: "Dwell in Jacob;" that is to say: Make your dwelling and residence in My predestined children, prefigured by Jacob, and not in the reprobate children of the Devil, prefigured by Esau.

Just as in the natural and corporal generation of children there are a father and a mother, so in the supernatural and spiritual generation there are a Father, Who is God, and a Mother, who is Mary. All the true children of God, the predestinate, have God for their Father and Mary for their Mother. He who has not Mary for his Mother has not God for his Father. This is the reason why the reprobate, such as heretics, schismatics and others, who hate our Blessed Lady or regard her with contempt and indifference, have not God for their Father,

Mancipia Publications

however much they boast of it, simply because they have not Mary for their Mother. For if they had her for their Mother, they would love and honor her as a true child naturally loves and honors the mother who has given him life.

The most infallible and indubitable sign by which we may distinguish a heretic, a man of bad doctrine, a reprobate, from one of the predestinate, is that the heretic and the reprobate have nothing but contempt and indifference for Our Lady, endeavoring by their words and examples to diminish the worship and love of her, openly or hiddenly, and sometimes by misrepresentation. Alas! God the Father has not told Mary to dwell in them, for they are Esaus.

God the Son wishes to form Himself, and, so to speak, to incarnate Himself in His members every day, by His dear Mother, and He says to her: "Take Israel for your inheritance." It is as if He had said: God the Father has given Me for an inheritance all the nations of the earth, all men, good and bad, predestinate and reprobate. The ones I will lead with a rod of gold, and the others with a rod of iron. Of the ones, I will be the Father and the Advocate; of the others, the Just Punisher; and of all, the Judge. But as for you, My dear Mother, you shall have for your heritage and possession only the predestinate, prefigured by Israel; and as their Mother, you shall bring them forth and take care of them; and as their sovereign, you shall conduct them, govern them and defend them.

"This man and that man is born in her," says the Holy Ghost through the Royal Psalmist. According to the explanation of some of the Fathers, the first man that is born in Mary is the Man-God, Jesus Christ; the second is a mere man, the child of God and Mary by adoption. If Jesus Christ, the Head of men, is born in her, then the predestinate, who are the members of that Head, ought also to be born in her, by a necessary consequence. One and the same mother does not bring forth into the world the head without the members, or the members without the head; for this would be a monster of nature. So in like manner, in the order of grace, the head and the members are born of one and the same Mother; and if a member of the Mystical Body of Jesus Christ—that is to say, one of the predestinate—were born of any other mother than Mary, who has produced the Head, he would not be one of the predestinate, nor a member of Jesus Christ, but simply a monster in the order of grace.

Besides this, Jesus being at present as much as ever the fruit of Mary—as Heaven and earth repeat thousands and thousands of times a day, "and blessed is the fruit of thy womb, Jesus"—it is certain that Jesus Christ is, for each man in particular who possesses Him, as truly the fruit and the work of Mary as He is for the whole world in general; so that if any one of the faithful has Jesus Christ formed in his heart, he can say boldly, "All thanks be to Mary! What I possess is her effect and her fruit, and without her I should never have had it." We can apply to her more than Saint Paul applied to himself the words: "I am in labor again with all the children of God, until Jesus Christ my Son be formed in them in the fullness of His age."

Saint Augustine, surpassing himself, and going beyond all I have yet said, affirms that all the predestinate, in order to be conformed to the image of the

Son of God, are in this world hidden in the womb of the most holy Virgin, where they are guarded, nourished, brought up and made to grow by that good Mother until she has brought them forth to glory after death, which is properly the day of their birth, as the Church calls the death of the just. O mystery of grace, unknown to the reprobate, and but little known even to the predestinate!

God the Holy Ghost wishes to form elect for Himself in her and by her, and He says to her: "Strike the roots," My Well-beloved and My Spouse, "of all your virtues in My elect," in order that they may grow from virtue to virtue and from grace to grace. I took so much complacence in you when you lived on earth in the practice of the most sublime virtues, that I desire still to find you on earth, without your ceasing to be in Heaven. For this end, reproduce yourself in My elect, that I may behold in them with complacence the roots of your invincible faith, of your profound humility, of your universal mortification, of your sublime prayer, of your ardent charity, of your firm hope and of all your virtues. You are always My spouse, as faithful, as pure and as fruitful as ever. Let your faith give Me My faithful, your purity, My virgins, and your fertility, My temples and My elect.

When Mary has struck her roots in a soul, she produces there marvels of grace, which she alone can produce, because she alone is the fruitful Virgin who never has had, and never will have, her equal in purity and in fruitfulness.

Mary has produced, together with the Holy Ghost, the greatest thing which has been or ever will be—a God-Man; and she will consequently produce the greatest saints that there will be in the end of time. The formation and the education of the great saints who shall come at the end of the world are reserved for her. For it is only that singular and miraculous Virgin who can produce, in union with the Holy Ghost, singular and extraordinary things.

When the Holy Ghost, her Spouse, has found Mary in a soul, He flies there. He enters there in His fullness; He communicates Himself to that soul abundantly, and to the full extent to which it makes room for His spouse. Nay, one of the greatest reasons why the Holy Ghost does not now do startling wonders in our souls is because He does not find there a sufficiently great union with His faithful and inseparable spouse. I say "inseparable" spouse, because since that Substantial Love of the Father and the Son has espoused Mary, in order to produce Jesus Christ, the Head of the elect, and Jesus Christ in the elect, He has never repudiated her, because she has always been fruitful and faithful.

Consequences
I. Mary Is Queen of All Hearts

We may evidently conclude, then, from what I have said, first of all, that Mary has received from God a great domination over the souls of the elect; for she cannot make her residence in them as God the Father ordered her to do, and, as their mother, form, nourish and bring them forth to eternal life, and have them as her inheritance and portion, and form them in Jesus Christ and Jesus Christ in them, and strike the roots of her virtues in their hearts and be the

Mancipia Publications

inseparable companion of the Holy Ghost in all His works of grace—she cannot, I say, do all these things unless she has a right and a domination over their souls by a singular grace of the Most High, Who, having given her power over His only and natural Son, has given it also to her over His adopted children, not only as to their bodies, which would be but a small matter, but also as to their souls.

Mary is the Queen of Heaven and earth by grace, as Jesus is the King of them by nature and by conquest. Now, as the kingdom of Jesus Christ consists principally in the heart or the interior of man—according to the words, "The kingdom of God is within you"—in like manner the kingdom of our Blessed Lady is principally in the interior of man; that is to say, his soul. And it is principally in souls that she is more glorified with her Son than in all visible creatures, and so we can call her, as the saints do, the Queen of All Hearts.

II. Mary Is Necessary to Men

In the second place we must conclude that, the most holy Virgin being necessary to God by a necessity which we call "hypothetical," in consequence of His will, she is far more necessary to men, in order that they may attain their last end. We must not confuse devotion to the Blessed Virgin with devotions to the other saints, as if devotion to her were not far more necessary than devotion to them, and as if devotion to her were a matter of supererogation.

1. Necessary to All Men to Attain Salvation

The learned and pious Jesuit, Suarez, the erudite and devout Justus Lipsius, doctor of Louvain, and many others have proved invincibly, from the sentiments of the Fathers (among others, Saint Augustine, Saint Ephrem, deacon of Edessa, Saint Cyril of Jerusalem, Saint Germanus of Constantinople, Saint John Damascene, Saint Anselm, Saint Bernard, Saint Bernardine, Saint Thomas and Saint Bonaventure), that devotion to our Blessed Lady is necessary to salvation, and that (even in the opinion of Oecolampadius and some other heretics) it is an infallible mark of reprobation to have no esteem and love for the holy Virgin; while on the other hand, it is an infallible mark of predestination to be entirely and truly devoted to her.

The figures and words of the Old and New Testaments prove this. The sentiments and the examples of the saints confirm it. Reason and experience teach and demonstrate it. Even the devil and his crew, constrained by the force of truth, have often been obliged to avow it in spite of themselves. Among all the passages of the holy Fathers and Doctors, of which I have made an ample collection in order to prove this truth, I shall for brevity's sake quote but one: "To be devout to you, O holy Virgin," says St. John Damascene, "is an arm of salvation which God gives to those whom He wishes to save."

I could bring forward here many anecdotes which prove the same thing, and among others one which is related in the chronicles of St. Francis. This same saint saw in ecstasy a great ladder ascending into Heaven, at the top of which stood the Blessed Virgin and by which it was shown him he must ascend to reach Heaven. There is another related in the chronicles of St. Dominic. There was an unfortunate heretic near Carcassonne, where St. Dominic was preaching the Rosary, who was possessed by a legion of fifteen thousand devils. These evil spirits were compelled, to their confusion, by the command of our Blessed Lady, to avow many great and consoling truths touching devotion to the Blessed Virgin; and they did this with so much force and so much clearness that it is impossible to read this authentic account and the eulogy which the devil made, in spite of himself, of devotion to the most holy Virgin Mary, without shedding tears of joy, however lukewarm we may be in our devotion to her.

2. Still More Necessary to Those Called to a Special Perfection

If devotion to the most holy Virgin Mary is necessary to all men simply for working out their salvation, it is still more so for those who are called to any special perfection; and I do not think anyone can acquire an intimate union with Our Lord and a perfect fidelity to the Holy Ghost without a very great union with the most holy Virgin, and a great dependence on her assistance.

It is Mary alone who has found grace before God without the aid of any other mere creature; it is only through her that all those who have since found grace before God have found it at all; and it is only through her that all those who shall come afterward shall find it. She was full of grace when she was greeted by the Archangel Gabriel, and she was superabundantly filled with grace by the Holy Ghost when He covered her with His unspeakable shadow; and she has so augmented this double plenitude from day to day and from moment to moment that she has reached a point of grace immense and inconceivable—in such wise that the Most High has made her the sole treasurer of His treasures and the sole dispenser of His graces to ennoble, to exalt and to enrich whom she wishes; to give entry to whom she wills into the narrow way of Heaven; to bring whom she wills, and in spite of all obstacles, through the narrow gate of life; and to give the throne, the scepter and the crown of king to whom she wills. Jesus is everywhere and always the Fruit and the Son of Mary; and Mary is everywhere the veritable tree who bears the Fruit of life, and the true Mother who produces it.

It is Mary alone to whom God has given the keys of the cellars of divine love and the power to enter into the most sublime and secret ways of perfection, and the power likewise to make others enter in there also. It is Mary alone who has given to the miserable children of Eve, the faithless, entry into the terrestrial paradise; that they may walk there agreeably with God, hide there securely against their enemies, feed themselves there deliciously, without further fear of death, on the fruit of the trees of life and of the knowledge of good and evil, and drink in long draughts the heavenly waters of that fair fountain which gushes forth there with abundance; or rather, since she is herself that terrestrial paradise, that virgin and blessed earth from which Adam and Eve, the sinners, have been driven, she gives no entry there except to those whom it is her pleasure to make saints.

Mancipia Publications

All the rich among the people, to make use of an expression of the Holy Ghost according to the explanation of Saint Bernard—all the rich among the people shall supplicate her face from age to age, and particularly at the end of the world; that is to say, the greatest saints, the souls richest in graces and virtues, shall be the most assiduous in praying to our Blessed Lady, and in having her always present as their perfect model for imitation and their powerful aid for help.

3. Especially Necessary to the Great Saints of the Latter Times

I have said that this would come to pass, particularly at the end of the world and indeed presently, because the Most High with His holy Mother has to form for Himself great saints who shall surpass most of the other saints in sanctity as much as the cedars of Lebanon outgrow the little shrubs, as has been revealed to a "holy soul" (Marie des Vallees) whose life has been written by M. de Renty.

These great souls, full of grace and zeal, shall be chosen to match themselves against the enemies of God, who shall rage on all sides; and they shall be singularly devout to our Blessed Lady, illuminated by her light, strengthened with her nourishment, led by her spirit, supported by her arm and sheltered under her protection, so that they shall fight with one hand and build with the other. With the one hand they shall fight, overthrow and crush the heretics with their heresies, the schismatics with their schisms, the idolaters with their idolatries and the sinners with their impieties. With the other hand they shall build the temple of the true Solomon and the mystical city of God, that is to say, the most holy Virgin, called by the Fathers the "Temple of Solomon" and the "City of God." By their words and their examples they shall draw the whole world to true devotion to Mary. This shall bring upon them many enemies, but shall also bring many victories and much glory for God alone. This is what God revealed to Saint Vincent Ferrer, the great apostle of his age, as he has sufficiently noted in one of his works.

This is what the Holy Ghost seems to have prophesied in the Fifty-eighth Psalm: "And they shall know that God will rule Jacob and all the ends of the earth; they shall return at evening and shall suffer hunger like dogs and shall go round about the city." This city which men shall find at the end of the world to convert themselves in, and to satisfy the hunger they have for justice, is the most holy Virgin, who is called by the Holy Ghost the "City of God."

Secret of Mary # 24-25

There are several true devotions to Our Lady: here I do not speak of those that are false.

Devotion without Special Practices

The first consists in fulfilling our Christian duties, avoiding mortal sin, acting more out of love than fear, praying to Our Lady now and then, honoring her as the Mother of God, yet without having any special devotion to her.

Third Day _____

Daily prayers during the Second Week: *Litany of the Holy Ghost* on page 160, the *Ave Maris Stella* on page 156, Saint Louis De Montfort's *Prayer to Mary* on page 157 and the Recitation of the *Rosary.*

Continuation of the holy Gospel according to Saint Luke 1:46-66

And Mary said: My soul doth magnify the Lord.

47. And my spirit hath rejoiced in God my Saviour.

48. Because He hath regarded the humility of His handmaid; for behold from henceforth all generations shall call me blessed.

49. Because He that is mighty, hath done great things to me; and holy is His name.

50. And His mercy is from generation unto generations, to them that fear Him.

51. He hath shewed might in His arm: He hath scattered the proud in the conceit of their heart.

52. He hath put down the mighty from their seat, and hath exalted the humble.

53. He hath filled the hungry with good things; and the rich He hath sent empty away.

54. He hath received Israel His servant, being mindful of His mercy:

55. As He spoke to our fathers, to Abraham and to His seed forever.

56. And Mary abode with her about three months; and she returned to her own house.

57. Now Elizabeth's full time of being delivered was come, and she brought forth a son.

58. And her neighbors and kinsfolks heard that the Lord had shewed His great mercy towards her, and they congratulated with her.

59. And it came to pass, that on the eighth day they came to circumcise the child, and they called him by his father's name Zachary.

60. And his mother answering, said: Not so; but he shall be called John.

61. And they said to her: There is no one of thy kindred that is called by this name.

62. And they made signs to his father, how he would have him called.

63. And demanding a writing table, he wrote, saying: John is his name. And they all wondered.

64. And immediately his mouth was opened, and his tongue *loosed*, and he spoke, blessing God.

65. And fear came upon all their neighbors; and all these things were noised abroad over all the hill country of Judea:

66. And all they that had heard them laid them upon their heart, saying: What an one, think ye, shall this child be? For the hand of the Lord was with him.

True Devotion #90-93; 105-114
Choice of True Devotion to the Blessed Virgin

Today, more than ever, we must take pains in choosing true devotion to our Blessed Lady, because, more than ever before, there are false devotions to our Blessed Lady which are easily mistaken for true ones. The devil, like a false coiner and a subtle and experienced sharper, has already deceived and destroyed so many souls by a false devotion to the Blessed Virgin that he makes a daily use of his diabolical experience to plunge many others by this same way into everlasting perdition; amusing them, lulling them to sleep in sin, under the pretext of some prayers badly said or of some outward practices which he inspires. As a false coiner does not ordinarily counterfeit anything but gold or silver, and very rarely other metals, because they are not worth the trouble, so the evil spirit does not for the most part counterfeit other devotions, but only those to Jesus and Mary—devotion to Holy Communion and to our Blessed Lady because they are among other devotions what gold and silver are among other metals.

It is then very important to recognize, first of all, false devotions to our Blessed Lady, in order to avoid them, and true devotion, in order to embrace it; secondly, which of the many practices of true devotion to our Blessed Lady is the most perfect, the most agreeable to her, the most glorious to God, and the most sanctifying for ourselves, so that we may adopt that one.

False Devotions to the Blessed Virgin and False Devotees

I find seven kinds of false devotees and false devotions to Our Lady, namely: 1. the critical devotees; 2. the scrupulous devotees; 3. the external devotees; 4. the presumptuous devotees; 5. the inconstant devotees; 6. the hypocritical devotees; 7. the interested devotees. *(N.B. According to the "Preparation for Total Consecration" only the critical devotees is examined. eds.)*

Critical Devotees

The critical devotees are, for the most part, proud scholars, rash and self-sufficient spirits, who have at heart some devotion to the holy Virgin, but who criticize nearly all the practices of devotion which simple people pay simply and holily to their good Mother, because these practices do not fall in with their own humor and fancy. They call in doubt all the miracles and pious stories recorded by authors worthy of faith, or drawn from the chronicles of religious orders: narratives which testify to us the mercies and the power of the most holy Virgin. They cannot see, without uneasiness, simple and humble people on their knees before an altar or an image of Our Lady, sometimes at the corner of a street, in order to pray to God there; and they even accuse them of idolatry, as if they adored the wood or the stone. They say that, for their part, they are not fond of these external devotions, and that they are not so credulous as to believe so many tales and stories that are told about Our Lady. When they are told how admirably the Fathers of the Church praised the Blessed Virgin, they either reply that the Fathers spoke as professional orators, with exaggeration; or they misinterpret their words.

These kinds of false devotees and of proud and worldly people are greatly to be feared. They do an infinite wrong to devotion to Our Lady; and they are but too successful in alienating people from it, under the pretext of destroying its abuses.

I. Characteristics

After having laid bare and condemned the false devotions to the most holy Virgin, we must, in a few words, give the characteristics of true devotion. It must be: 1. interior, 2. tender, 3. holy, 4. constant, and 5. disinterested.

1. Interior

True devotion to Our Lady is interior; that is, it comes from the mind and the heart. It flows from the esteem we have for her, the high idea we have formed of her greatness, and the love which we have for her.

2. Tender

It is tender; that is, full of confidence in her, like a child's confidence in his loving mother. This confidence makes the soul have recourse to her in all its bodily and mental necessities, with much simplicity, trust and tenderness. It implores the aid of its good Mother at all times, in all places and above all things: in its doubts, that it may be enlightened; in its wanderings, that it may be brought into the right path; in its temptations, that it may be supported; in its weaknesses, that it may be strengthened; in its falls, that it may be lifted up; in its discouragements, that it may be cheered; in its scruples, that they may be taken away; in the crosses, toils and disappointments of life, that it may be consoled under them. In a word, in all the evils of body and mind, the soul ordinarily has recourse to Mary, without fear of annoying her or displeasing Jesus Christ.

3. Holy

True devotion to Our Lady is holy; that is to say, it leads the soul to avoid sin and to imitate the virtues of the Blessed Virgin, particularly her profound humility, her lively faith, her blind obedience, her continual prayer, her universal mortification, her divine purity, her ardent charity, her heroic patience, her angelic sweetness and her divine wisdom. These are the ten principal virtues of the most holy Virgin.

4. Constant

True devotion to Our Lady is constant. It confirms the soul in good, and does not let it easily abandon its spiritual exercises. It makes it courageous in opposing the world in its fashions and maxims, the flesh in its wearinesses and passions, and the devil in his temptations; so that a person truly devout to our Blessed Lady is neither changeable, irritable, scrupulous nor timid. It is not that such a person does not fall, or change sometimes in the sensible feeling of devotion. But when he falls, he rises again by stretching out his hand to his good Mother. When he loses the taste and relish of devotion, he does not become disturbed because of that; for the just and faithful client of Mary lives by the faith (Heb. 10:38) of Jesus and Mary, and not by natural sentiment.

Mancipia Publications

5. Disinterested

Lastly, true devotion to Our Lady is disinterested; that is to say, it inspires the soul not to seek itself but only God, and God in His holy Mother. A true client of Mary does not serve that august Queen from a spirit of lucre and interest, nor for his own good, whether temporal or eternal, corporal or spiritual, but exclusively because she deserves to be served, and God alone in her. He does not love Mary just because she obtains favors for him, or because he hopes she will, but solely because she is so worthy of love. It is on this account that he loves and serves her as faithfully in his disgusts and drynesses as in his sweetnesses and sensible fervors. He loves her as much on Calvary as at the marriage of Cana.

Oh, how agreeable and precious in the eyes of God and of His holy Mother is such a client of our Blessed Lady, who has no self-seeking in his service of her!

But in these days how rare is such a sight! It is that it may be less rare that I have taken my pen in hand to put on paper what I have taught with good results, in public and in private, during my missions for many years.

I have now said many things about the most holy Virgin; but I have many more to say, and there are infinitely more which I shall omit, either from ignorance, inability or want of time, in unfolding the plan for forming a true client of Mary and a true disciple of Jesus Christ.

Oh, but my labor will have been well expended if this little writing, falling into the hands of a soul of good dispositions—a soul well-born of God and of Mary, and not of blood, nor of the will of the flesh, nor of the will of man— should unfold to him, and should by the grace of the Holy Ghost inspire him with the excellence and the value of that true and solid devotion to our Blessed Lady which I am going presently to describe. If I knew that my guilty blood could serve in engraving upon anyone's heart the truths which I am writing in honor of my true Mother and Sovereign Mistress, of whose children and slaves I am the least, I would use my blood instead of ink to form the letters, in the hope of finding some good souls who, by their fidelity to the practice which I teach, should compensate my dear Mother and Mistress for the losses which she has suffered through my ingratitude and infidelities.

I feel myself more than ever encouraged to believe and to hope for the fulfillment of all that I have deeply engraven upon my heart and have asked of God these many years, namely, that sooner or later the Blessed Virgin shall have more children, servants and slaves of love than ever; and that by this means, Jesus Christ, my dear Master, shall reign in hearts more than ever.

I clearly foresee that raging beasts shall come in fury to tear with their diabolical teeth this little writing and him whom the Holy Ghost has made use of to write it—or at least to smother it in the darkness and silence of a coffer, that it may not appear. They shall even attack and persecute those who shall read it and carry it out in practice. But what matter? On the contrary, so much the better! This very foresight encourages me, and makes me hope for great success, that is to say, for a great squadron of brave and valiant soldiers of Jesus and Mary, of both sexes, to combat the world, the devil and corrupted nature, in those more-than-ever perilous times which are about to come. "He who reads, let him understand." "He who can take it, let him take it."

Secret of Mary #26-27

The second consists in entertaining for Our Lady more perfect feelings of esteem and love, of confidence and veneration. It leads us to join the Confraternities of the Holy Rosary and of the Scapular, to recite the five decades or the fifteen decades of the Rosary, to honor Mary's images and altars, to publish her praises and to enroll ourselves in her sodalities. This devotion is good, holy and praiseworthy if we keep ourselves free from sin; but it is not so perfect as the next, nor so efficient in severing our soul from creatures or in detaching us from ourselves, in order to be united to Jesus Christ.

The third devotion of Our Lady, known and practiced by very few persons, is the one I am now about to disclose to you, predestinate soul.

"...True devotion to Our Lady
is disinterested;
that is to say, it inspires the soul
not to seek itself
but only God, and
God in His holy Mother."

Happy and a thousand times happy
is the generous soul
that consecrates itself entirely
to Jesus through Mary as a slave of love
after it has shaken off by Baptism
the tyrannical slavery of the Devil!

Fourth Day ───────────

Daily prayers during the Second Week: Litany of the Holy Ghost on page 160,
the *Ave Maris Stella* on page 156, Saint Louis De Montfort's *Prayer to
Mary* on page 157 and the Recitation of the *Rosary.*

Continuation of the holy Gospel according to Saint Luke 1:67-80

And Zachary his father was filled with the Holy Ghost; and he prophesied,
saying:

68. Blessed be the Lord God of Israel: because He hath visited and
wrought the redemption of His people:

69. And hath raised up a horn of salvation to us, in the house of David His
servant:

70. As He spoke by the mouth of His holy prophets, who are from the
beginning:

71. Salvation from our enemies, and from the hand of all that hate us:

72. To perform mercy to our fathers, and to remember His holy testament,

73. The oath, which He swore to Abraham our father, that He would grant
to us;

74. That, being delivered from the hand of our enemies, we may serve Him
without fear,

75. In holiness and justice before Him, all our days.

76. And thou, child, shalt be called the prophet of the Highest: for thou
shalt go before the face of the Lord to prepare His ways:

77. To give knowledge of salvation to His people, unto the remission of
their sins:

78. Through the bowels of the mercy of our God, in which the Orient from
on high hath visited us:

79. To enlighten them that sit in darkness, and in the shadow of death: to
direct our feet into the way of peace.

80. And the child grew, and was strengthened in spirit; and was in the
deserts until the day of his manifestation to Israel.

True Devotion #115-134
II. Practices
1. Common practices, both interior and exterior.

There are several interior practices of true devotion to the Blessed Virgin.
Here are the principal ones, stated compendiously: (1) to honor her as the
worthy Mother of God, with the worship of hyperdulia; that is to say, to esteem
her and honor her above all the other saints, as the masterpiece of grace, and
the first after Jesus Christ, true God and true Man; (2) to meditate on her
virtues, her privileges and her actions; (3) to contemplate her grandeurs; (4) to
make acts of love, of praise, of gratitude to her; (5) to invoke her cordially; (6)
to offer ourselves to her and unite ourselves with her; (7) to do all our actions

with the view of pleasing her; (8) to begin, to continue and to finish all our actions by her, in her, with her and for her, in order that we may do them by Jesus Christ, in Jesus Christ, with Jesus Christ and for Jesus Christ our Last End. We will presently explain this last practice.

True devotion to Our Lady also has several exterior practices, of which the following are the principal ones: (1) to enroll ourselves in her confraternities and enter her congregations; (2) to join the religious orders instituted in her honor; (3) to proclaim her praises; (4) to give alms, to fast and to undergo outward and inward mortifications in her honor; (5) to wear her liveries, such as the Rosary, the Scapular or the little chain; (6) to recite with attention, devotion and modesty the holy Rosary, composed of fifteen decades of *Hail Marys* in honor of the fifteen principal mysteries of Jesus Christ; or five decades, which is one third of the Rosary, either in honor of the five Joyful Mysteries, which are the Annunciation, the Visitation, the Nativity of Jesus Christ, the Purification, and the Finding of Our Lord in the Temple; or in honor of the five Sorrowful Mysteries, which are the Agony of Our Lord in the Garden of Olives, His Scourging, His Crowning with Thorns, His Carrying of the Cross, and His Crucifixion; or in honor of the five Glorious Mysteries, which are the Resurrection, the Ascension, the Descent of the Holy Ghost at Pentecost, the Assumption of our Blessed Lady, body and soul, into Heaven, and her Coronation by the Three Persons of the Most Holy Trinity. We may also say a chaplet of six or seven decades in honor of the years which we believe Our Lady lived on earth; or the Little Crown of the Blessed Virgin, composed of three *Our Fathers* and twelve *Hail Marys*, in honor of her crown of twelve stars or privileges; or the Office of Our Lady, so universally received and recited in the Church; or the little Psalter of the holy Virgin, which Saint Bonaventure composed in her honor, and which is so tender and so devout that one cannot say it without being moved by it; or fourteen *Our Fathers* and *Hail Marys* in honor of her fourteen joys; or some other prayers, hymns and canticles of the Church, such as the *Salve Regina*, the *Alma*, the *Ave Regina Coelorum*, or the *Regina Coeli*, according to the different seasons; or the *Ave Maris Stella*, the *O Gloriosa Domina*, the *Magnificat*, or some other practices of devotion, of which books are full; (7) to sing, or have sung, spiritual canticles in her honor; (8) to make a number of genuflections or reverences, while saying, for example, every morning, sixty or a hundred times, *Ave Maria, Virgo Fidelis* ("Hail Mary, Faithful Virgin"), to obtain from God through her the grace to be faithful to the graces of God during the day; and then again in the evening, *Ave Maria, Mater Misericordiae* ("Hail Mary, Mother of Mercy") to ask pardon of God through her for the sins that we have committed during the day; (9) to take care of her confraternities, to adorn her altars, to crown and ornament her images; (10) to carry her images, or to have them carried, in procession, and to carry a picture or an image of her about our own persons, as a mighty arm against the evil spirit; (11) to have copies of her name or picture made and placed in churches, or in houses, or on the gates and entrances into cities, churches and houses; (12) to consecrate ourselves to her in a special and solemn manner.

Mancipia Publications

There are numerous other practices of true devotion toward the Blessed Virgin which the Holy Ghost has inspired in saintly souls and which are very sanctifying; they can be read at length in the *Paradise Opened to Philagius* of Father Barry, the Jesuit, in which he has collected a great number of devotions which the saints have practiced in honor of Our Lady—devotions which serve marvelously to sanctify our souls, provided they are performed as they ought to be, that is to say, (1) with a good and pure intention to please God only, to unite ourselves to Jesus Christ as to our Last End, to edify our neighbor; (2) with attention and without voluntary distraction; (3) with devotion, equally avoiding precipitation and negligence; (4) with modesty, and a respectful and edifying posture of the body.

2. Its perfect practice

But after all, I loudly protest that, having read nearly all the books which profess to treat of devotion to Our Lady, and having conversed familiarly with the best and wisest of men of these latter times, I have never known nor heard of any practice of devotion toward her at all equal to the one which I now wish to unfold; demanding from the soul, as it does, more sacrifices for God, ridding the soul more of itself and of its self-love, keeping it more faithfully in grace and grace more faithfully in it, uniting it more perfectly and more easily to Jesus Christ; and finally, being more glorious to God, more sanctifying to the soul and more useful to our neighbor than any other of the devotions to her.

As the essential of this devotion consists in the interior which it ought to form, it will not be equally understood by everybody. Some will stop at what is exterior in it, and will go no further, and these will be the greatest number. Some, in small number, will enter into its inward spirit; but they will only mount one step. Who will mount to the second step? Who will get as far as the third? Lastly, who will so advance as to make this devotion his habitual state? He alone to whom the spirit of Jesus Christ shall have revealed this secret, the faultlessly faithful soul whom He shall conduct there Himself, to advance from virtue to virtue, from grace to grace, from light to light, until he arrives at the transformation of himself into Jesus Christ, and to the plenitude of His age on earth and of His glory in Heaven.

Nature of Perfect Devotion to the Blessed Virgin or Perfect Consecration to Jesus Christ

All our perfection consists in being conformed, united and consecrated to Jesus Christ; and therefore the most perfect of all devotions is, without any doubt, that which the most perfectly conforms, unites and consecrates us to Jesus Christ. Now, Mary being the most conformed of all creatures to Jesus Christ, it follows that, of all devotions, that which most consecrates and conforms the soul to Our Lord is devotion to His holy Mother, and that the more a soul is consecrated to Mary, the more it is consecrated to Jesus.

Hence it comes to pass that the most perfect consecration to Jesus Christ is nothing else but a perfect and entire consecration of ourselves to the Blessed

Virgin, and this is the devotion which I teach; or, in other words, a perfect renewal of the vows and promises of holy Baptism.

A Perfect and Entire Consecration of Oneself to the Blessed Virgin

This devotion consists, then, in giving ourselves entirely to Our Lady, in order to belong entirely to Jesus through her. We must give her, (1) our body, with all its senses and its members; (2) our soul, with all its powers; (3) our exterior goods of fortune, whether present or to come; (4) our interior and spiritual goods, which are our merits and our virtues, grace and glory; and this we must do without the reserve of so much as one farthing, one hair, or one least good action; and we must do it also for all eternity; and we must do it, further, without pretending to, or hoping for, any other recompense for our offering and service except the honor of belonging to Jesus Christ through Mary and in Mary—as though that sweet Mistress were not (as she always is) the most generous and the most grateful of creatures.

Here we must note that there are two things in the good works we perform, namely, satisfaction and merit; in other words, their satisfactory or impetratory value, and their meritorious value. The satisfactory or impetratory value of a good action is that action inasmuch as it satisfies for the pain due to sin, or obtains some new grace; the meritorious value, or the merit, is the good action inasmuch as it merits grace now and eternal glory hereafter. Now, in this consecration of ourselves to Our Lady, we give her all the satisfactory, impetratory and meritorious value of our actions; in other words, the satisfactions and the merits of all our good works. We give her all our merits, graces and virtues—not to communicate them to others, for our merits, graces and virtues are, properly speaking, incommunicable, and it is only Jesus Christ Who, in making Himself our surety with His Father, is able to communicate His merits—but we give her them to keep them, augment them and embellish them for us, as we shall explain by and by. Our satisfactions, however, we give her to communicate to whom she likes, and for the greatest glory of God.

It follows from this that:

1. By this devotion we give to Jesus Christ in the most perfect manner, inasmuch as it is by Mary's hands, all we can give Him, and far more than by any other devotions in which we give Him either a part of our time, or a part of our good works, or a part of our satisfactions and mortifications; because here everything is given and consecrated to Him, even the right of disposing of our interior goods and of the satisfactions which we gain by our good works day after day. This is more than we do even in a religious order. In religious orders we give God the goods of fortune by the vow of poverty, the goods of the body by the vow of chastity, our own will by the vow of obedience, and sometimes the liberty of the body by the vow of cloister. But we do not by these vows give Him the liberty or the right to dispose of the value of our good works; and we do not strip ourselves, as far as a Christian man can do so, of that which is dearest and most precious, namely, our merits and our satisfactions.

2. A person who is thus voluntarily consecrated and sacrificed to Jesus

Mancipia Publications

Christ through Mary can no longer dispose of the value of any of his good actions. All he suffers, all he thinks, all the good he says or does, belongs to Mary, in order that she may dispose of it according to the will of her Son and His greatest glory—without, however, that dependence interfering in any way with the obligations of the state we may be in at present or may be placed in for the future; for example, without interfering with the obligations of a priest who, by his office or otherwise, ought to apply the satisfactory and impetratory value of the Holy Mass to some private person. For we make the offering of this devotion only according to the order of God and the duties of our state.

3. We consecrate ourselves at one and the same time to the most holy Virgin and to Jesus Christ; to the most holy Virgin as to the perfect means which Jesus Christ has chosen whereby to unite Himself to us, and us to Him; and to Our Lord as to our Last End, to Whom, as our Redeemer and our God, we owe all we are.

A Perfect renewal of the Vows of Holy Baptism

I have said that this devotion may rightly be called a perfect renewal of the vows or promises of holy Baptism.

For every Christian, before his Baptism, was the slave of the devil, seeing that he belonged to him. He has in his Baptism, by his own mouth or by his sponsor's, solemnly renounced Satan, his pomps and his works; and he has taken Jesus Christ for his Master and Sovereign Lord, to depend upon Him in the quality of a slave of love. That is what we do by the present devotion. We renounce, as is expressed in the formula of consecration the devil, the world, sin and self; and we give ourselves entirely to Jesus Christ by the hands of Mary. Nay, we even do something more; for in Baptism, we ordinarily speak by the mouth of another, our godfather or godmother, and so we give ourselves to Jesus Christ not by ourselves but through another. But in this devotion we do it by ourselves, voluntarily, knowing what we are doing.

Moreover, in holy Baptism we do not give ourselves to Jesus by the hands of Mary, at least not in an explicit manner; and we do not give Him the value of our good actions. We remain entirely free after Baptism, either to apply them to whom we please or to keep them for ourselves. But by this devotion we give ourselves to Our Lord explicitly by the hands of Mary, and we consecrate to Him the value of all our actions.

Men, says Saint Thomas, make a vow at their Baptism to renounce the devil and all his pomps. This vow, says Saint Augustine, is the greatest and most indispensable of all vows. It is thus also that canonists speak: "The principal vow is the one we make at Baptism." Yet who has kept this great vow? Who is it that faithfully performs the promises of holy Baptism? Have not almost all Christians swerved from the loyalty which they promised Jesus in their Baptism? Whence can come this universal disobedience, except from our forgetfulness of the promises and obligations of holy Baptism, and from the fact that hardly anyone ratifies, of himself, the contract he made with God by those who stood sponsors for him?

This is so true that the Council of Sens, convoked by order of Louis the Debonair to remedy the disorders of Christians, which were then so great, judged that the principal cause of that corruption of morals arose from the oblivion and the ignorance in which men lived of the obligations of holy Baptism; and it could think of no better means for remedying so great an evil than to persuade Christians to renew the vows and promises of Baptism.

The *Catechism of the Council of Trent*, the faithful interpreter of that holy Council, exhorts the parish priests to do the same thing, and to induce the people to remind themselves, and to believe, that they are bound and consecrated as slaves to Our Lord Jesus Christ, their Redeemer and their Lord. These are its words: "The parish priest shall exhort the faithful people so that they may know that it is most just ... that we should devote and consecrate ourselves forever to our Redeemer and Lord as His very slaves."

Now, if the Councils, the Fathers and even experience show us that the best means of remedying the irregularities of Christians is by making them call to mind the obligations of their Baptism, and persuading them to renew now the vows they made then, is it not only right that we should do it in a perfect manner, by this devotion and consecration of ourselves to Our Lord through His holy Mother? I say "in a perfect manner," because in thus consecrating ourselves to Him, we make use of the most perfect of all means, namely, the Blessed Virgin.

Objections and Answers

No one can object to this devotion as being either a new or an indifferent one. It is not new, because the Councils, the Fathers and many authors both ancient and modern speak of this consecration to Our Lord, or renewal of the vows and promises of Baptism, as of a thing anciently practiced, and which they counsel to all Christians. Neither is it a matter of indifference, because the principal source of all disorders, and consequently of the eternal perdition of Christians, comes from their forgetfulness and indifference about this practice.

But some may object that this devotion, in making us give to Our Lord, by Our Lady's hands, the value of all our good works, prayers, mortifications and alms, puts us in a state of incapacity for assisting the souls of our parents, friends and benefactors.

I answer them as follows:

1. That it is not credible that our parents, friends and benefactors should suffer from the fact of our being devoted and consecrated without exception to the service of Our Lord and His holy Mother. To think this would be to think unworthily of the goodness and power of Jesus and Mary, who know well how to assist our parents, friends and benefactors, out of our own little spiritual revenue or by other ways.

2. This practice does not hinder us from praying for others, whether dead or living, although the application of our good works depends on the will of our Blessed Lady. On the contrary, it is this very thing which will lead us to pray with more confidence; just as a rich person who has given all his wealth to his

prince in order to honor him the more, would beg the prince all the more confidently to give an alms to one of his friends who should ask for it. It would even be a source of pleasure to the prince to be given an occasion of proving his gratitude toward a person who had stripped himself to clothe him, and impoverished himself to honor him. We must say the same of our Blessed Lord and of Our Lady. They will never let themselves be outdone in gratitude.

Someone may perhaps say, "If I give to our Blessed Lady all the value of my actions to apply to whom she wills, I may have to suffer a long time in Purgatory."

This objection, which comes from self-love and ignorance of the generosity of God and His holy Mother, refutes itself. A fervent and generous soul who gives God all he has, without reserve, so that he can do nothing more; who lives only for the glory and reign of Jesus Christ, through His holy Mother, and who makes an entire sacrifice of himself to bring it about—will this generous and liberal soul, I say, be more punished in the other world because it has been more liberal and more disinterested than others? Far, indeed, will that be from the truth! Rather, it is toward that soul, as we shall see by what follows, that Our Lord and His holy Mother are the most liberal in this world and in the other, in the orders of nature, grace and glory.

But we must now, as briefly as we can, run over the motives which ought to recommend this devotion to us, the marvelous effects it produces in the souls of the faithful, and its practices.

Secret of Mary #28-29

It consists in giving oneself entirely and as a slave to Mary, and to Jesus through Mary; and after that to do all that we do, through Mary, with Mary, in Mary and for Mary. I shall now explain these words.

We should choose a special feast day on which we give, consecrate and sacrifice to Mary voluntarily, lovingly and without constraint, entirely and without reserve: our body and soul, our exterior property, such as house, family and income; and also our interior and spiritual possessions; namely, our merits, graces, virtues, and satisfactions.

It should be observed here, that by this devotion the soul sacrifices to Jesus, through Mary, all that it holds most dear, things of which even no religious Order would require the sacrifice; namely, the right to dispose of ourselves, of the value of our prayers and alms, of our mortifications and satisfactions. The soul leaves everything to be feely disposed of by Our Lady so that she may apply it all according to her own will for the greater glory of God, which she alone knows perfectly.

Fifth Day _____

Daily prayers during the Second Week: Litany of the Holy Ghost on page 160, the *Ave Maris Stella* on page 156, Saint Louis De Montfort's *Prayer to Mary* on page 157 and the Recitation of the *Rosary*.

Gospel according to Saint John 2:1-25

And the third day, there was a marriage in Cana of Galilee: and the mother of Jesus was there.

2. And Jesus also was invited, and His disciples, to the marriage.

3. And the wine failing, the mother of Jesus said to Him: They have no wine.

4. And Jesus said to her: Woman, what is that to Me and to thee? My hour is not yet come.

5. His mother said to the waiters: Whatsoever He shall say to you, do.

6. Now there were set there six waterpots of stone, according to the manner of the purifying of the Jews, containing two or three measures apiece.

7. Jesus said to them: Fill the waterpots with water. And they filled them up to the brim.

8. And Jesus said to them: Draw out now, and carry to the chief steward of the feast and they carried it.

9. And when the chief steward had tasted the water made wine, and knew not whence it was, but the waiters knew who had drawn the water; the chief steward called the bridegroom,

10. And said to him: Every man at first sets forth good wine, and when men have well drunk, then that which is worse. But thou has kept the good wine until now.

11. This beginning of miracles did Jesus in Cana of Galilee; and manifested His glory, and His disciples believed in Him.

12. After this He went down to Capharnaum, He and His mother, and His brethren, and His disciples: and they remained there not many days.

13. And the pasch of the Jews was at hand, and Jesus went up to Jerusalem.

14. And He found in the temple them that sold oxen and sheep and doves, and the changers of money, sitting.

15. And when He had made, as it were, a scourge of little cords, He drove them all out of the temple, the sheep also and the oxen, and the money of the changers He poured out, and the tables He overthrew.

16. And to them that sold doves He said: Take these things hence, and make not the house of My Father a house of traffic.

17. And His disciples remembered, that it was written: The zeal of Thy house has eaten me up.

18. The Jews, therefore, answered, and said to Him: What sign does Thou show unto us, seeing Thou does these things?

19. Jesus answered, and said to them: Destroy this temple, and in three days I will raise it up.

20. The Jews then said: Six and forty years was this temple in building;

Mancipia Publications

and will Thou raise it up in three days?

21. But He spoke of the temple of His body.

22. When therefore He was risen again from the dead, His disciples remembered, that He had said this, and they believed the scripture, and the word that Jesus had said.

23. Now when He was at Jerusalem, at the pasch, upon the festival day, many believed in His name, seeing His signs which He did.

24. But Jesus did not trust Himself unto them, for that He knew all men,

25. And because He needed not that any should give testimony of man: for He knew what was in man.

True Devotion #135-168
Motives of this perfect Consecration—It devotes us Entirely to the Service of God

The first motive, which shows us the excellence of this consecration of ourselves to Jesus Christ by the hands of Mary.

If we can conceive on earth no employment more lofty than the service of God—if the least servant of God is richer, more powerful and more noble than all the kings and emperors of this earth, unless they also are the servants of God—what must be the riches, the power and the dignity of the faithful and perfect servant of God, who is devoted to His service entirely and without reserve, to the utmost extent possible? Such is the faithful and loving slave of Jesus in Mary who has given himself up entirely to the service of that King of Kings, by the hands of His holy Mother, and has reserved nothing for himself. Not all the gold of earth nor all the beauties of the heavens can repay him.

The other congregations, associations and confraternities erected in honor of Our Lord and His holy Mother, which do such immense good in Christendom, do not make us give everything without reserve. They prescribe to their members only certain practices and actions to satisfy their obligations. They leave them free for all other actions and moments and occupations. But this devotion makes us give to Jesus and Mary, without reserve, all our thoughts, words, actions and sufferings, every moment of our life, in such wise that whether we wake or sleep, whether we eat or drink, whether we do great actions or very little ones, it is always true to say that whatever we do, even without thinking of it, is, by virtue of our offering—at least if it has not been intentionally retracted—done for Jesus and Mary. What a consolation this is!

Moreover, as I have already said, there is no other practice equal to this for enabling us to rid ourselves easily of a certain proprietorship which imperceptibly creeps into our best actions. Our good Jesus gives us this great grace in recompense for the heroic and disinterested action of giving over to Him, by the hands of His holy Mother, all the value of our good works. If He gives a hundredfold even in this world to those who, for His love, quit outward and temporal and perishable goods, what will that hundredfold be which He will give to the man who sacrifices for Him even his inward and spiritual goods!

Jesus, our great Friend, has given Himself to us without reserve, body and soul, virtues, graces and merits. "He has bought the whole of me with the whole of Himself," says Saint Bernard. Is it not then a simple matter of justice and of gratitude that we should give Him all that we can give Him? He has been the first to be liberal toward us; let us, at least, be the second; and then, in life and death and throughout all eternity, we shall find Him still more liberal. "With the liberal He will be liberal."

It makes us imitate the example of Jesus Christ and of the Holy Trinity and practice Humility

The second motive, which shows us how just it is in itself, and how advantageous to Christians, to consecrate themselves entirely to the Blessed Virgin by this practice, in order to belong more perfectly to Jesus Christ.

This good Master did not disdain to shut Himself up in the womb of the Blessed Virgin, as a captive and as a loving slave, and later to be subject and obedient to her for thirty years. It is here, I repeat, that the human mind loses itself, when it seriously reflects on the conduct of the Incarnate Wisdom Who willed to give Himself to men—not directly, though He might have done so, but through the Blessed Virgin. He did not will to come into the world at the age of a perfect man, independent of others, but like a poor little babe, dependent on the care and support of this holy Mother. He is that Infinite Wisdom Who had a boundless desire to glorify God His Father and to save men; and yet He found no more perfect means, no shorter way to do it, than to submit Himself in all things to the Blessed Virgin, not only during the first eight, ten or fifteen years of His life, like other children, but for thirty years! He gave more glory to God His Father during all that time of submission to and dependence on our Blessed Lady than He would have given Him if He had employed those thirty years in working miracles, in preaching to the whole world and in converting all men—all of which He would have done, could He have thereby contributed more to God's glory. Oh, how highly we glorify God when, after the example of Jesus, we submit ourselves to Mary!

Having, then, before our eyes an example so plain and so well known to the whole world, are we so senseless as to imagine that we can find a more perfect or a shorter means of glorifying God than that of submitting ourselves to Mary, after the example of her Son?

Let us recall here, as a proof of the dependence we ought to have on our Blessed Lady, what I have said above in bringing forward the example which the Father, the Son and the Holy Ghost give of this dependence. The Father has not given, and does not give, His Son, except by her; He has no children but by her, and communicates no graces but through her. The Son has not been formed for the whole world in general, except by her; and He is not daily formed and engendered except by her, in union with the Holy Ghost; neither does He communicate His merits and His virtues except through her. The Holy Ghost has not formed Jesus Christ except by her; neither does He form the members of Our Lord's Mystical Body, except by her; and through her alone does He

78

dispense His favors and His gifts. After so many and such pressing examples of the Most Holy Trinity, can we without extreme blindness dispense with Mary, can we fail to consecrate ourselves to her and depend on her for the purpose of going to God and sacrificing ourselves to God?

Here are some passages of the Fathers which I have chosen to prove what has just been said: "Mary has two sons, a God-Man and a pure man; she is Mother of the first corporally, of the second spiritually."

"This is the will of God, Who wished us to have all things through Mary; if, therefore, there is in us any hope, any grace, any salutary gift, we know it comes to us through her."

"All the gifts, virtues and graces of the Holy Ghost are distributed by Mary, to whom she wishes, when she wishes, the way she wishes and as much as she wishes."

"Since you were unworthy to receive the divine graces, they were given to Mary, so that whatever you would have, you would receive through her."

God, says Saint Bernard, seeing that we are unworthy to receive His graces immediately from His own hand, gives them to Mary, in order that we may have through her whatever He wills to give us; and He also finds His glory in receiving, through the hands of Mary, the gratitude, respect and love which we owe Him for His benefits. It is most just, then, that we imitate this conduct of God, in order, as the same Saint Bernard says, that grace return to its Author by the same channel through which it came: "That grace should return to the giver by the same channel through which it came."

This is precisely what our devotion does. We offer and consecrate all we are and all we have to the Blessed Virgin in order that Our Lord may receive through her mediation the glory and the gratitude which we owe Him. We

*Never will anyone
who says his Rosary every day
be led astray.
This is a statement that I would
gladly sign with my blood.*

acknowledge ourselves unworthy and unfit to approach His Infinite Majesty by ourselves; and it is on this account that we avail ourselves of the intercession of the most holy Virgin.

Moreover, this devotion is a practice of great humility, which God loves above all the other virtues. A soul which exalts itself abases God; a soul which abases itself exalts God. God resists the proud and gives His grace to the humble. If you abase yourself, thinking yourself unworthy to appear before Him and to draw nigh to Him, He descends and lowers Himself to come to you, to take pleasure in you and to exalt you in spite of yourself. On the contrary, when you are bold enough to approach God without a mediator, God flies from you and you cannot reach Him. Oh, how He loves humility of heart! It is to this humility that this devotion induces us, because it teaches us never to draw nigh, of ourselves, to Our Lord, however sweet and merciful He may be, but always to avail ourselves of the intercession of our Blessed Lady, whether it be to appear before God, or to speak to Him, or to draw near to Him, or to offer Him anything, or to unite and consecrate ourselves to Him.

It Obtains for Us the Good Offices of the Blessed Virgin
I. Mary Gives Herself to Her Slave of Love

The most holy Virgin, who is a Mother of sweetness and mercy, and who never lets herself be outdone in love and liberality, seeing that we give ourselves entirely to her, to honor and to serve her, and for that end strip ourselves of all that is dearest to us, in order to adorn her, meets us in the same spirit. She also gives her whole self, and gives it in an unspeakable manner, to him who gives all to her. She causes him to be engulfed in the abyss of her graces. She adorns him with her merits; she supports him with her power; she illuminates him with her light; she inflames him with her love; she communicates to him her virtues: her humility, her faith, her purity and the rest. She makes herself his bail, his supplement, and his dear all toward Jesus. In a word, as that consecrated person is all Mary's, so Mary is all his, after such a fashion that we can say of that perfect servant and child of Mary what Saint John the Evangelist said of himself, that he took the holy Virgin for his own: "The disciple took her for his own."

It is this which produces in the soul, if it is faithful, a great distrust, contempt and hatred of self, and a great confidence in and self-abandonment to the Blessed Virgin, its good Mistress. A man no longer, as before, relies on his own dispositions, intentions, merits, virtues and good works; because, having made an entire sacrifice of them to Jesus Christ by that good Mother, he has but one treasure now, where all his goods are laid up, and that is no longer in himself, for his treasure is Mary.

This is what makes him approach Our Lord without servile or scrupulous fear, and pray to Him with great confidence. This is what makes him share the sentiments of the devout and learned Abbot Rupert, who, alluding to the victory that Jacob gained over the angel, said to our Blessed Lady these beautiful words: "O Mary, my Princess, Immaculate Mother of the God-Man, Jesus

Christ, I desire to wrestle with that man, namely, the Divine Word, not armed with my own merits but with yours."

Oh, how strong and mighty we are with Jesus Christ when we are armed with the merits and intercession of the worthy Mother of God, who, as Saint Augustine says, has lovingly vanquished the Most High.

II. Mary Purifies Our Good Works, Embellishes Them and Makes Them Acceptable to Her Son

As by this practice we give to Our Lord, by His Mother's hands, all our good works, that good Mother purifies them, embellishes them and makes them acceptable to her Son.

1. She purifies them of all the stain of self-love, and of that imperceptible attachment to created things which slips unnoticed into our best actions. As soon as they are in her most pure and fruitful hands, those same hands, which have never been sullied or idle and which purify whatever they touch, take away from the present which we give her all that was spoiled or imperfect about it.

2. She embellishes our works, adorning them with her own merits and virtues. It is as if a peasant, wishing to gain the friendship and benevolence of the king, went to the queen and presented her with a fruit which was his whole revenue, in order that she might present it to the king. The queen, having accepted the poor little offering from the peasant, would place the fruit on a large and beautiful dish of gold, and so, on the peasant's behalf, would present it to the king. Then the fruit, however unworthy in itself to be a king's present, would become worthy of his majesty because of the dish of gold on which it rested and the person who presented it.

3. She presents these good works to Jesus Christ; for she keeps nothing of what is given her for herself, as if she were our last end. She faithfully passes it all on to Jesus. If we give to her, we give necessarily to Jesus. If we praise her or glorify her, she immediately praises and glorifies Jesus. As of old when Saint Elizabeth praised her, so now when we praise her and bless her, she sings: "My soul doth magnify the Lord."

She persuades Jesus to accept these good works, however little and poor the present may be for that Saint of Saints and that King of Kings. When we present anything to Jesus by ourselves, and relying on our own efforts and dispositions, Jesus examines the offering, and often rejects it because of the stains it has contracted through self-love, just as of old He rejected the sacrifices of the Jews when they were full of their own will. But when we present Him anything by the pure and virginal hands of His well-beloved, we take Him by His weak side, if it is allowable to use such a term. He does not consider so much the thing that is given Him as the Mother who presents it. He does not consider so much whence the offering comes, as by whom it comes. Thus Mary, who is never repelled but always well received by her Son, makes everything she presents to Him, great or small, acceptable to His Majesty. Mary has but to present it for Jesus to accept it and be pleased with it. Saint Bernard used to give to those whom he conducted to perfection this great counsel: "When you want to offer anything to God, take care to offer it by the most agreeable and worthy hands of Mary, unless you wish to have it rejected."

Is not this what nature itself suggests to the little with regard to the great, as we have already seen? Why should not grace lead us to do the same thing with regard to God, who is infinitely exalted above us and before whom we are less than atoms—especially since we have an advocate so powerful that she is never refused; so ingenious that she knows all the secret ways of winning the heart of God; and so good and charitable that she repels no one, however little and wretched he may be.

I shall speak further on of the true figure of the truths in the story of Jacob and Rebecca.

It Is an Excellent Means of Procuring God's Greater Glory

This devotion, faithfully practiced, is an excellent means of making sure that the value of all our good works shall be employed for the greater glory of God. Scarcely anyone acts for that noble end, although we are all under an obligation to do so. Either we do not know where the greater glory of God is to be found, or we do not wish to find it. But our Blessed Lady, to whom we cede the value and merit of our good works, knows most perfectly where the greater glory of God is to be found; and inasmuch as she never does anything except for the greater glory of God, a perfect servant of that good Mistress, who is wholly consecrated to her, may say with the hardiest assurance that the value of all his actions, thoughts and words is employed for the greater glory of God, unless he purposely revokes his offering. Is there any consolation equal to this for a soul who loves God with a pure and disinterested love, and who prizes the glory and interest of God far beyond his own?

It Leads Us to Union With Our Lord

This devotion is an *easy, short, perfect and secure* way of attaining union with Our Lord, in which union the perfection of a Christian consists.

I.   It Is an Easy Way

It is the way which Jesus Christ Himself trod in coming to us, and in which there is no obstacle in reaching Him. It is true that we can attain divine union by other roads; but it is by many more crosses and strange deaths, and with many more difficulties, which we shall find it hard to overcome. We must pass through obscure nights, through combats, through strange agonies, over craggy mountains, through cruel thorns and over frightful deserts. But by the path of Mary we pass more gently and more tranquilly.

We do find, it is true, great battles to fight, and great hardships to master; but that good Mother makes herself so present and so near to her faithful servants, to enlighten them in their darknesses and their doubts, to strengthen them in their fears, and to sustain them in their struggles and their difficulties, that in truth this virginal path to find Jesus Christ is a path of roses and honey

Mancipia Publications

compared with the other paths. There have been some saints, but they have been in small numbers, who have walked upon this sweet path to go to Jesus, because the Holy Ghost, faithful Spouse of Mary, by a singular grace disclosed it to them. Such were Saint Ephrem, Saint John Damascene, Saint Bernard, Saint Bernardine, Saint Bonaventure, Saint Francis de Sales, and others. But the rest of the saints, who are the greater number, although they have all had devotion to our Blessed Lady, nevertheless have either not at all, or at least very little, entered upon this way. That is why they have had to pass through ruder and more dangerous trials.

How is it, then, some of the faithful servants of Mary will say to me, that the faithful servants of this good Mother have so many occasions of suffering, nay, even more than others who are not so devout to her? They are contradicted, they are persecuted, they are calumniated, the world cannot endure them; or again, they walk in interior darkness and in deserts where there is not the least drop of the dew of Heaven. If this devotion to our Blessed Lady makes the road to Jesus easier, how is it that they who follow it are the most despised of men?

I reply that it is quite true that the most faithful servants of the Blessed Virgin, being also her greatest favorites, receive from her the greatest graces and favors of Heaven, which are crosses. But I maintain that it is also the servants of Mary who carry these crosses with more ease, more merit and more glory. That which would stay the progress of another a thousand times over, or perhaps would make him fall, does not once stop their steps, but rather enables them to advance; because that good Mother, all full of grace and of the unction of the Holy Ghost, prepares her servants' crosses with so much maternal sweetness and pure love as to make them gladly acceptable, no matter how bitter they may be in themselves; and I believe that a person who wishes to be devout, and to live piously in Jesus Christ, and consequently to suffer persecutions and carry his cross daily, either will never carry great crosses, or will not carry them joyously or perseveringly, without a tender devotion to Our Lady, which is the sweetmeat and confection of crosses; just as a person would not be able to eat unripe fruits without a great effort which he could hardly keep up, unless they had been preserved in sugar.

II. It Is a Short Way

This devotion to our Blessed Lady is a short road to find Jesus Christ, both because it is a road from which we do not stray, and because, as I have just said, it is a road we tread with joy and facility, and consequently with promptitude. We make more progress in a brief period of submission to and dependence on Mary than in whole years of following our own will and of relying upon ourselves. A man obedient and submissive to Mary shall sing the signal victories which he shall gain over his enemies. They will try to hinder his advancing, or to make him retrace his steps or fall; this is true. But with the support, the aid and the guidance of Mary, he shall advance with giant strides toward Jesus, without falling, without drawing back one step, without even slackening his pace, along the same path by which he knows that Jesus also came to us with giant strides and in the briefest space of time.

Why do you think that Jesus lived so few years on earth, and of those few years, spent nearly all of them in subjection and obedience to His Mother? The truth is that, being perfected in a short time, He lived a long time—longer than Adam, whose fall He had come to repair, although the patriarch lived above nine hundred years. Jesus Christ lived a long time because He lived in complete subjection to His holy Mother, and closely united with her, in order that He might thus obey His Father. For (1) the Holy Ghost says that a man who honors his mother is like a man who lays up a treasure; that is to say, he who honors Mary, his Mother, to the extent of subjecting himself to her and obeying her in all things, will soon become exceedingly rich, because he is every day amassing treasures by the secret of that touchstone: "He who honors his mother is as one who lays up a treasure;" (2) because, according to a mystical interpretation of the inspired text, "My old age is to be found in the mercy of the bosom," it is in the bosom of Mary, which has surrounded and engendered a perfect man, and has had the capacity of containing Him Whom the whole universe could neither contain nor comprehend—it is, I say, in the bosom of Mary that they who are youthful become elders in light, in holiness, in experience and in wisdom, and that we arrive in a few years at the fullness of the age of Jesus Christ.

III. It Is a Perfect Way

This practice of devotion to our Blessed Lady is also a perfect path by which to go and unite ourselves to Jesus; because the divine Mary is the most perfect and the most holy of creatures, and because Jesus, Who has come to us most perfectly, took no other road for His great and admirable journey. The Most High, the Incomprehensible, the Inaccessible, He Who is, has willed to come to us, little worms of earth who are nothing. How has He done this? The Most High has come down to us perfectly and divinely, by the humble Mary, without losing anything of His divinity and sanctity. So it is by Mary that the very little ones are to ascend perfectly and divinely, without any fear, to the Most High. The Incomprehensible has allowed Himself to be comprehended and perfectly contained by the little Mary, without losing anything of His immensity. So also it is by the little Mary that we must let ourselves be contained and guided perfectly without any reserve. The Inaccessible has drawn near to us and has united Himself closely, perfectly and even personally to our humanity, by Mary, without losing anything of His majesty. So also it is by Mary that we must draw near to God and unite ourselves perfectly and closely to His Majesty without fear of being repulsed. In a word, He Who is has willed to come to that which is not, and to make that which is not, become He Who is; and He has done this perfectly in giving Himself and subjecting Himself entirely to the young Virgin Mary, without ceasing to be in time He Who is from all eternity. In like manner, it is by Mary that we, who are nothing, can become like to God by grace and glory, by giving ourselves to her so perfectly

Mancipia Publications

and entirely as to be nothing in ourselves, but everything in her, without fear of delusion.

Make for me, if you will, a new road to go to Jesus, and pave it with all the merits of the blessed, adorn it with all their heroic virtues, illuminate and embellish it with all the lights and beauties of the angels, and let all the angels and saints be there themselves, to escort, defend and sustain those who are ready to walk there; and yet in truth, in simple truth, I say boldly, and I repeat that I say truly, I would prefer to this new, perfect path the immaculate way of Mary. "He made my way blameless." It is the way without stain or spot, without original or actual sin, without shadow or darkness. When my sweet Jesus comes a second time on earth in His glory, as it is most certain He will do, to reign there, He will choose no other way for His journey than the divine Mary, by whom He came the first time so surely and so perfectly. But there will be a difference between His first and His last coming. The first time He came secretly and hiddenly; the second time He will come gloriously and resplendently. But both times He will have come perfectly, because both times He will have come by Mary. Alas! Here is a mystery which is not understood. "Here let all tongues be mute."

IV. It Is a Secure Way

This devotion to our Blessed Lady is also a secure way to go to Jesus and to acquire perfection by uniting ourselves to Him.

1. It is a secure way, because the practice which I am teaching is not new. Father Boudon, who died a short time ago in the odor of sanctity, says in a book which he composed on this devotion that it is so ancient that we cannot fix precisely the date of its beginning. It is, however, certain that for more than seven hundred years we find traces of it in the Church.

Saint Odilon, the Abbot of Cluny, who lived about the year 1040, was one of the first who publicly practiced it in France, as is told in his life.

Peter Cardinal Damian relates that in the year 1016 Blessed Marino, his brother, made himself a slave of the Blessed Virgin in the presence of his director in a most edifying manner. He put a rope around his neck, took the discipline, and laid on the altar a sum of money, as a token of his devotedness and consecration to Our Lady; and he continued this devotion so faithfully during his whole life that he deserved to be visited and consoled at his death by his good Mistress, and to receive from her mouth the promise of paradise in recompense for his services. Caesarius Bollandus mentions an illustrious knight, Vautier de Birbac, a near relative of the Duke of Louvain, who about the year 1300 consecrated himself to the Blessed Virgin.

This devotion was also practiced by several private individuals up to the seventeenth century, when it became public.

Father Simon de Roias, of the Order of the Most Holy Trinity, known as the Order of Redemption of Captives, and preacher of Philip III, made this devotion popular in Spain and Germany; and at the request of Philip III, obtained of Gregory XV ample indulgences for those who practiced it.

Father de Los Rios, the Augustinian, devoted himself, with his intimate friend, Father de Roias, to spreading this devotion throughout Spain and Germany both by preaching and by writing. He composed a thick volume called *Hierarchia Mariana,* in which he treats with as much piety as learning of the antiquity, excellence and solidity of this devotion.

In the seventeenth century the Theatine Fathers established this devotion in Italy, Sicily and Savoy. Father Stanislaus Phalacius, the Jesuit, furthered this devotion wonderfully in Poland.

Father de Los Rios, in his work just cited, quotes the names of princes, princesses, bishops and cardinals of different kingdoms, who embraced this devotion.

Cornelius à Lapide, as praiseworthy for his piety as for his profound erudition, having been commissioned by several bishops and theologians to examine this devotion, did so with great thoroughness and deliberation, and praised it in a manner which we might have expected from his well-known piety; and many other distinguished persons have followed his example.

The Jesuit Fathers, always zealous in the service of our Blessed Lady, in the name of the Sodalists of Cologne presented a little treatise on this devotion to Duke Ferdinand of Bavaria, who was then Archbishop of Cologne. He approved it, granted permission for its printing, and exhorted all the parish priests and religious of his diocese to promote this solid devotion as much as they could.

Cardinal de Berulle, whose memory is held in veneration throughout all France, was one of the most zealous in spreading this devotion in that country, in spite of all the calumnies and persecutions which he suffered from critics and freethinkers. They accused him of novelty and superstition. They wrote and published a libel against him, in order to defame him; and they, or rather the Devil by their ministry, made use of a thousand artifices to hinder his spreading the devotion in France. But that great and holy man only answered their calumnies by his patience; and he met the objections contained in their libel by a short treatise in which he most convincingly refuted them. He showed them that the devotion was founded on the example of Jesus Christ, on the obligations which we have toward Him, and on the vows which we have made in holy Baptism. It was chiefly by means of this last reason that he shut his adversaries' mouths, making them see that this consecration to the holy Virgin, and to Jesus Christ by her hands, is nothing else than a perfect renewal of the vows and promises of Baptism. He has said many beautiful things about this practice, which can be read in his works.

We may also see in Father Boudon's book the different Popes who have approved this devotion, the theologians who have examined it, the persecutions it has undergone and has overcome, and the thousands of persons who have embraced it, without any Pope ever having condemned it. Indeed, we cannot see how it could be condemned without overturning the foundations of Christianity.

It is clear, then, that this devotion is not new; and that if it is not common, that is because it is too precious to be relished and practiced by everyone.

2. This devotion is a secure means of going to Jesus Christ, because it is the very characteristic of our Blessed Lady to conduct us surely to Jesus, just as it is the very characteristic of Jesus to conduct us surely to the Eternal Father. Spiritual persons therefore, must not fall into the false belief that Mary can be a hindrance to them in attaining divine union; for is it possible that she who has found grace before God for the whole world in general and for each one in particular, should be a hindrance to a soul in finding the great grace of union with Him? Can it be possible that she who has been full and superabounding with graces, so united and transformed that it has been a kind of necessity that He should be incarnate in her, should be a stumbling-block in the way of a soul's perfect union with God?

It is quite true that the view of other creatures, however holy, may perhaps at certain times retard divine union. But this cannot be said of Mary, as I have remarked before and shall never weary of repeating. One reason why so few souls come to the fullness of the age of Jesus Christ is that Mary, who is as much as ever the Mother of the Son, and as much as ever the fruitful spouse of the Holy Ghost, is not sufficiently formed in their hearts. He who wishes to have the fruit well ripened and well formed must have the tree that produces it; he who wishes to have the fruit of life, Jesus Christ, must have the tree of life, which is Mary; he who wishes to have in himself the operation of the Holy Ghost must have His faithful and inseparable spouse, the divine Mary, who makes Him fertile and fruit-bearing, as we have said elsewhere.

Be persuaded, then, that the more you look at Mary in your prayers, contemplations, actions and sufferings, if not with a distinct and definite view, at least with a general and imperceptible one, the more perfectly will you find Jesus Christ, who is always, with Mary, great, powerful, active and incomprehensible—more than in Heaven or in any other creature. Thus, so far from the divine Mary, all absorbed in God, being an obstacle to the perfect in attaining union with God, there has never been up to this time, and there never will be, any creature who will aid us more efficaciously in this great work; either by the graces she will communicate to us for this purpose—for as a saint has said, "No one can be filled with the thought of God except by her"—or by the protection she will afford us against the illusions and trickeries of the evil spirit.

Where Mary is, there the evil spirit is not. One of the most infallible marks we can have of our being conducted by the good spirit is our being very devout to Mary, thinking often of her and speaking often of her. This last is the thought of a saint, who adds that as respiration is a certain sign the body is not dead, the frequent thought and loving invocation of Mary is a certain sign the soul is not dead by sin.

As it is Mary alone, says the Church (and the Holy Ghost Who guides the Church), who makes all heresies come to naught—"Thou alone hast destroyed all heresies in the whole world"—we may be sure that, however critics may grumble, no faithful client of Mary will ever fall into heresy or illusions, at least formal ones. He may very well err materially, take falsehood for truth, and the evil spirit for the good; and yet he will do even this less readily than others. But sooner or later he will acknowledge his material fault and error; and when he knows it, he will not be in any way self-opinionated by continuing to believe and maintain what he had once thought true.

Whoever, then, wishes to put aside the fear of illusion, which is the besetting timidity of men of prayer, and to advance in the way of perfection and surely and perfectly find Jesus Christ, let him embrace with great-heartedness—"with a great heart and willing mind"—this devotion to our Blessed Lady which perhaps he has not known before; let him enter into this excellent way which was unknown to him and which I now point out: "I show you a more excellent way." It is a path trodden by Jesus Christ, the Incarnate Wisdom, our sole Head. One of His members cannot make a mistake in passing by the same road.

It is an easy road, because of the fullness of the grace and unction of the Holy Ghost which fills it to overflowing. No one wearies there; no one walking there ever has to retrace his steps. It is a short road which leads us to Jesus in a little time. It is a perfect road, where there is no mud, no dust, not the least spot of sin. Lastly, it is a secure road, which conducts us to Jesus Christ and life eternal in a straight and secure manner, without turning to the right hand or to the left. Let us, then, set forth upon that road and walk there day and night, until we come to the fullness of the age of Jesus Christ.

Secret of Mary #28-29

It consists in giving oneself entirely and as a slave to Mary, and to Jesus through Mary; and after that to do all that we do, through Mary, with Mary, in Mary and for Mary. I shall now explain these words.

We should choose a special feast day on which we give, consecrate and sacrifice to Mary voluntarily, lovingly and without constraint, entirely and without reserve: our body and soul, our exterior property, such as house, family and income; and also our interior and spiritual possessions; namely, our merits, graces, virtues, and satisfactions.

It should be observed here, that by this devotion the soul sacrifices to Jesus, through Mary, all that it holds most dear, things of which even no religious order would require the sacrifice; namely, the right to dispose of ourselves, of the value of our prayers and alms, of our mortifications and satisfactions. The soul leaves everything to be freely disposed of by Our Lady so that she may apply it all according to her own will for the greater glory of God, which she alone knows perfectly.

Mancipia Publications

Sixth Day _____

Daily prayers during the Second Week: Litany of the Holy Ghost on page 160, the *Ave Maris Stella* on page 156, Saint Louis De Montfort's *Prayer to Mary* on page 157 and the Recitation of the *Rosary*.

Gospel according to Saint Luke 2:1-24

And it came to pass that in those days there went out a decree from Caesar Augustus, that the whole world should be enrolled.

2. This enrolling was first made by Cyrinus, the governor of Syria.

3. And all went to be enrolled, every one into his own city.

4. And Joseph also went up from Galilee, out of the city of Nazareth into Judea, to the city of David, which is called Bethlehem: because he was of the house and family of David,

5. To be enrolled with Mary his espoused wife, who was with child.

6. And it came to pass, that when they were there, her days were accomplished, that she should be delivered.

7. And she brought forth her firstborn Son, and wrapped Him up in swaddling clothes, and laid Him in a manger; because there was no room for them in the inn.

8. And there were in the same country shepherds watching, and keeping the night-watches over their flock.

9. And behold an angel of the Lord stood by them, and the brightness of God shone round about them, and they feared with a great fear.

10. And the angel said to them: Fear not; for, behold, I bring you good tidings of great joy, that shall be to all the people;

11. For this day is born to you a Saviour, Who is Christ the Lord, in the city of David.

12. And this shall be a sign unto you: You shall find the Infant wrapped in swaddling clothes, and laid in a manger.

13. And suddenly there was with the angel a multitude of the heavenly army, praising God, and saying:

14. Glory to God in the highest; and on earth peace to men of good will.

15. And it came to pass, after the angels departed from them into Heaven, the shepherds said one to another: Let us go over to Bethlehem, and let us see this word that is come to pass, which the Lord hath showed to us.

16. And they came with haste; and they found Mary and Joseph, and the Infant lying in the manger.

17. And seeing, they understood of the word that had been spoken to them concerning this Child.

18. And all that heard, wondered; and at those things that were told them by the shepherds.

19. But Mary kept all these words, pondering them in her heart.

20. And the shepherds returned, glorifying and praising God, for all the things they had heard and seen, as it was told unto them.

21. And after eight days were accomplished, that the Child should be circumcised, His name was called Jesus, which was called by the angel, before He was conceived in the womb.

22. And after the days of her purification, according to the law of Moses, were accomplished, they carried Him to Jerusalem, to present Him to the Lord:

23. As it is written in the law of the Lord: Every male opening the womb shall be called holy to the Lord;

24. And to offer a sacrifice, according as it is written in the law of the Lord, a pair of turtle doves, or two young pigeons.

True Devotion 169-182
It gives us great interior liberty

This practice of devotion gives to those who make use of it faithfully a great interior liberty, which is the liberty of the children of God. Since, by this devotion, we make ourselves slaves of Jesus Christ and consecrate ourselves entirely to Him in this capacity, our good Master, in recompense for the loving captivity in which we put ourselves, (1) takes from the soul all scruple and servile fear, which are capable only of cramping, imprisoning or confusing it; (2) He enlarges the heart with firm confidence in God, making it look upon Him as a Father; and (3) He inspires us with a tender and filial love.

Without stopping to prove these truths with arguments, I shall be content to relate here what I have read in the life of Mother Agnes of Jesus, a Dominican nun of the convent of Langeac, in Auvergne, who died there in the odor of sanctity in the year 1634. When she was only seven years old, and was suffering from great spiritual anguish, she heard a voice which told her that if she wished to be delivered from her anguish, and to be protected against all her enemies, she was as quickly as possible to make herself the slave of Jesus and His most holy Mother. She had no sooner returned to the house than she gave herself up entirely to Jesus and His Mother in this capacity, although up to that time she did not so much as know what the devotion meant. Taking an iron chain, she put it around her body and wore it until her death. After this, all her anguish and scruples ceased, and she experienced great peace and dilation of heart. This is what brought her to teach the devotion to many persons who made great progress in it among others, Father Olier, the founder of Saint Sulpice, as well as many priests and ecclesiastics of the same seminary. One day Our Lady appeared to her and put around her neck a chain of gold, to show her the joy she had at Mother Agnes' having made herself her Son's slave and her own; and Saint Cecilia, who accompanied Our Lady in that apparition, said to the religious: "Happy are the faithful slaves of the Queen of Heaven: for they shall enjoy true liberty." "To serve thee is liberty."

It Procures Great Blessings for Our Neighbor

Another consideration which may bring us to embrace this practice is the great good which our neighbor receives from it. For by this practice we exercise charity toward him in an eminent manner, seeing that we give him by Mary's hands all that is most precious to ourselves namely, the satisfactory and impetratory value of all our good works, without excepting the least good thought or the least little suffering. We agree that all the satisfactions we may have acquired, or may acquire up to the moment of our death, should be employed at Our Lady's will either for the conversion of sinners or for the deliverance of souls from Purgatory.

Is this not loving our neighbor perfectly? Is this not being a true disciple of Jesus Christ, who is always to be recognized by his charity? Is this not the way to convert sinners, without any fear of vanity; and to deliver souls from Purgatory, with scarcely doing anything but what we are obliged to do by our state of life?

To understand the excellence of this motive, we must understand also how great a good it is to convert a sinner or to deliver a soul from Purgatory. It is an infinite good, greater than creating Heaven and earth; because we give to a soul the possession of God. If by this practice we deliver but one soul in our life from Purgatory, or convert but one sinner, would not that be enough to induce a truly charitable man to embrace it?

But we must remark that, inasmuch as our good works pass through the hands of Mary, they receive an augmentation of purity, and consequently of merit, and of satisfactory and impetratory value. On this account they become more capable of solacing the souls in Purgatory and of converting sinners than if they did not pass through the virginal and liberal hands of Mary. It may be little that we give by Our Lady; but, in truth, if it is given without self-will and with a disinterested charity, that little becomes very mighty to turn away the wrath of God and to draw down His mercy. It would be no wonder if, at the hour of death, it should be found that a person faithful to this practice should by means of it have delivered many souls from Purgatory and converted many sinners, though he should have done nothing more than the ordinary actions of his state of life. What joy at his judgment! What glory in his eternity!

It Is an Admirable Means of Perseverance

Lastly, that which in some sense most persuasively draws us to this devotion to Our Lady is that it is an admirable means of persevering and being faithful in virtue. Whence comes it that the majority of the conversions of sinners are not durable? Whence comes it that we relapse so easily into sin? Whence comes it that the greater part of the just, instead of advancing from virtue to virtue and acquiring new graces, often lose the little virtue and the little grace they have? This misfortune comes, as I have shown before from the fact that man is so corrupt, so feeble and so inconstant, and yet trusts in himself, relies on his own strength and believes himself capable of safeguarding the treasure of his graces, virtues and merits.

But by this devotion, we entrust all that we possess to the Blessed Virgin, who is faithful; we take her for the universal depositary of all our goods of nature and of grace. It is in her fidelity that we trust; it is on her power that we lean; it is on her mercy and charity that we build, in order that she may preserve and augment our virtues and merits, in spite of the Devil, the world and the flesh, who put forth all their efforts to take them from us. We say to her as a good child to his mother, and a faithful servant to her mistress: "Keep that which is committed to your trust. My good Mother and Mistress, I acknowledge that up to this time I have, through your intercession received more graces from God than I deserve; and my sad experience teaches me that I carry this treasure in a very frail vessel, and that I am too weak and too miserable to keep it safely of myself: 'I am very young and despised'; I beseech you therefore, receive in trust all that I possess, and keep it for me by your fidelity and power. If you keep it for me, I shall lose nothing; if you hold me up, I shall not fall; if you protect me, I shall be sheltered from my enemies."

Listen to what Saint Bernard says in order to encourage us to adopt this practice: "When Mary holds you up, you do not fall; when she protects you, you need not fear; when she leads you, you do not tire, when she is favorable to you, you arrive at the harbor of safety." Saint Bonaventure seems to say the same thing still more clearly. "The Blessed Virgin," he says, "is not only retained in the plenitude of the saints, but she also retains and keeps the saints in their plenitude, so that it may not diminish. She prevents their virtues from being dissipated, their merits from perishing, their graces from being lost, the Devil from harming them, and even Our Lord from punishing them when they sin."

Our Blessed Lady is the faithful Virgin who by her fidelity to God repairs the losses which the faithless Eve has caused by her infidelity. It is she who obtains for those who attach themselves to her the graces of fidelity to God and perseverance. It is for this reason that a saint compares her to a firm anchor which holds her servants fast and hinders them from being shipwrecked in the agitated sea of this world, where so many persons perish simply through not being fastened to that anchor. "We fasten our souls," says he, "to thy hope, as to an abiding anchor." It is to her that the saints who have saved themselves have been the most attached and have done their best to attach others, in order to persevere in virtue. Happy, then, a thousand times happy, are the Christians who are now fastened faithfully and entirely to her, as to a firm anchor! The violence of the storms of this world will not make them founder, nor sink their heavenly treasures! Happy those who enter into Mary, as into the ark of Noah! The waters of the deluge of sin, which drown so great a portion of the world, shall do no harm to them; for "They who work in me shall not sin," says Mary, together with the Divine Wisdom. Blessed are the faithless children of the unhappy Eve, if only they attach themselves to the faithful Mother and Virgin who "remains always faithful and never belies herself." "She always loves those who love her" not only with an affective love, but with an effectual and efficacious one, by hindering them, through a great abundance of graces, from drawing back in the pursuit of virtue, from falling in the road, and from losing the grace of her Son.

This good Mother, out of pure charity, always receives whatever we

92

deposit with her—and what she has once received as depository, she is obliged in justice, by virtue of the contract of trusteeship, to keep safe for us; just as a person with whom I had left a thousand dollars in trust would be under the obligation of keeping them safe for me, so that if, by his negligence, they were lost, he would in justice be responsible to me for them. But the faithful Mary cannot let anything which has been entrusted to her be lost through her negligence. Heaven and earth could pass away sooner than that she could be negligent and faithless to those who trust in her.

Poor children of Mary, your weakness is extreme, your inconstancy is great, your inward nature is very much corrupted. You are drawn (I grant it) from the same corrupt mass as all the children of Adam and Eve. Yet do not be discouraged because of that. Console yourselves and exult in having the secret which I teach you—secret unknown to almost all Christians, even the most devout.

Leave not your gold and silver in your coffers, which have already been broken open by the evil spirits who have robbed you. These coffers are too little, too weak, too old, to hold a treasure so precious and so great. Put not the pure and clear water of the fountain into your vessels, all spoilt and infected by sin. If the sin is there no longer, at least the odor of it is, and so the water will be spoilt. Put not your exquisite wines into your old casks, which have had bad wine in them; else even these wines will be spoilt and perhaps break the casks, and be spilled on the ground.

Though you, predestinate souls, understand me well enough, I will speak yet more openly. Trust not the gold of your charity, the silver of your purity, the waters of your heavenly graces, nor the wines of your merits and virtues, to a torn sack, an old and broken coffer, a spoilt and corrupted vessel, like yourselves, else you will be stripped by the robbers—that is to say, the demons—who are seeking and watching night and day for the right time to do it; and you will infect by your own bad odor of self-love, self-confidence and self-will, every most pure thing which God has given you.

Pour, pour into the bosom and the heart of Mary all your treasures, all your graces, all your virtues. She is a spiritual vessel, she is a vessel of honor, she is a singular vessel of devotion. Since God Himself has been shut up in person, with all His perfections, in that vessel, it has become altogether spiritual, and the spiritual abode of the most spiritual souls. It has become honorable and the throne of honor for the grandest princes of eternity. It has become wonderful in devotion, and a dwelling the most illustrious for sweetness, for graces and for virtues. It has become rich as a house of gold, strong as a tower of David, and pure as a tower of ivory.

Oh, how happy is the man who has given everything to Mary, and has entrusted himself to Mary, and lost himself in her, in everything and for everything! He belongs all to Mary, and Mary belongs all to him. He can say boldly with David: "Mary is made for me;" or with the beloved disciple: "I have taken her for my own;" or with Jesus Christ: "All that I have is thine, and all that thou hast is Mine."

If any critic who reads this shall take it into his head that I speak here exaggeratedly, and with an extravagance of devotion, alas! he does not understand me—either because he is a carnal man who has no relish for spiritual things; or because he is a worldling who cannot receive the Holy Ghost; or because he is proud and critical, condemning and despising whatever he does not understand himself. But the souls which are not born of blood, nor of flesh, nor of the will of man, but of God and Mary, understand me and relish me—and it is for these that I also write.

Nevertheless, I say now, both for the former and for the latter, in returning from this digression, that the divine Mary, being the most gracious and liberal of all pure creatures, never lets herself be outdone in love and liberality. As a holy man said of her, for an egg she gives an ox; that is to say, for a little that is given to her, she gives much of what she has received from God. Hence, if a soul gives itself to her without reserve, she gives herself to that soul without reserve, if only we put our confidence in her without presumption, and on our side labor to acquire virtues and to bridle our passions.

Then let the faithful servants of the Blessed Virgin say boldly with Saint John Damascene, "Having confidence in you, O Mother of God, I shall be saved; being under your protection, I shall fear nothing; with your help I shall give battle to my enemies and put them to flight; for devotion to you is an arm of salvation which God gives to those whom it is His will to save."

Secret of Mary #33-34

By this devotion we also place our merits in the hands of Our Lady, but only that she may preserve, augment and embellish them, because we cannot communicate to one another either the merits of sanctifying grace or those of glory. However, we give her all our prayers and good works inasmuch as they have an impetratory and satisfactory value, that she may distribute and apply them to whom she pleases. If, after having thus consecrated ourselves to Our Lady, we desire to relieve a soul in Purgatory, to save a sinner, or to assist a friend by our prayers, our almsdeeds, our mortifications and sacrifices, we must humbly ask it of Our Lady, abiding, however, by her decision, which remains unknown to us; and we must be fully persuaded that the value of our actions, being dispensed by the same hand which God Himself makes use of to distribute to us His graces and gifts, cannot fail to be applied for His greater glory.

I have said that this devotion consists in giving ourselves to Mary as slaves. But notice that there are three kinds of slavery. The first is the slavery of nature; in this sense all men, good and bad alike, are slaves of God. The second is the slavery of constraint; the devils and the damned are slaves of God in this second sense. The third is the slavery of love and of free will; and this is the one by which we must consecrate ourselves to God through Mary. It is the most perfect way for us human creatures to give ourselves to God our Creator.

Mancipia Publications

Seventh Day —————————

Daily prayers during the Second Week: Litany of the Holy Ghost on page 160,
the *Ave Maris Stella* on page 156, Saint Louis De Montfort's *Prayer to
Mary* on page 157 and the Recitation of the *Rosary.*

Continuation of the holy Gospel according to Saint Luke 2:25-52

And behold there was a man in Jerusalem named Simeon, and this man
was just and devout, waiting for the consolation of Israel; and the Holy Ghost
was in him.

26. And he had received an answer from the Holy Ghost, that he should not
see death before he had seen the Christ of the Lord.

27. And he came by the Spirit into the temple. And when His parents
brought in the Child Jesus, to do for Him according to the custom of the law,

28. He also took Him into his arms, and blessed God, and said:

29. Now Thou dost dismiss Thy servant, O Lord, according to Thy word in
peace:

30. Because my eyes have seen Thy salvation,

31. Which Thou hast prepared before the face of all peoples:

32. A light to the revelation of the Gentiles, and the glory of Thy people
Israel.

33. And His father and mother were wondering at those things, which were
spoken concerning Him.

34. And Simeon blessed them, and said to Mary His mother: Behold this
Child is set for the fall and for the resurrection of many in Israel, and for a sign
which shall be contradicted;

35. And thy own soul a sword shall pierce, that out of many hearts,
thoughts may be revealed.

36. And there was one Anna, a prophetess, the daughter of Phanuel, of the
tribe of Aser; she was far advanced in years, and had lived with her husband
seven years from her virginity.

36. And she was a widow until fourscore and four years; who departed not
from the temple, by fastings and prayers serving night and day.

38. Now she, at the same hour coming in, confessed to the Lord; and spoke
of Him to all that looked for the redemption of Israel.

39. And after they had performed all things according to the law of the
Lord, they returned into Galilee, to their city Nazareth.

40. And the Child grew, and waxed strong, full of wisdom; and the grace
of God was in Him.

41. And His parents went every year to Jerusalem, at the solemn day of
the pasch,

42. And when He was twelve years old, they going up into Jerusalem,
according to the custom of the feast,

43. And having fulfilled the days, when they returned, the Child Jesus
remained in Jerusalem; and His parents knew it not.

Manual for the Total Consecration to Mary

44. And thinking that He was in the company, they came a day's journey, and sought Him among their kinsfolks and acquaintance.

45. And not finding Him, they returned into Jerusalem seeking Him.

46. And it came to pass, that, after three days, they found Him in the temple, sitting in the midst of the doctors, hearing them and asking them questions.

47. And all that heard Him were astonished at His wisdom and His answers.

48. And seeing Him, they wondered. And His mother said to Him: Son, why hast Thou done so to us? Behold, Thy father and I have sought Thee sorrowing.

49. And He said to them: How is it that you sought Me? Did you not know, that I must be about My Father's business?

50. And they understood not the word, that He spoke unto them.

51. And He went down with them, and came to Nazareth, and was subject to them. And His mother kept all these words in her heart.

52. And Jesus advanced in wisdom and age, and grace with God and men.

True Devotion #213-225
Wonderful Effects of This Devotion

My dear brother, be sure that if you are faithful to the interior and exterior practices of this devotion which I will point out, the following effects will take place in your soul.

—First Effect—Knowledge and Contempt of Self

By the light which the Holy Ghost will give you through His dear spouse, Mary, you will understand your own evil, your corruption and your incapacity for anything good. In consequence of this knowledge, you will despise yourself. You will think of yourself only with horror. You will regard yourself as a snail that spoils everything with its slime; or a toad that poisons everything with its venom; or as a spiteful serpent seeking only to deceive. In other words, the humble Mary will communicate to you a portion of her profound humility, which will make you despise yourself—despise nobody else, but love to be despised yourself.

—Second Effect—Participation in Mary's Faith

Our Blessed Lady will give you also a portion of her faith, which was the greatest of all faiths that ever were on earth, greater than the faith of all the patriarchs, prophets, apostles and saints put together. Now that she is reigning in Heaven, she no longer exercises this faith, because she sees all things clearly in God by the light of glory. Nevertheless, with the consent of the Most High, in entering into glory she did not lose her faith. She kept it for her faithful servants in the Church Militant. The more, then, that you gain the favor of that august Princess and faithful Virgin, the more will you act by pure faith; a pure faith which will make you care hardly at all about sensible consolations and extraordinary favors; a lively faith animated by charity, which will enable you to perform all your actions from the motive of pure love; a faith firm and immovable as a rock, through which you will rest quiet and constant in the midst of storms and hurricanes; a faith active and piercing, which like a mysterious pass-key, will give you entrance into all the mysteries of Jesus, into the last ends of man, and into the Heart of God Himself; a courageous faith, which will enable you to undertake and carry out without hesitation great things for God and for the salvation of souls; lastly, a faith which will be your blazing torch, your divine life, your hidden treasure of divine wisdom and your omnipotent arm; which you will use to enlighten those who are in the darkness of the shadow of death, to inflame those who are lukewarm and who have need of the heated gold of charity, to give life to those who are dead in sin, to touch and overthrow, by your meek and powerful words, the hearts of marble and the cedars of Lebanon; and finally, to resist the devil and all the enemies of salvation.

—Third Effect—Deliverance from Scruples, Cares and Fears

This Mother of fair love will take away from your heart all scruple and all disorder of servile fear. She will open and enlarge it to run the way of her Son's commandments with the holy liberty of the children of God. She will introduce into it pure love, of which she has the treasure, so that you shall no longer be guided by fear, as hitherto, in your dealings with the God of charity, but by love alone. You will look on Him as your good Father, Whom you will be incessantly trying to please, and with Whom you will converse confidently, as a child with its tender father. If, unfortunately, you offend Him, you will at once humble yourself before Him. You will ask His pardon with great lowliness, but at the same time you will stretch your hand out to Him with simplicity, and you will raise yourself up lovingly, without trouble or disquietude, and go on your way to Him without discouragement.

—Fourth Effect—Great Confidence in God and Mary

Our Blessed Lady will fill you with great confidence in God and in herself: (1) because you will not be approaching Jesus by yourself, but always by that good Mother; (2) because, as you have given her all your merits, graces and satisfactions to dispose of at her will, she will communicate to you her virtues and will clothe you in her merits, so that you will be able to say to God with confidence: "Behold Mary Thy handmaid; be it done unto me according to Thy word;" (3) because, as you have given yourself entirely to her, body and soul, she, who is liberal with the liberal, and more liberal even than the liberal, will in return give herself to you in a marvelous but real manner, so that you may say to her with assurance: "I am thine, holy Virgin; save me;" or as I have said before with the beloved disciple: "I have taken thee, holy Mother, for my own." You may also say with Saint Bonaventure: "My loving and redeeming Mistress, I will have confidence and will not fear, because you are my strength and my praise in the Lord ... I am altogether yours, and all that I have belongs to you!" And in another place: "O glorious Virgin, blessed above all created things! I will put you as a seal upon my heart, because your love is as strong as death." "Lord, my heart and my eyes have no right to extol themselves, or to be proud, or to seek great and wonderful things. Yet even at that, I am not humble; but I have lifted up and encouraged my soul by confidence; I am like a child, weaned from the pleasures of earth and resting on its mother's lap; and it is on that lap that all good things come to me." What will still further increase your confidence in her is that you will have less confidence in yourself. You have given her in trust all you have of good about you, that she may have it and keep it; and so all the trust you once had in yourself has become an increase of confidence in her, who is your treasure. Oh, what confidence and what consolation is this for a soul who can say that the treasure of God, where He was pleased to put all He had most precious, is his own treasure also! It was a saint who said she is the treasure of the Lord.

—Fifth Effect—Communication of the Soul and Spirit of Mary

The soul of our Blessed Lady will communicate itself to you, to glorify the Lord. Her spirit will enter into the place of yours, to rejoice in God her salvation, provided only that you are faithful to the practices of this devotion. "Let the soul of Mary be in each of us to glorify the Lord: let the spirit of Mary be in each of us to rejoice in God." Ah! when will the happy time come, said a holy man of our own days who was all absorbed in Mary—Ah! when will the happy time come when the divine Mary will be established Mistress and Queen of all hearts, in order that she may subject them fully to the empire of her great and holy Jesus? When will souls breath Mary as the body breathes air? When that time comes, wonderful things will happen in those lowly places where the Holy Ghost, finding His dear spouse, as it were, reproduced, in souls, shall come in with abundance, and fill them to overflowing with His gifts, and particularly with the gift of wisdom, to work miracles of grace. My dear brother, when will that happy time, that age of Mary, come, when many souls, chosen and procured from the Most High by Mary, shall lose themselves in the abyss of her interior, shall become living copies of Mary, to love and glorify Jesus? That time will not come until men shall know and practice this devotion which I am teaching. "That Thy reign may come, let the reign of Mary come.

—Sixth Effect—Transformation of the Faithful Soul by Mary into the Likeness of Jesus Christ

If Mary, who is the tree of life, is well cultivated in our soul by fidelity to the practices of this devotion, she will bear her fruit in her own time, and her fruit is none other than Jesus Christ. How many devout souls do I see who seek Jesus Christ, some by one way or by one practice, and others by other ways and other practices; and often times, after they have toiled much throughout the night, they say, "We have toiled all night, and have taken nothing!" We may say to them: "You have labored much and gained little"; Jesus is yet feeble in you. But by that immaculate way of Mary and that divine practice which I am teaching, we toil during the day, we toil in a holy place, we toil but little. There is no night in Mary, because there is no sin nor even the slightest shade. Mary is a holy place, and the holy of holies where saints are formed and molded.

Take notice, if you please, that I say the saints are molded in Mary. There is a great difference between making a figure in relief by blows of hammer and chisel, and making a figure by throwing it into a mold. Statuaries and sculptors labor much to make figures in the first manner; but to make them in the second manner, they work little and do their work quickly.

Saint Augustine calls our Blessed Lady "the mold of God"—the mold fit to cast and mold gods. He who is cast in this mold is presently formed and molded in Jesus Christ, and Jesus Christ in him. At a slight expense and in a short time he will become God, because he has been cast in the same mold which has formed a God.

It seems to me that I can very aptly compare directors and devout persons, who wish to form Jesus Christ in themselves or others by practices different from this one, to sculptors who trust in their own professional skill, ingenuity or art, and so give an infinity of hammerings and chiselings to a hard stone or a piece of badly polished wood, to make an image of Jesus Christ out of it. Sometimes they do not succeed in giving anything like the natural expression of Jesus, either from having no knowledge or experience of the Person of Jesus, or from some blow awkwardly given, which has spoiled the work. But those who embrace the secret of grace which I am revealing to them I may rightly compare to founders and casters who have discovered the beautiful mold of Mary, where Jesus was naturally and divinely formed; and without trusting in their own skill, but only in the goodness of the mold, they cast themselves and lose themselves in Mary, to become the faithful portraits of Jesus Christ.

Oh, beautiful and true comparison! But who will comprehend it? I desire that you may, my dear brother. But remember that we cast in a mold only what is melted and liquid; that is to say, you must destroy and melt down in yourself the old Adam to become the new one in Mary.

—Seventh Effect— The Greater Glory of God

By this practice, faithfully observed, you will give Jesus more glory in a month than by any other practice, however difficult, in many years; and I give the following reasons for it:

1. Because, doing your actions by our Blessed Lady, as this practice teaches you, you abandon your own intentions and operations, although good and known, to lose yourself, so to speak, in the intentions of the Blessed Virgin, although they are unknown. Thus you enter by participation into the sublimity of her intentions, which are so pure that she gives more glory to God by the least of her actions—for example, in twirling her distaff or pointing her needle—than Saint Lawrence by his cruel martyrdom on the gridiron, or even all the saints by all their heroic actions put together. It was thus that, during her sojourn here below, she acquired such an unspeakable aggregate of graces and merits that it were easier to count the stars of the firmament, the drops of water in the sea or the grains of sand upon its shore, than her merits and graces. Thus

it was that she gave more glory to God than all the angels and saints have given Him or ever will give Him. O prodigy of a Mary! Thou canst not help but do prodigies of grace in souls that wish to lose themselves altogether in thee!

2. Because the soul in this practice counts as nothing whatever it thinks or does of itself, and puts its trust and takes its pleasures only in the dispositions of Mary, when it approaches Jesus or even speaks to Him. Thus it practices humility far more than the souls who act of themselves and trust, with however imperceptible a complacency, in their own dispositions. But if the soul acts more humbly, it therefore more highly glorifies God, who is perfectly glorified only by the humble and those that are little and lowly in heart.

3. Because our Blessed Lady, being pleased, out of great charity, to receive the present of our actions in her virginal hands, gives them an admirable beauty and splendor. Moreover, she offers them herself to Jesus Christ, and it is evident that Our Lord is thus more glorified by them than if we offered them by our own criminal hands.

4. Lastly, because you never think of Mary without Mary's thinking of God for you. You never praise or honor Mary without Mary's praising and honoring God with you. Mary is altogether relative to God; and indeed, I might well call her the relation to God. She only exists with reference to God. She is the echo of God that says nothing, repeats nothing, but God. If you say "Mary," she says "God." Saint Elizabeth praised Mary, and called her blessed, because she had believed. Mary, the faithful echo of God, at once intoned: "My soul doth magnify the Lord."

That which Mary did then, she does daily now. When we praise her, love her, honor her or give anything to her, it is God Who is praised, God Who is loved, God Who is glorified, and it is to God that we give, through Mary and in Mary.

Secret of Mary #33-34

Notice again, that there is a great difference between a servant and a slave. A servant claims wages for his services; a slave has a right to none. A servant is free to leave his master when he likes—he serves him only for a time; a slave belongs to his master for life and has no right to leave him. A servant does not give to his master the right of life and death over him; a slave gives himself up entirely, so that his master can put him to death, without being molested by the law. It is easily seen, then, that he who is a slave by constraint is rigorously dependent on his master. Strictly speaking, a man must be dependent in that sense only on his Creator. Hence we do not find that kind of slavery among Christians, but only among pagans.

But happy and a thousand times happy is the generous soul that consecrates itself entirely to Jesus through Mary as a slave of love after it has shaken off by Baptism the tyrannical slavery of the devil!

Mancipia Publications

Knowledge of Jesus Christ

Second Period — Third Week

During the third week they should apply themselves to the study of Jesus Christ. They can meditate upon what we have said about Him, and say the prayer of Saint Augustine which they will find in this manual. They can, with the same saint, repeat a hundred times a day: "Lord, that I may know Thee!" or: "Lord, that I may see Who Thou art!"

What is to be studied in Chirst? First the Man-God, His grace and glory; then His rights to sovereign dominion over us; since, after having renounced Satan and the world, we have taken Jesus Christ for our Lord. What next shall be the object of our study? His exterior actions and also His interior life; namely, the virtues and acts of His Sacred Heart: His association with Mary in the mysteries of the Annunciation and Incarnation, during His infancy and hidden life, at the feast of Cana and on Calvary.

Daily Prayers during the Third Week are the: Litany of the Holy Ghost, the *Ave Maris Stella, Litany of the Holy Name of Jesus* or *Litany of the Sacred Heart. Saint Louis De Montfort's prayer to Jesus, O Jesus Living in Mary,* and the *Prayer of Saint Augustine.*

Spiritual Exercises during the Third Week are: Acts of love of God, thanksgiving for the blessings of Jesus, contrition and resolution.

(N. B., During this third week of preparation there are two Scripture readings for each day, you may choose which ever you prefer, you do not have to read both.)

First Day _____

Daily Prayers during the Third Week: Litany of the Holy Ghost on page 160, the *Ave Maris Stella* on page 156, the *Litany of the Holy Name of Jesus* or *Litany of the Sacred Heart,* on pages 163 or 165, respectively. Saint Louis De Montfort's *Prayer to Jesus* page 158, *O Jesus Living in Mary* on page 159, and the *Prayer of Saint Augustine* on page 158.

Gospel according to Saint John 13

Before the festival day of the pasch, knowing that His hour was come, that He should pass out of this world to the Father: having loved His own who were in the world, He loved them unto the end.

2. And when supper was done, (the Devil having now put into the heart of Judas Iscariot, the son of Simon, to betray Him,)

3. Knowing that the Father had given Him all things into His hands, and that He came from God, and goes to God;

4. He rose from supper, and laid aside His garments, and having taken a towel, girded Himself.

5. After that, He put water into a basin, and began to wash the feet of the disciples, and to wipe them with the towel wherewith He was girded.

6. He came therefore to Simon Peter. And Peter said to Him: Lord, do Thou wash my feet?

7. Jesus answered, and said to him: 'What I do thou know not now; but thou shall know hereafter.

8. Peter said to Him: Thou shall never wash my feet. Jesus answered him: If I wash thee not, thou shall have no part with Me.

9. Simon Peter said to Him: Lord, not only my feet, but also my hands and my head,

10. Jesus said to him: He that is washed, needs not but to wash his feet, but is clean wholly. And you are clean, but not all.

11. For He knew who he was that would betray Him; therefore He said: You are not all clean.

12. Then after He had washed their feet, and taken His garments, being set down again, He said to them: Know you what I have done to you?

13. You call Me Master, and Lord; and you say well, for so I am.

14. If then I being your Lord and Master, have washed your feet; you also ought to wash one another's feet.

15. For I have given you an example, that as I have done to you, so you do also.

16. Amen, amen I say to you: The servant is not greater than his lord; neither is the apostle greater than he that sent him.

17. If you know these things, you shall be blessed if you do them.

18. I speak not of you all: I know whom I have chosen. But that the scripture may be fulfilled: He that eats bread with Me, shall lift up his heel against Me.

19. At present I tell you, before it come to pass: that when it shall come to pass, you may believe that I am He.

20. Amen, amen I say to you, he that receives whomsoever I send, receives Me; and he that receives Me, receives Him that sent Me.

21. When Jesus had said these things, He was troubled in spirit; and He testified, and said: Amen, amen I say to you, one of you shall betray Me.

22. The disciples therefore looked one upon another, doubting of whom He spoke.

23. Now there was leaning on Jesus' bosom one of His disciples, whom Jesus loved.

24. Simon Peter therefore beckoned to him, and said to him: Who is it of whom He speaks?

25. He therefore, leaning on the breast of Jesus, said to Him: Lord, who is it?

26. Jesus answered: He it is to whom I shall reach bread dipped. And when He had dipped the bread, He gave it to Judas Iscariot, the son of Simon.

27. And after the morsel, Satan entered into him. And Jesus said to him: That which thou do, do quickly.

28. Now no man at the table knew to what purpose He said this unto him.

29. For some thought, because Judas had the purse, that Jesus had said to him: Buy those things which we have need of for the festival day: or that he should give something to the poor.

30. He therefore having received the morsel, went out immediately. And it was night.

31. When he therefore was gone out, Jesus said: Now is the Son of man glorified, and God is glorified in Him.

32. If God be glorified in Him, God also will glorify Him in Himself; and immediately will He glorify Him.

33. Little children, yet a little while I am with you. You shall seek Me; and as I said to the Jews: Whither I go you cannot come; so I say to you now.

34. A new commandment I give unto you: That you love one another, as I have loved you, that you also love one another.

35. By this shall all men know that you are My disciples, if you have love one for another.

36. Simon Peter said to Him: Lord, where go Thou? Jesus answered: Where I go, thou cannot follow Me now; but thou shall follow hereafter.

37. Peter said to Him: Why cannot I follow Thee now? I will lay down my life for Thee.

38. Jesus answered him: Will thou lay down thy life for Me? Amen, amen I say to thee, the cock shall not crow, till thou deny Me thrice.

Gospel according to Saint Matthew 26: 1-20

And it came to pass, when Jesus had ended all these words, He said to His disciples:

2. You know that after two days shall be the pasch, and the Son of man

Mancipia Publications

shall be delivered up to be crucified:

3. Then were gathered together the chief priests and ancients of the people into the court of the high priest, who was called Caiphas:

4. And they consulted together, that by subtlety they might apprehend Jesus, and put Him to death.

5. But they said: Not on the festival day, lest perhaps there should be a tumult among the people.

6. And when Jesus was in Bethania, in the house of Simon the leper,

7. There came to Him a woman having an alabaster box of precious ointment, and poured it on His head as He was at table.

8. And the disciples seeing it, had indignation, saying: To what purpose is this waste?

9. For this might have been sold for much, and given to the poor.

10. And Jesus knowing, said to them: Why do you trouble this woman? For she hath wrought a good work upon Me.

11. For the poor you have always with you: but Me you have not always.

12. For she in pouring this ointment upon My body, hath done it for My burial.

13. Amen I say to you, wheresoever this gospel shall be preached in the whole world, that also which she has done, shall be told for a memory of her.

14. Then went one of the twelve, who was called Judas Iscariot, to the chief priests.

15. And said to them: What will you give me, and I will deliver Him unto you? But they appointed him thirty pieces of silver.

16. And from thenceforth he sought opportunity to betray Him.

17. And on the first day of the Azymes, the disciples came to Jesus, saying: Where wilt Thou that we prepare for You to eat the pasch?

18. But Jesus said: Go into the city to a certain man, and say to him: The Master says, My time is near at hand, with you I make the pasch with My disciples.

19. And the disciples did as Jesus apointed to them, and they prepared the pasch.

20. But when it was evening, He sat down with His twelve disciples.

Imitation of Christ, Book 2, Chapter 7
Of the Love of Jesus above All Things

Blessed is he who knows what it is to love Jesus and to despise himself for the sake of Jesus.

We must quit what we love for this Beloved, because Jesus will be loved alone above all things.

The love of things created is deceitful and inconstant.

The love of Jesus is faithful and enduring.

He that cleaves to creatures shall fall with them.

He that embraces Jesus shall stand firm forever.

Love Him and keep Him for thy friend, Who, when all go away, will not leave thee nor suffer thee to perish in the end.

Thou must at last be separated from all things else, whether thou wilt or not.

2. Keep thyself with Jesus both in life and death and commit thyself to His care, Who alone can help thee when all others fail.

Thy Beloved is of such a nature that He will admit of no other, but will have thy heart to Himself, and sit there like a king upon his own throne.

If thou could but purge thyself well from affection to creatures, Jesus would willingly dwell with thee.

Thou wilt find all that in a manner lost, which thou has placed in men out of Jesus.

Do not trust or rely upon a frail reed; "for all flesh is grass and all the glory thereof shall fade as the flower of the field."

3. Thou wilt soon be deceived if thou only regard the outward show of men.

For if thou seek thy comfort and thy gain in others, thou wilt often meet with loss.

If in all things thou seek Jesus, doubtless thou wilt find Jesus.

But if thou seek thyself thou wilt indeed find thyself, to thine own ruin.

For a man does himself more harm if he seek not Jesus, than the whole world and all his enemies could do him.

Imitation of Christ, Book 2, Chapter 11
Of the Small Number of the Lovers of the Cross of Jesus

Jesus has now many lovers of His heavenly Kingdom but few that are willing to bear His Cross.

He has many that are desirous of comfort, but few of tribulation.

He finds many companions of His table, but few of His abstinence.

All desire to rejoice with Him, few are willing to suffer with Him.

Many follow Jesus to the breaking of bread, but few to the drinking of the chalice of His Passion.

Many reverence His miracles, but few follow the ignominy of His cross.

Many love Jesus as long as they meet with no adversity.

Many praise Him and bless Him as long as they receive consolation from Him.

But if Jesus hide Himself, and leave them for a little while, they either fall into complaints or excessive dejection.

2. But they that love Jesus for Jesus' sake and not for any comfort of their own, bless Him no less in tribulation and anguish of heart than in the greatest consolation.

And if He should never give them His comfort, yet would they always praise Him and always give Him thanks.

3. Oh, how much is the pure love of Jesus able to do when it is not mixed with any self-interest or self-love.

Are not all those to be called hirelings who are always seeking

Mancipia Publications

consolation?

Are they not proved to be rather lovers of themselves than of Christ who are always thinking of their own profit and gain?

Where shall we find a man that is willing to serve God gratis?

4. Seldom do we find anyone so spiritual as to be stripped of all things.

For who shall be able to find the man that is truly poor in spirit and stripped of all affection to all created things? His price is from afar and from the uttermost coasts.

If a man give his whole substance it is yet nothing.

And if he do great penance it is yet little.

And if he attain to all knowledge he is far off still.

And if he have great virtue and exceeding fervent devotion there is still much wanting to him, to wit, one thing which is chiefly necessary for him.

And what is that? That, having left all things else, he leave also himself and wholly go out of himself and retain nothing of self-love.

And when he shall have done all things which he knows should be done, let him think that he has done nothing.

5. Let him not make great account of that which may appear much to be esteemed, but let him in truth acknowledge himself to be an unprofitable servant, as Truth itself has said: "When you shall have done all the things that are commanded you, say: We are unprofitable servants."

Then may he be truly poor and naked in spirit and may say with the Prophet: "I am alone and poor."

Yet no one is indeed richer than such a man, none more powerful, none more free, who knows how to leave himself and all things and place himself in the very lowest place.

True Devotion #60-67

Having spoken thus far of the necessity of devotion to the Most Holy Virgin, I must now show in what this devotion consists. This I will do, with God's help, after I shall have first laid down some fundamental truths which shall throw light on that grand and solid devotion which I desire to disclose.

First Truth—Jesus Christ is the Last End of Devotion to Mary

Jesus Christ Our Saviour, true God and true Man, ought to be the last end of all our other devotions, else they are false and delusive. Jesus Christ is the Alpha and the Omega, the beginning and the end of all things. We labor not, as the Apostle says, except to render every man perfect in Jesus Christ; because it is in Him alone that the whole plentitude of the Divinity dwells together with all the other plentitudes of graces, virtues and perfections. It is in Him alone that we have been blessed with all spiritual benediction; and He is our only Master, Who has to teach us; our only Lord on Whom we ought to depend; our only Head to Whom we must be united; our only Model to Whom we should conform ourselves; our only Physician Who can heal us; our only Shepherd

Who can feed us; our only Way Who can lead us; our only Truth Whom we must believe; our only Life Who can animate us; and our only All in all things Who can satisfy us. There has been no other name given under Heaven except the name of Jesus, by which we can be saved. God has laid no other foundation of our salvation, our perfection or our glory, than Jesus Christ. Every building which is not built on that firm rock is founded upon the moving sand, and sooner or later infallibly will fall. Every one of the faithful who is not united to Him as a branch to the stock of the vine, shall fall, shall wither and shall be fit only to be cast into the fire. Outside of Him there exists nothing but error, falsehood, iniquity, futility, death and damnation. But if we are in Jesus Christ and Jesus Christ in us, we have no condemnation to fear. Neither the angels of Heaven nor the men of earth nor the devils of hell nor any other creature can injure us; because they cannot separate us from the love of God, which is Jesus Christ. By Jesus Christ, with Jesus Christ, in Jesus Christ, we can do all things; we can render all honor and glory to the Father in the unity of the Holy Ghost; and we can become perfect ourselves and be to our neighbor a good odor of eternal life.

If, then, we establish solid devotion to Our Blessed Lady, it is only to establish more perfectly devotion to Jesus Christ, and to provide an easy and secure means for finding Jesus Christ. If devotion to Our Lady removed us from Jesus Christ, we should have to reject it as an illusion of the devil; but so far from this being the case, devotion to Our Lady is, on the contrary, necessary for us, as I have already shown, and will show still further hereafter, as a means of finding Jesus Christ perfectly, of loving Him tenderly, of serving Him faithfully.

I here turn for one moment to Thee, O sweet Jesus, to complain lovingly to Thy Divine Majesty that the greater part of Christians, even the most learned, do not know the necessary union there is between Thee and Thy holy Mother. You, Lord, are always with Mary, and Mary is always with You, and she cannot be without You, else she would cease to be what she is. She is so transformed into You by grace that she lives no more, she is as though she were not. It is You only, My Jesus, Who lives and reigns in her more perfectly than in all the angels and the blessed. Ah! if we knew the glory and the love which You receive from this admirable creature, we should have very different thoughts both of You and her from what we have now. She is so intimately united with You that it were easier to separate the light from the sun, the heat from the fire; nay, it were easier to separate from You all the angels and saints than the divine Mary, because she loves You more ardently and glorifies You more perfectly than all the other creatures put together.

After that, my sweet Master, is it not an astonishingly pitiable thing to see the ignorance and the darkness of all men here below in regard to Your holy Mother? I speak not so much of idolaters and pagans, who knowing You not, care not to know her. I speak not even of heretics and schismatics, who care not to be devout to Your holy Mother, being separated as they are from You and Your Holy Church; but I speak of Catholic Christians, and even of doctors

108

among Catholics who make profession of teaching truths to others, and yet know not You nor Your holy Mother, except in a speculative, dry, barren and indifferent manner. These gentlemen speak but rarely of Your holy Mother and of the devotion we ought to have to her, because they fear, so they say, lest we should abuse it, and do some injury to You in honoring Your holy Mother too much. If they hear or see anyone devout to Our Blessed Lady, speaking often of his devotion to that good Mother in a tender, strong and persuasive way, and as a secure means without delusion, as a short road without danger, as an immaculate way without imperfection, and as a wonderful secret for finding and loving You perfectly, they cry out against him and give him a thousand false reasons by way of proving to him that he ought not to talk so much of Our Blessed Lady; that there are great abuses in that devotion; and that we must direct our energies to destroy these abuses, and to speak of You, rather than to incline the people to devotion to Our Blessed Lady, whom they already love sufficiently.

We hear them sometimes speak of devotion to Our Blessed Lady, not for the purpose of establishing it and persuading men to embrace it, but to destroy the abuses which are made of it; and all the while these teachers are without piety or tender devotion towards You, simply because they have none for Mary. They regard the Rosary and the Scapular as devotions proper for weak and ignorant minds, without which men can save themselves; and if there falls into their hands any poor client of Our Lady who says his Rosary, or has any other practice of devotion toward her, they soon change his spirit and his heart. Instead of the Rosary, they counsel him the seven Penitential Psalms. Instead of devotion to the holy Virgin, they counsel him devotion to Jesus Christ.

O my sweet Jesus, have these people got Your spirit? Do they please You in acting thus? Does it please You, when for fear of displeasing You we neglect doing our utmost to please Your Mother? Does devotion to Your holy Mother hinder devotion to Yourself? Does she attribute to herself the honor we pay her? Does she head a faction of her own? Is she a stranger who has no connection with You? Does it displease You that we should try to please her? Do we separate or alienate ourselves from Your love by giving ourselves to her and honoring her?

Yet, my sweet Master, the greater part of the learned could not discourage devotion to Your holy Mother more, and could not show more indifference to it, even if all that I have just said were true. Thus have they been punished for their pride! Keep me, Lord—keep me from their sentiments and their practices, and give me some share of the sentiments of gratitude, esteem, respect and love which You have in regard to Your holy Mother, so that the more I imitate and follow her, the more I may love and glorify You.

So, as if up to this point I had still said nothing in honor of Your holy Mother, give me now the grace to praise Thee worthily—in spite of all her enemies, who are Yours as well; and grant me to say loudly with the saints, "Let not that man presume to look for the mercy of God who offends His holy Mother."

Manual for the Total Consecration to Mary

Make me love You ardently, so that I may obtain of Thy mercy a true devotion to Thy holy Mother, and inspire the whole earth with it; and for that end, receive the burning prayer which I offer to Thee with Saint Augustine and Thy other true friends: "Thou art Christ, my holy Father, my tender God, my great King, my good Shepherd, my one Master, my best Helper, my most Beautiful and my Beloved, my living Bread, my Priest forever, my Leader to my country, my true Light, my holy Sweetness, my straight Way, my excellent Wisdom, my pure Simplicity, my pacific Harmony, my whole Guard, my good Portion, my everlasting Salvation.

Christ Jesus, my sweet Lord, why have I ever loved, why in my whole life have I ever desired anything except Thee, Jesus my God? Where was I when I was not in Thy mind with Thee? Now, from this time forth, do ye, all my desires, grow hot, and flow out upon the Lord Jesus: run, ye have been tardy thus far; haste whither ye are going, seek Whom ye are seeking. O Jesus, may he who loves Thee not, be anathema; may he who loves Thee not, be filled with bitterness!

"O sweet Jesus, may every good feeling that is fitted for Thy praise, love Thee, delight in Thee, admire Thee. God of my heart and my Portion, Christ Jesus, may my heart faint away in spirit and mayest Thou be my life within me! May the live coal of Thy love grow hot within my spirit, and break forth into a perfect fire; may it burn incessantly on the altar of my heart; may it glow in my innermost being; may it blaze in hidden recesses of my soul; and in the day of my consummation, may I be found consummated with Thee. Amen."

Nothing is sweeter than love;
nothing stronger, nothing higher,
nothing more generous,
nothing more pleasant, nothing fuller or
better in Heaven or on earth;
for love proceeds from God and cannot
rest but in God above all things created.

Mancipia Publications

Second Day _____

Daily Prayers during the Third Week: Litany of the Holy Ghost on page 160, the *Ave Maris Stella* on page 156, the *Litany of the Holy Name of Jesus* or *Litany of the Sacred Heart,* on pages 163 or 165, respectively. Saint Louis De Montfort's *Prayer to Jesus* page 158, *O Jesus Living in Mary* on page 159, and the *Prayer of Saint Augustine* on page 158.

Gospel according to Saint John 14

Let not your heart be troubled. You believe in God, believe also in Me.

2. In my Father's house there are many mansions. If not, I would have told you: because I go to prepare a place for you.

3. And if I shall go, and prepare a place for you, I will come again, and will take you to Myself; that where I am, you also may be.

4. And where I go you know, and the way you know.

5. Thomas said to Him: Lord, we know not were Thou go; and how can we know the way?

6. Jesus said to him: I am the way, and the truth, and the life. No man comes to the Father, but by Me.

7. If you had known Me, you would without doubt have known My Father also: and from henceforth you shall know Him, and you have seen Him.

8. Philip said to Him: Lord, show us the Father, and it is enough for us.

9. Jesus said to Him: Have I been so long a time with you; and have you not known Me? Philip, he that sees Me sees the Father also. How say thou show us the Father?

10. Do you not believe, that I am in the Father, and the Father in Me? The words that I speak to you, I speak not of Myself. But the Father Who abides in Me, He does the works.

11. Believe you not that I am in the Father, and the Father in Me?

12. Otherwise believe for the very works' sake. Amen, amen I say to you, he that believes in Me, the works that I do, he also shall do; and greater than these shall he do.

13. Because I go to the Father: and whatsoever you shall ask the Father in My name, that will I do: that the Father may be glorified in the Son.

14. If you shall ask Me anything in My name, that I will do.

15. If you love me, keep My commandments.

16. And I will ask the Father, and He shall give you another Paraclete, that He may abide with you forever.

17. The Spirit of truth, whom the world cannot receive, because it sees Him not nor knows Him: but you shall know Him; because He shall abide with you, and shall be in you.

18. I will not leave you orphans, I will come to you.

19. Yet a little while: and the world sees Me no more. But you see Me: because I live, and you shall live.

20. In that day you shall know, that I am in My Father, and you in Me, and I in you.

21. He that has My commandments, and keeps them; he it is that loves Me. And he that loves Me, shall be loved of My Father: and I will love him, and will manifest Myself to him.

22. Judas said to Him, not the Iscariot: Lord, how is it, that thou will manifest Thyself to us, and not to the world?

23. Jesus answered, and said to him: If anyone love Me, he will keep my word, and My Father will love him, and We will come to him, and will make Our abode with him.

24. He that loves Me not, keeps not My words. And the word which you have heard, is not Mine; but the Father's Who sent Me.

25. These things have I spoken to you, abiding with you.

26. But the Paraclete, the Holy Ghost, Whom the Father will send in My name, He will teach you all things, and bring all things to your mind, whatsoever I shall have said to you.

27. Peace I leave with you, My peace I give unto you: not as the world gives, do I give unto you. Let not your heart be troubled, nor let it be afraid.

28. You have heard that I said to you I go away, and I come unto you. If you loved Me, you would indeed be glad, because I go to the Father: for the Father is greater than I.

29. And now I have told you before it comes to pass: that when it shall come to pass, you may believe.

30. I will not now speak many things with you. For the prince of this world comes, and in Me he has not anything.

31. But that the world may know, that I love the Father: and as the Father has given Me commandment, so do I: Arise, let us go hence.

Gospel according to Saint John 15

I am the true vine; and My Father is the husbandman.

2. Every branch in Me, that bears not fruit, He will take away: and every one that bears fruit, He will purge it, that it may bring forth more fruit.

3. Now you are clean by reason of the word, which I have spoken to you.

4. Abide in Me, and I in you. As the branch cannot bear fruit of itself, unless it abide in the vine, so neither can you, unless you abide in Me.

5. I am the vine; you the branches: he that abides in Me, and I in him, the same bears much fruit: for without Me you can do nothing.

6. If any one abide not in Me, he shall be cast forth as a branch, and shall wither, and they shall gather him up, and cast him into the fire, and he burns.

7. If you abide in Me, and My words abide in you, you shall ask whatever you will, and it shall be done unto you.

8. In this is My Father glorified; that you bring forth very much fruit, and become My disciples.

9. As the Father has loved Me, I also have loved you. Abide in My love.

10. If you keep My commandments, you shall abide in My love; as I also have kept My Father's commandments, and do abide in His love.

Mancipia Publications

11. These things I have spoken to you, that My joy may be in you, and your joy may be filled.

12. This is My commandment, that you love one another, as I have loved you.

13. Greater love than this no man has, that a man lay down his life for his friends.

14. You are My friends, if you do the things that I command you.

15. I will not now call you servants: for the servant knows not what his lord does. But I have called you friends: because all things whatsoever I have heard of My Father, I have made known to you.

16. You have not chosen Me : but I have chosen you; and have appointed you, that you should go, and should bring forth fruit; and your fruit should remain: that whatsoever you shall ask of the Father in My name, He may give it to you.

17. These things I command you, that you love one another.

18. If the world hate you, know, that it has hated Me before you.

19. If you had been of the world, the world would love its own: but because you are not of the world, but I have chosen you out of the world, therefore the world hates you.

20. Remember My word that I said to you: The servant is not greater than His master. If they have persecuted Me, they will also persecute you: if they have kept My word, they will keep yours also.

21. But all these things they will do to you for My name's sake: because they know not Him that sent Me.

22. If I had not come, and spoken to them, they would not have sin; but now they have no excuse for their sin.

23. He that hates Me, hates my Father also.

24. If I had not done among them the works that no other man has done, they would not have sin; but now they have both seen and hated both Me and My Father.

25. But that the word may be fulfilled which is written in their law: They hated Me without cause.

26. But when the Paraclete comes, Whom I will send you from the Father, the Spirit of truth, Who proceeds from the Father, He shall give testimony of Me.

27. And you shall give testimony, because you are with Me from the beginning.

Imitation of Christ, Book 2, Chapter 12
Of the Royal Way of The Holy Cross

To many this seems a hard saying: "Deny yourself, take up your cross, and follow Jesus."

But it will be much harder to bear that last word: "Depart from me, you cursed, into everlasting fire."

For they that at present willingly hear and follow the word of the cross shall not then be afraid of eternal condemnation.

This sign of the cross will be in Heaven when the Lord shall come to judge.

Then all the servants of the cross, who in their lifetime have conformed themselves to Him that was crucified, shall come to Christ their judge with great confidence.

2. Why then art you afraid to take up your cross, which leads to a kingdom?

In the cross is salvation; in the cross is life; in the cross is protection from your enemies.

In the cross is infusion of heavenly sweetness; in the cross is strength of mind; in the cross is joy of spirit.

In the cross is the height of virtue; in the cross is the perfection of sanctity.

There is no health of the soul nor hope of eternal life but in the cross.

Take up, therefore, your cross and follow Jesus, and you shall go into life everlasting.

He is gone before you carrying His own Cross; and He died for you upon the Cross that you may also bear your cross and love to die on the cross.

Because if you die with Him you shall also live with Him, and if you art His companion in suffering you shall also partake in His glory. (2 Cor. 1: 7)

3. Behold the cross is all and in dying to yourself all consists, and there is no other way to life and to true internal peace but the holy way of the cross and of daily mortification.

Go where you will, seek what you will, and you shall not find a higher way above, nor a safer way below than the way of the holy cross.

Dispose and order all things according as you will and as seems best to you, and you will still find something to suffer, either willingly or unwillingly, and so you shall still find the cross.

For either you shall feel pain in the body, or sustain in your soul tribulation of spirit.

4. Sometimes you shall be left by God, other times you shall be afflicted by your neighbor, and what is more, you shall often be a trouble to yourself.

Neither can you be delivered or eased by any remedy or comfort, but as long as it shall please God you must bear it.

For God would have you learn to suffer tribulation without comfort, and wholly to submit yourself to Him, and to become more humble by tribulation.

No man has so lively a feeling of the Passion of Christ as he who has happened to suffer such things.

The cross, therefore, is always ready and everywhere waits for you.

You cannot escape it, wheresoever you run; for wheresoever you go you carry yourself with you and shall always find yourself.

Turn yourself upwards, or turn yourself downwards; turn yourself without, or turn yourself within, and everywhere you shall find the cross.

And everywhere you must of necessity have patience if you desire inward peace and would merit an eternal crown.

Mancipia Publications

5. If you carry the cross willingly, it will carry you and bring you to your desired end; to that place where there will be an end of suffering, though here there will be no end.

If you carry it unwillingly you make it a burden to you and load yourself the more, and nevertheless you must bear it.

If you fling away one cross, without doubt you shall find another and perhaps a heavier.

6. Do you think to escape that which no mortal ever could avoid? What saint was there ever in the world without his cross and afflictions? Our Lord Jesus Christ Himself was not one hour of His life without suffering: "It behooved Christ to suffer," said He, "and rise again from the dead, and so enter into His glory."

And why do you pretend to seek another way than this royal way, which is the way of the holy cross?

7. The whole life of Christ was a cross and a martyrdom, and do you seek rest and joy?

You err, you err, if you seek any other thing than to suffer tribulations; for this whole mortal life is full of miseries and beset on all sides with crosses.

And the higher a person is advanced in spirit the heavier crosses shall he often meet with, because the pain of his banishment increases in proportion to his love.

8. Yet this man, in many ways afflicted, is not without some allay of comfort, because he is sensible of the great profit which he reaps by bearing the cross.

For while he willingly resigns himself to it, all the burden of tribulation is converted into an assured hope of comfort from God.

And the more the flesh is brought down by affliction the more the spirit is strengthened by inward grace.

And it sometimes gains such strength through affection to tribulation and adversity, by loving to be conformable to the Cross of Christ, as not to be willing to be without suffering and affliction; because it is confident that it is so much the more acceptable to God, as it shall be able to bear more and greater things for Him.

This is not man's power, but the grace of Christ, which can and does effect such great things in frail flesh, that what it naturally abhors and flies, even this, through fervor of spirit, it now embraces and loves.

9. To bear the cross, to love the cross, to chastise the body, and bring it under subjection; to fly honors, to be willing to suffer reproaches, to despise one's self and wish to be despised; to bear all adversities and losses, and to desire no prosperity in this world, are not according to man's natural inclination.

If you look upon yourself, you can do nothing of this of yourself.

But if you confide in the Lord, strength will be given you from Heaven, and the world and the flesh shall be made subject to you.

Neither shall you fear your enemy, the Devil, if you be armed with faith and signed with the Cross of Christ.

10. Set yourself, then, like a good and faithful servant of Christ, to bear manfully the Cross of your Lord, crucified for the love of you.

Prepare yourself to suffer many adversities and divers evils in this miserable life; for so it will be with you wherever you are, and so indeed will you find it wheresoever you may hide yourself.

It must be so, and there is no remedy against the tribulation of evil and sorrow but to bear them patiently.

Drink of the chalice of your Lord lovingly if you desire to be His friend and to have part with Him.

Leave consolations to God, to do with them as best please Him.

But prepare yourself to bear tribulations, and account them the greatest consolations; for the sufferings of this life bear no proportion to the glory to come, although you alone could suffer them all.

11. When you shall arrive this far, that tribulation becomes sweet and savory to you for the love of Christ, then think that it is well with you, for you have found a paradise upon earth.

As long as suffering appears grievous to you and you seek to fly from it, so long will it be ill with you, and the tribulation from which you fly will everywhere follow you.

12. If you set yourself to what you ought, that is to suffer and die to yourself, it will quickly be better with you and you shall find peace.

Although you should have been rapt up to the third heaven with Saint Paul, (2 Cor. 12:2) you are not thereby assured that you shall suffer no adversity. "I," said Jesus, "will show him how great things he must suffer for My name."

To suffer therefore, is what waits for you, if you will love Jesus and constantly serve Him.

13. Would to God you were worthy to suffer something for the name of Jesus! How great a glory would be laid up for you, how great joy would it be to all the saints of God and how great edification to your neighbors.

All recommend patience, but alas! how few there are that desire to suffer.

With good reason ought you willingly to suffer a little for Christ, since many suffer greater things for the world.

14. Know for certain that you must lead a dying life and the more a man dies to himself the more he begins to live to God.

No man is fit to comprehend heavenly things who has not resigned himself to suffer adversities for Christ.

Nothing is more acceptable to God, nothing more wholesome for you in this world than to suffer willingly for Christ.

And if you were to choose, you ought to wish rather to suffer adversities for Christ than to be delighted with many comforts, because you would be more like unto Christ and more conformable to all the saints.

For our merit and the advancement of our state consist, not in having many sweetnesses and consolations, but rather in bearing great afflictions and tribulations.

15. If, indeed, there had been anything better and more beneficial to man's salvation than suffering, Christ certainly would have showed it by word and example.

For He manfully exhorts both His disciples that followed Him and all that desire to follow Him to bear the cross, saying: "If any one will come after Me, let him deny himself and take up his cross and follow Me."

So that when we have read and searched all let this be the final conclusion, that "Through many tribulations we must enter into the kingdom of God."

True Devotion
#183
Of all the truths which I have been explaining with regard to our Blessed Lady and her children and servants, the Holy Ghost gives us an admirable figure in the Scriptures. (Gen. 27) It is in the story of Jacob, who received the blessing of his father Isaac through the skill and pains of his mother Rebecca.
#212
Furthermore, after Mary has heaped her favors upon her children and faithful servants, and has obtained for them the blessing of the heavenly Father and union with Jesus Christ, she preserves them in Jesus and Jesus in them. She takes care of them, watches over them always, for fear they should lose the grace of God and fall into the snares of their enemies. "She retains the saints in their fullness," says Saint Bonaventure, and makes them persevere to the end, as we have seen.

This is the interpretation of the story of Jacob and Esau, that great and ancient figure of predestination and reprobation, so unknown and so full of mysteries.

Mary...produces in the soul
wherein she dwells, purity of heart and body,
purity of intention and of purpose and fruitfulness
in good works.... She will cause Jesus Christ to
live in that soul, and the soul to live in constant
union with Jesus Christ.

Third Day _____

Daily Prayers during the Third Week: Litany of the Holy Ghost on page 160, the *Ave Maris Stella* on page 156, the *Litany of the Holy Name of Jesus* or *Litany of the Sacred Heart,* on pages 163 or 165, respectively. Saint Louis De Montfort's *Prayer to Jesus* page 158, *O Jesus Living in Mary* on page 159, and the *Prayer of Saint Augustine* on page 158.

Gospel according to Saint John 16

These things have I spoken to you, that you may not be scandalized.

2. They will put you out of the synagogues: yea, the hour comes, that whosoever kills you, will think that he does a service to God.

3. And these things will they do to you; because they have not known the Father, nor Me.

4. But these things I have told you, that when the hour shall come, you may remember that I told you of them.

5. But I told you not these things from the beginning, because I was with you. And now I go to Him that sent Me, and none of you ask Me: Where goest Thou?

6. But because I have spoken these things to you, sorrow has filled your heart.

7. But I tell you the truth: it is expedient to you that I go: for if I go not, the Paraclete will not come to you; but if I go, I will send Him to you.

8. And when He is come, He will convince the world of sin, and of justice, and of judgment.

9. Of sin: because they believed not in Me.

10. And of justice: because I go to the Father; and you shall see Me no longer.

11. And of judgment: because the prince of this world is already judged.

12. I have yet many things to say to you: but you cannot bear them now.

13. But when He, the Spirit of truth, is come, He will teach you all truth. For He shall not speak of Himself; but what things soever He shall hear, He shall speak; and the things that are to come, He shall show you.

14. He shall glorify Me; because He shall receive of Mine and shall show it to you.

15. All things whatsoever the Father has, are Mine. Therefore I said, that He shall receive of Mine, and show it to you.

16. A little while, and now you shall not see Me; and again a little while, and you shall see Me: because I go to the Father.

17. Then some of His disciples said one to another: What is this that He says to us: A little while, and you shall not see Me; and again a little while, and you shall see Me, and, because I go to the Father?

18. They said therefore: What is this that He says, a little while? We know not what He speaks.

19. And Jesus knew that they had a mind to ask Him; and He said to them: Of this do you inquire among yourselves, because I said: A little while, and you

shall not see Me; and again a little while, and you shall see Me?

20. Amen, amen I say to you, that you shall lament and weep, but the world shall rejoice; and you shall be made sorrowful, but your sorrow shall be turned into joy.

21. A woman, when she is in labor, has sorrow, because her hour is come; but when she has brought forth the child, she remembers no more the anguish, for joy that a man is born into the world.

22. So also you now indeed have sorrow; but I will see you again, and your heart shall rejoice; and your joy no man shall take from you.

23. And in that day you shall not ask Me anything. Amen, amen I say to you: if you ask the Father anything in My name, He will give it you.

24. Hitherto you have not asked anything in My name. Ask, and you shall receive; that your joy may be full.

25. These things I have spoken to you in proverbs. The hour comes, when I will no more speak to you in proverbs, but will show you plainly of the Father.

26. In that day you shall ask in My name; and I say not to you, that I will ask the Father for you:

27. For the Father Himself loves you, because you have loved Me, and have believed that I came out from God.

28. I came forth from the Father, and am come into the world: again I leave the world, and I go to the Father.

29. His disciples say to Him: Behold, now Thou speak plainly, and speak no proverb.

30. Now we know that Thou know all things, and Thou need not that any man should ask Thee. By this we believe that Thou came forth from God.

31. Jesus answered them: Do you, now believe?

32. Behold, the hour comes, and it is now come, that you shall be scattered every man to his own, and shall leave Me alone; and yet I am not alone, because the Father is with Me.

33. These things I have spoken to you, that in Me, you may have peace. In the world you shall have distress: but have confidence, I have overcome the world.

Continuation of the holy Gospel according to Saint Matthew 26:42-58

Again the second time, He went and prayed, saying: My Father, if this chalice may not pass away, but I must drink it, Thy will be done.

43. And again He came and found them sleeping: for their eyes were heavy.

44. And leaving them, He went again: and He prayed the third time, saying the selfsame word.

45. Then He came to His disciples, and said to them: Sleep now and take your rest; behold the hour is at hand, and the Son of man shall be betrayed into the hands of sinners.

46. Rise, let us go: behold he is at hand that will betray Me.

47. As He spoke, behold Judas, one of the twelve, came, and with him a

great multitude with swords and clubs, sent from the chief priests and the ancients of the people.

48. And he that betrayed Him, gave them a sign, saying: Whomsoever I shall kiss, that is He, hold Him fast.

49. And forthwith coming to Jesus, he said: Hail, Rabbi. And he kissed Him.

50. And Jesus said to him: Friend, why art thou come? Then they came up, and laid hands on Jesus, and held Him.

51. And behold one of them that were with Jesus stretching forth his hand, drew out his sword: and striking the servant of the high priest, cut off his ear.

52. Then Jesus said to him: Put up again your sword into its place: for all that take the sword shall perish with the sword.

53. Think thou that I cannot ask my Father, and He will give me presently more than twelve legions of angels?

54. How then shall the scriptures be fulfilled, that so it must be done?

55. In that same hour Jesus said to the multitudes: You are come out as it were to a robber with swords and clubs to apprehend Me. I sat daily with you, teaching in the temple, and you laid not hands on Me.

56. Now all this was done, that the scriptures of the prophets might be fulfilled. Then the disciples all leaving Him fled.

57. But they holding Jesus led Him to Caiphas the high priest, where the scribes and the ancients were assembled.

58. And Peter followed Him afar off, even to the court of the high priest. And going in, he sat with the servants, that he might see the end.

Imitation of Christ Book 3, Chapter 5
The Wonderful Effects of Divine Love
DISCIPLE

I bless Thee, O heavenly Father, Father of my Lord Jesus Christ; because Thou has vouchsafed to be mindful of so poor a wretch as I am.

O Father of mercies and God of all comfort, (2 Cor. 1:3) I give thanks to Thee, Who sometimes are pleased to cherish with Thy consolation, me who am unworthy of any comfort.

I bless Thee and glorify Thee forevermore, together with Thine only-begotten Son and the Holy Ghost, the Comforter to all eternity.

O Lord God, my holy Lover, when Thou shall come into my heart all that is within me will be filled with joy. (Prov. 23:5)

Thou art my Glory and the Joy of my heart.

Thou art my Hope and my Refuge in the day of my trouble. (Ps. 58:17)

2. But because I am as yet weak in love and imperfect in virtue, therefore do I stand in need of being strengthened and comforted by Thee. For this reason visit me often and instruct me in Thy holy discipline.

Free me from evil passions and heal my heart of all disorderly affections, that being healed and well purified in my interior, I may become fit to love, courageous to suffer and constant to persevere.

Mancipia Publications

3. Love is an excellent thing, a great good indeed, which alone makes light all that is burdensome and equally bears all that is unequal.

For it carries a burden without being burdened and makes all that which is bitter sweet and savory.

The love of Jesus is noble and generous; it spurs us on to do great things and excites us to desire always that which is most perfect.

Love will tend upwards and is not to be detained by things beneath.

Love will be at liberty and free from all worldly affections, lest its interior sight be hindered, lest it suffer itself to be entangled with any temporal interest or cast down by losses.

Nothing is sweeter than love; nothing stronger, nothing higher, nothing more generous, nothing more pleasant, nothing fuller or better in Heaven or on earth; for love proceeds from God and cannot rest but in God above all things created.

4. The lover flies, runs and rejoices, he is free and not held.

He gives all for all and has all in all, because he rests in one sovereign Good above all, from Whom all good flows and proceeds.

He looks not at the gifts, but turns himself to the giver above all goods.

Love often knows no measure, but is inflamed above all measure.

Love feels no burden, values no labors, would willingly do more than it can; complains not of impossibility, because it conceives that it may and can do all things.

It is able therefore to do anything and it performs and effects many things where he that loves not faints and lies down.

5. Love watches, and sleeping, slumbers not.

When weary is not tired; when straitened is not constrained; when frightened is not disturbed, but like a lively flame and a torch all on fire it mounts upwards and securely passes through all opposition.

Whosoever loves knows the cry of this voice.

A loud cry in the ears of God is the ardent affection of the soul, which says, O my God, my love, Thou are all mine and I am all Thine. (Cant. 2:16)

6. Give increase to my love, that I may learn to taste with the interior mouth of the heart how sweet it is to love and to swim and to be dissolved in love. (Ps. 33:9)

Let me be possessed by love, going above myself through excess of fervor and ecstasy.

Let me sing the canticle of love, let me follow Thee my Beloved on high, let my soul lose herself in Thy praises, rejoicing exceedingly in Thy love.

Let me love Thee more than myself and myself only for Thee, and all others in Thee, who truly love Thee as the law of love commands, which shines forth from Thee.

7. Love is swift, sincere, pious, pleasant, and delightful; strong, patient, faithful, prudent, longsuffering, courageous, and never seeking itself.

For where a man seeks himself there he falls from love.

Love is circumspect, humble, and upright, not soft, not light, not intent upon vain things; is sober, chaste, stable, quiet, and keeps a guard over all the senses.

Love is submissive and obedient to superiors, in its own eyes mean and contemptible, devout and thankful to God; always trusting and hoping in Him, even when it tastes not the relish of God's sweetness, for there is no living in love without some pain or sorrow.

8. Whosoever is not ready to suffer all things and to stand resigned to the will of his Beloved, is not worthy to be called a lover.

He that loves must willingly embrace all that is hard and bitter, for the sake of his Beloved, and never suffer himself to be turned away from Him by any contrary occurrences whatsoever.

True Devotion #226, 231-242

Although what is essential in this devotion consists in the interior, we must not fail to unite to the inward practice certain external observances. "We must do the one, yet not leave the other undone;" because the outward practices, well performed, aid the inward ones; and because they remind man, who is always guided by his senses, of what he has done or ought to do; and also because they are suitable for edifying our neighbor, who sees them; these are things which inward practices cannot do. Let no worldling, then, or critic, intrude here to say that because true devotion is in the heart, we must avoid external devotion; or that devotion ought to be hidden, and that there may be vanity in showing it. I answer, with my Master, that men should see our good works, that they may glorify our Father Who is in Heaven; not, as Saint Gregory says, that we ought to perform our actions and exterior devotions to please men and get praise— that would be vanity; but that we should sometimes do them before men with the view of pleasing God, and glorifying Him thereby, without caring either for the contempt or the praise of men.

I will allude only briefly to some exterior practices, which I call "exterior" not because we do not perform them interiorly, but because they have something outward about them to distinguish them from those which are purely inward.

I. The Preparatory Exercises and Consecration

At the end of the three weeks they should go to confession and Communion, with the intention of giving themselves to Jesus Christ in the quality of slaves of love, by the hands of Mary. After Communion, which they should try to make according to the method given on page 169, they should recite the formula of their consecration, which they will also find on page 167. They ought to write it, or have it written, unless they have a printed copy of it; and they should sign it the same day on which they have made it.

It would be well also that on that day they should pay some tribute to Jesus Christ and our Blessed Lady, either as a penance for their past unfaithfulness to the vows of their Baptism, or as a testimony of their dependence on the dominion of Jesus and Mary. This tribute ought to be according to the devotion and ability of each one, such as a fast, a mortification, an alms or a candle. If they had but a pin to give in homage, and gave it with a good heart, it would be enough for Jesus, who looks only at the good will.

Once a year at least, and on the same day, they should renew the same consecration, observing the same practices during the three weeks.

They might also, once a month or even once a day, renew all they have done, in these few words: "I am all Thine and all that I have is Thine, O most loving Jesus, through Mary, Thy most holy Mother."

II. Recitation of the Little Crown of the Blessed Virgin

They may recite every day of their life—without, however, making a burden of it—the *Little Crown of the Blessed Virgin*, composed of three *Our Fathers* and twelve *Hail Marys*, in honor of Our Lady's twelve privileges and grandeurs. This is a very ancient practice and it has its foundation in Holy Scripture. Saint John saw a woman crowned with twelve stars, clothed with the sun, and with the moon under her feet; and this woman, according to the interpreters, was the most holy Virgin.

There are many ways of saying this *Crown* well, but it would take too long to enter upon them, the Holy Ghost will teach them to those who are the most faithful to this devotion. Nevertheless, to say it quite simply, we should begin by saying: "Grant that I may praise thee, holy Virgin; give me strength against thy enemies." After that, we should say the *Apostles' Creed*, then an *Our Father* with four *Hail Marys* and then one *Glory be to the Father*; then another *Our Father*, four *Hail Marys*, and *Glory be to the Father*, and so on with the rest; and at the end we should say the *Sub Tuum Praesidium* ("We fly to thy patronage...").

III. The Wearing of Little Chains

It is a most glorious and praiseworthy thing, and very useful to those who have thus made themselves slaves of Jesus in Mary, that they should wear, as a sign of their loving slavery, little iron chains, blessed with the proper blessing.

It is perfectly true that these external insignia are not essential, and a person who has embraced this devotion may very well go without them; nevertheless, I cannot refrain from warmly praising those who, after having shaken off the shameful chains of the slavery of the Devil, in which original sin, and perhaps actual sin, had bound them, have voluntarily surrendered themselves to the glorious slavery of Jesus Christ, and glory with Saint Paul in being in chains for Christ, chains a thousand times more glorious and precious, though of iron, than all the golden ornaments of emperors.

Once there was nothing more infamous on earth than the cross, and now that wood is the most glorious boast of Christianity. Let us say the same of the irons of slavery. There was nothing more ignominious among the ancients; there is nothing more shameful even now among the heathens. But among Christians, there is nothing more illustrious than the chains of Jesus; for they unchain us and preserve us from the infamous fetters of sin and the Devil. They set us at liberty and chain us to Jesus and Mary; not by compulsion and constraint, like galley-slaves, but by charity and love, like children. "I will draw them to Me," says God by the mouth of the prophet, "by the chains of love." (Osee 11:14) These chains are as strong as death (Cant. 8:6), and in a certain sense even stronger than death in those who are faithful in carrying these glorious chains to their death. For though death destroys their bodies by bringing them to corruption, it does not destroy the chains of their slavery, which, being of iron, do not corrode so easily. Perhaps, on the day of the resurrection of the body, at the Last Judgment, these chains shall be around their bones, and shall be a part of their glory, and be transmuted into chains of light and splendor. Happy then, a thousand times happy, the illustrious slaves of Jesus who wear their chains even to the tomb!

The following are the reasons for wearing these little chains:

First, to remind the Christian of the vows and promises of his Baptism, of the perfect renewal he has made of them by this devotion, and of the strict obligation under which he is to be faithful to them. As man, who shapes his course more often by the senses than by pure faith, easily forgets his obligations toward God unless he has some outward thing to remind him of them, these little chains serve marvelously to remind the Christian of the chains of sin and the slavery of the Devil from which Baptism has delivered him, and of the dependence on Jesus which he has vowed to Him in Baptism, and of the ratification of it which he has made by the renewal of his vows. One of the reasons why so few Christians think of their baptismal vows, and live with as much license as if they had promised no more to God than the heathen, is that they do not wear any external sign to remind them of their vows.

Secondly, to show that we are not ashamed of the servitude and slavery of Jesus Christ, and that we renounce the slavery of the world, of sin and of the Devil.

Thirdly, to protect ourselves against the chains of sin and of the Devil; for we must wear either "the chains of sinners or the chains of charity and salvation."

O my dear brother, let us break the chains of sin and sinners, of the world and worldliness, of the Devil and his ministers; and let us cast far from us their depressing yoke. (Ps. 2:3) Let us put our feet, to use the terms of the Holy Ghost, into His glorious fetters and our necks into His chains. (Ecclus. 6:25) Let us shoulder and carry the Divine Wisdom [that is, Jesus Christ] and let us never weary of His chains. You will remark that the Holy Ghost, before saying these words, prepares a soul for them, lest it should reject His important counsel. See His words: "Hearken, My son, and receive a counsel of understanding and reject not My counsel." (Ecclus. 6:24)

You would wish, my very dear friend, that I should here unite myself to the Holy Ghost to give you the same counsel as His: "His chains are chains of salvation." (Ecclus. 6:31) As Jesus Christ on the cross must draw all to Himself, whether they will it or not, He will draw the reprobate by the chains of

Mancipia Publications

their sins, that He may chain them like galley-slaves and devils to His eternal anger and revengeful justice. But He will, and particularly in these latter times, draw the predestinate by the chains of charity: "I will draw all things to Myself" (Jn. 12:32); "I will draw them with the bands of love." (Osee 11:4) These loving slaves of Jesus Christ, "the chained of Christ" (Eph. 3:1; Philem. 9), can wear their chains on their feet or on their arms, around their body or around their neck. Father Vincent Caraffa, seventh Superior General of the Jesuits, who died in the odor of sanctity in the year 1643, used to wear an iron band around his feet as a mark of his servitude; and he said that his only regret was that he could not publicly drag a chain. Mother Agnes of Jesus, of whom we have spoken before, used to wear an iron chain around her body. Others have worn it around their neck in penance for the pearl necklaces which they had worn in the world; while others have worn it around their arms to remind themselves, in their manual labors, that they were slaves of Jesus Christ.

Fourth Day ——————

Daily Prayers during the Third Week: Litany of the Holy Ghost on page 160, the *Ave Maris Stella* on page 156, the *Litany of the Holy Name of Jesus* or *Litany of the Sacred Heart,* on pages 163 or 165, respectively. Saint Louis De Montfort's *Prayer to Jesus* page 158, *O Jesus Living in Mary* on page 159, and the *Prayer of Saint Augustine* on page 158.

Gospel According to Saint John 17

These things Jesus spoke, and lifting up His eyes to Heaven, He said: Father, the hour is come, glorify Thy Son, that Thy Son may glorify Thee.

2. As Thou has given Him power over all flesh, that He may give eternal life to all whom Thou has given Him.

3. Now this is eternal life: That they may know Thee, the only true God, and Jesus Christ, Whom Thou has sent.

4. I have glorified Thee on the earth; I have finished the work which Thou gave Me to do.

5. And now glorify Thou Me, O Father with Thyself, with the glory which I had, before the world was, with Thee.

6. I have manifested Thy name to the men whom Thou has given Me out of the world. Thine they were, and to Me Thou has given them; and they have kept Thy word.

7. Now they have known, that all things which Thou has given Me, are from Thee;

8. Because the words which Thou gave Me, I have given to them. And they have received them, and have known in very deed that I came out from Thee; and they have believed that Thou did send Me.

9. I pray for them. I pray not for the world, but for them whom Thou has

given Me; because they are Thine.

10. And all My things are Thine, and Thine are Mine; and I am glorified in them.

11. And now I am not in the world, and these are in the world, and I come to Thee. Holy Father, keep them in Thy name whom Thou has given Me; that they may be one, as We also are.

12. While I was with them, I kept them in Thy name. Those whom Thou gave Me have I kept; and none of them is lost but the son of perdition, that the scripture may be fulfilled.

13. And now I come to Thee; and these things I speak in the world, that they may have My joy filled in themselves.

14. I have given them Thy word, and the world has hated them, because they are not of the world, as I also am not of the world.

15. I pray not that Thou should take them out of the world, but that Thou should keep them from evil.

16. They are not of the world, as I also am not of the world.

17. Sanctify them in truth. Thy word is truth.

18. As Thou has sent Me into the world, I also have sent them into the world.

19. And for them do I sanctify Myself, that they also may be sanctified in truth.

20. And not for them only do I pray, but for them also who through their word shall believe in Me,

21. That they all may be one, as Thou, Father, in Me, and I in Thee; that they also may be one in Us; that the world may believe that Thou has sent Me.

22. And the glory which Thou has given Me, I have given to them; that they may be one, as We also are one,

23. I in them, and Thou in Me; that they may be made perfect in one; and the world may know that Thou has sent Me, and has loved them, as Thou has also loved Me.

24. Father, I will that where I am, they also whom Thou has given Me may be with Me; that they may see My glory which Thou has given Me, because Thou has loved Me before the creation of the world.

25. Just Father, the world has not known Thee; but I have known Thee: and these have known that Thou has sent Me.

26. And I have made known Thy name to them, and will make it known; that the love wherewith Thou has loved Me, may be in them, and I in them.

Gospel according to Saint John 18

When Jesus had said these things, He went forth with His disciples over the brook Cedron, where there was a garden, into which He entered with His disciples.

2. And Judas also, who betrayed Him, knew the place; because Jesus had often resorted there together with His disciples.

3. Judas therefore having received a band of soldiers and servants from the

Mancipia Publications

chief priests and the Pharisees, came there with lanterns and torches and weapons.

4. Jesus therefore, knowing all things that should come upon Him, went forth, and said to them; Whom seek ye?

5. They answered Him: Jesus of Nazareth. Jesus said to them: I am He. And Judas also, who betrayed Him, stood with them.

6. As soon therefore as He had said to them: I am He; they went backward, and fell to the ground.

7. Again therefore He asked them: Whom seek ye? And they said, Jesus of Nazareth.

8. Jesus answered, I have told you that I am He. If therefore you seek Me, let these go their way,

9. That the word might be fulfilled which He said: "Of them whom Thou has given Me, I have not lost any one."

10. Then Simon Peter, having a sword, drew it, and struck the servant of the high priest, and cut off his right ear. And the name of the servant was Malchus.

11. Jesus therefore said to Peter: Put up thy sword into the scabbard. The chalice which My Father has given Me, shall I not drink it?

12. Then the band and the tribune, and the servants of the Jews, took Jesus, and bound Him:

13. And they led Him away to Annas first, for he was father-in-law to Caiphas, who was the high priest of that year.

14. Now Caiphas was he who had given the counsel to the Jews; That it was expedient that one man should die for the people.

15. And Simon Peter followed Jesus, and so did another disciple. And that disciple was known to the high priest, and went in with Jesus into the court of the high priest.

16. But Peter stood at the door without. The other disciple therefore, who was known to the high priest, went out, and spoke to the portress, and brought in Peter.

17. The maid therefore that was portress, said to Peter: Art not thou also one of this man's disciples? He said: I am not.

18. Now the servants and ministers stood at a fire of coals, because it was cold, and warmed themselves. And with them was Peter also, standing, and warming himself.

19. The high priest therefore asked Jesus of His disciples, and of His doctrine.

20. Jesus answered him: I have spoken openly to the world: I have always taught in the synagogue, and in the temple, where all the Jews resort; and in secret I have spoken nothing.

21. Why ask thou Me? Ask them who have heard what I have spoken unto them: behold they know what things I have said.

22. And when He had said these things, one of the servants standing by, gave Jesus, a blow, saying: Answer Thou the high priest so?

23. Jesus answered him: If I have spoken evil, give testimony of the evil;

but if well, why strike thou Me?

24. And Annas sent Him bound to Caiphas the high priest.

25. And Simon Peter was standing, and warming himself. They said therefore to him: Art not thou also one of His disciples? He denied it, and said: I am not.

26. One of the servants of the high priest (a kinsman to him whose ear Peter cut off) said to him: Did not I see thee in the garden with Him?

27. Again therefore Peter denied; and immediately the cock crew.

28. Then they led Jesus from Caiphas to the governor's hall. And it was morning; and they went not into the hall, that they might not be defiled, but that they might eat the pasch.

29. Pilate therefore went out to them, and said: What accusation bring you against this man?

30. They answered, and said to him: If He were not a malefactor, we would not have delivered Him up to thee.

31. Pilate therefore said to them: Take Him you, and judge Him according to your law. The Jews therefore said to him: It is not lawful for us to put any man to death;

32. That the word of Jesus might be fulfilled, which He said, signifying what death He should die.

33. Pilate therefore went into the hall again, and called Jesus, and said to Him: Art Thou the king of the Jews?

34. Jesus answered: Say thou this thing of thyself, or have others told it thee of Me?

35. Pilate answered: Am I a Jew? Thy own nation, and the chief priests, have delivered Thee up to me: what has Thou done?

36. Jesus answered: My kingdom is not of this world. If My kingdom were of this world, My servants would certainly strive that I should not be delivered to the Jews: but now My kingdom is not from hence.

37. Pilate therefore said to Him: Art Thou a king then? Jesus answered: Thou say that I am a king. For this was I born, and for this came I into the world; that I should give testimony to the truth. Every one that is of the truth, hears My voice.

38. Pilate said to Him: What is truth? And when he said this, he went out again to the Jews, and said to them: I find no cause in Him.

39. But you have a custom that I should release one unto you at the pasch: will you, therefore, that I release unto you the king of the Jews?

40. Then cried they all again, saying: Not this man, but Barabbas. Now Barabbas was a robber.

Gospel according to Saint Matthew 26: 59-75

And the chief priests and the whole council sought false witness against Jesus, that they might put Him to death.

60. And they found not, whereas many false witnesses had come in. And

128

last of all there came two false witnesses;

61. And they said: This man said, I am able to destroy the temple of God, and after three days to rebuild it.

62. And the high priest rising up, said to Him: Answer Thou nothing to the things which these witness against Thee?

63. But Jesus held His peace. And the high priest said to Him: I adjure You by the living God, that You tell us if You are the Christ, the Son of God.

64. Jesus said to him: You have said it. Nevertheless I say to you, hereafter you shall see the Son of man sitting on the right hand of the power of God and coming in the clouds of heaven.

65. Then the high priest rent his garments, saying: He has blasphemed; what further need have we of witnesses? Behold, now you have heard the blasphemy.

66. What think you? But they answering, said: He is guilty of death.

67. Then they spat in His face, and buffeted Him: and others struck His face with the palms of their hands,

68. Saying: Prophesy unto us, O Christ, who is he that struck You?

69. But Peter sat without in the court. And there came to him a servant maid, saying: You also were with Jesus the Galilean.

70. But he denied before them all, saying: I know not what you are saying.

71. And as he went out of the gate, another maid saw him, and she said to them that were there: This man also was with Jesus of Nazareth.

72. And again he denied with an oath, I know not the man.

73. And after a little while they came that stood by, and said to Peter: Surely you also are one of them: for even your speech discovers you.

74. Then he began to curse and to swear that he knew not the man. And immediately the cock crew.

75. And Peter remembered the word of Jesus which He had said: Before the cock crow, you will deny Me three times. And going forth, he wept bitterly.

Imitation of Christ Book 3, Chapter 6
The Proof of a True Lover
CHRIST

My son, thou are not as yet a valiant and prudent lover.

DISCIPLE

Why, O Lord?

CHRIST

Because you fall off from what you have begun, upon meeting with a little adversity and too greedily seek after consolation.

A valiant lover stands his ground in temptations and yields not to the crafty persuasions of the enemy.

As he is pleased with Me in prosperity so I displease him not when I send adversity.

2. A prudent lover considers not so much the gift of the lover as the love of the giver.

He looks more at the good will than the value, and prizes his Beloved above all His gifts.

A generous lover rests not in the gift, but in Me above every gift.

All is not lost if sometimes thou has not that sense of devotion towards Me or My saints which thou would have.

That good and delightful affection, which thou sometimes perceive, is the effect of present grace and a certain foretaste of thy heavenly country, but thou must not rely too much upon it, because it goes and comes.

But to fight against the evil motions of the mind which arise, and to despise the suggestions of the Devil is a sign of virtue and of great merit.

3. Let not, therefore, strange fancies trouble thee, of what kind so ever they be that are suggested to thee.

Keep thy resolution firm and thine intention upright towards God.

Neither is it an illusion that sometimes thou are rapt into an ecstasy and presently return to the accustomed weakness of thy heart.

For these thou rather suffer against thy will than procure, and as long as you are displeased with them and resist them it is merit and not loss.

4. Know that the old enemy strives by all means to hinder thy desire after good and to divert thee from every devout exercise, namely from the veneration of the saints, from the pious meditation of My Passion, from the profitable remembrance of thy sins, from keeping a guard upon thine own heart and from a firm purpose of advancing in virtue.

He suggests to thee many evil thoughts that he may wear thee out, and frighten thee that he may withdraw thee from prayer and the reading of devout books.

He is displeased with humble confession, and if he could he would cause thee to omit Communion.

Give no credit to him, value him not, although he often lays his deceitful snares in thy way.

Charge him with it when he suggests wicked and unclean things and say to him:

Begone, unclean spirit; be ashamed, miserable wretch; you are very filthy indeed to suggest such things as these to me.

Depart from me, thou wicked impostor, thou shall have no share in me, but my Jesus will be with me as a valiant warrior and thou shall be confounded.

I would rather die and undergo any torment whatsoever than yield to thy suggestions.

Be silent, I will hear no more of thee, although thou so often strive to be troublesome to me. "The Lord is my light and my salvation, whom shall I fear? The Lord is the protector of my life, of whom shall I be afraid?" (Ps. 26:1)

"If armies in camp should stand together against me, my heart shall not fear. The Lord is my helper and my Redeemer." (Ps. 69:6)

5. Fight like a good soldier, and if sometimes you fall through frailty rise up again with greater strength than before, confiding in My more abundant grace, but take great care and yield not to any vain complacency and pride.

Mancipia Publications

Through this many are led into error and sometimes fall into incurable blindness.

Let this fall of the proud, who foolishly rely on their own strength, serve thee for a warning and keep thee always humble.

Imitation of Christ Book 3, Chapter 56
We Ought to Deny Ourselves and Imitate Christ by the Cross
CHRIST

Son, as much as thou can go out of thyself, so much will thou be able to enter into Me.

As desiring nothing abroad brings peace at home, so relinquishing thyself joins thee interiorly to God.

I will have thee learn the perfect renunciation of thyself, according to My will, without contradiction or complaint.

Follow Me: I am the way, the truth, and the life. Without the way there is no going; without the truth there is no knowing; without the life there is no living.

I am the way which thou must follow; the truth which thou must believe; the life for which thou must hope.

I am the way inviolable, the truth infallible, and the life interminable.

I am the straightest way, the sovereign truth, the true life, the blessed life, and uncreated life.

If thou continue in My way thou shall know the truth, and the truth shall deliver thee, and thou shall attain to life everlasting.

2. If thou will enter into life, keep the Commandments.

If thou will know the truth, believe Me.

If thou will be perfect, sell all things.

If thou will be My disciple, deny thyself.

If thou will possess a blessed life, despise this present life.

If thou will be exalted in Heaven, humble thyself in this world.

If thou will reign with Me, bear the cross with Me.

For none but the servants of the cross find the way of bliss and true light.

DISCIPLE

3. Lord Jesus, forasmuch as Thy way is narrow, and despised by the world, grant that I may follow Thee, and be despised by the world.

For the servant is not greater than his lord, neither is the disciple above his master.

Let Thy servant meditate on Thy life, for there is my salvation and true holiness.

Whatever I read or hear besides does not recreate nor fully delight me.

CHRIST

4. Son, now thou know those things and has read them all, happy shall thou be if thou fulfill them.

"He that has My commandments, and keeps them, he it is that loves Me; and I will love him, and will manifest Myself unto him," and "I will make him sit with Me in the kingdom of My Father."

DISCIPLE

5. Lord Jesus, as Thou has said and has promised, so may it be indeed, and may it be my lot to merit it.

I have received the cross, I have received it from Thy hand; I will bear it, yes, I will bear it until death, as Thou has laid it upon me.

Indeed the life of a good religious man is a cross, but it is a cross that conducts him to Paradise.

We have now begun, it is not lawful to go back, nor may we leave off.

6. Take courage, my brethren, let us go forward together, Jesus will be with us.

For the sake of Jesus we took up His cross; for the sake of Jesus let us persevere on the cross.

He will be our Helper, Who is our Captain and our Leader.

Behold our King marches before us, Who will fight for us.

Let us follow Him manfully; let no one shrink through fear; let us be ready to die valiantly in battle, and not stain our glory by flying from the standard of the cross.

True Devotion #243-248
IV. Special Devotion to the Mystery of the Incarnation

Those who undertake this holy slavery should have a special devotion to the great mystery of the Incarnation of the Word (March 25th). Indeed, the Incarnation is the mystery proper of this practice, inasmuch as it is a devotion inspired by the Holy Ghost: first, to honor and imitate the ineffable dependence which God the Son was pleased to have on Mary, for His Father's glory and our salvation—which dependence particularly appears in this mystery wherein Jesus is a captive and a slave in the bosom of the divine Mary, and depends on her for all things; secondly, to thank God for the incomparable graces He has given Mary, and particularly for having chosen her to be His most holy Mother, which choice was made in this mystery. These are the two principal ends of the slavery of Jesus in Mary.

Have the goodness to observe that I generally say, "the slave of Jesus in Mary," "the slavery of Jesus in Mary." I might, in good truth, as many have done before, say the "slave of Mary," "the slavery of the holy Virgin;" but I think it better to say "the slave of Jesus in Mary," as Father Tronson, Superior General of the Seminary of Saint Sulpice, renowned for his rare prudence and consummate piety, counseled to an ecclesiastic who consulted him on the subject. The following were the reasons:

First, as we are living in an age of intellectual pride, and there are all around us numbers of puffed-up scholars and conceited and critical spirits who have plenty to say against the best established and most solid practices of piety, it is better for us not to give them any needless occasion of criticism. Hence it is better for us to say, "the slavery of Jesus in Mary," and call ourselves the slaves of Jesus Christ rather than the slaves of Mary, taking the denomination

Mancipia Publications

of our devotion rather from its Last End, which is Jesus Christ, than from the road and the means to the end, which is Mary; though I repeat that in truth we may do either, as I have done myself. For example, a man who goes from Orleans to Tours by way of Amboise may very well say that he is going to Amboise, or that he is going to Tours; that he is a traveler to Amboise and a traveler to Tours; with this difference, however, that Amboise is but his straight road to Tours and that Tours is only the last end and term of his journey.

A second reason is that the principal mystery we celebrate and honor in this devotion is the mystery of the Incarnation, wherein we can see Jesus only in Mary, and incarnate in her bosom. Hence it is more to the purpose to speak of the slavery of Jesus in Mary, and of Jesus residing and reigning in Mary, according to that beautiful prayer of so many great men: "O Jesus, living in Mary, come and live in us in Thy spirit of sanctity," etc.

Another reason is that this manner of speaking sets forth still more the intimate union between Jesus and Mary. They are so intimately united that the one is altogether in the other. Jesus is altogether in Mary and Mary is altogether in Jesus; or rather, she exists no more, but Jesus alone is in her, and it were easier to separate the light from the sun than Mary from Jesus; so that we might call Our Lord, "Jesus of Mary," and our Blessed Lady, "Mary of Jesus."

Time would not permit me to stop now to explain the excellences and grandeurs of the mystery of Jesus living and reigning in Mary; in other words, of the Incarnation of the Word. I will content myself with saying these few words: We have here the first mystery of Jesus Christ—the most hidden, the most exalted and the least known. It is in this mystery that Jesus, in His Mother's womb—which is for that very reason called by the saints "the cabinet of the secrets of God"—has, in concert with Mary, chosen all the elect. It is in this mystery that He has wrought all the other mysteries of His life by the acceptance which He made of them. "When He cometh into the world, He saith: ...Behold, I come to do Thy will, O God." (Heb. 10:5-9) Hence this mystery is an abridgment of all mysteries and contains the will and grace of all. Finally, this mystery is the throne of the mercy, of the liberality and of the glory of God. It is the throne of His mercy for us because, as we cannot approach Jesus but through Mary, we can see Jesus and speak to Him only by means of her. Jesus, Who always hears His dear Mother, always grants His grace and mercy to poor sinners. "Let us go therefore with confidence to the throne of grace." (Heb. 4:16) It is the throne of His liberality toward Mary, because while the New Adam dwelt in that true terrestrial paradise, He worked so many miracles in secret that neither angels nor men can comprehend them. It is on this account that the saints call Mary the "magnificence of God"—as if God were magnificent only in Mary. It is the throne of His glory for His Father, because it is in Mary that Jesus Christ has calmed His Father, angered against men, and that He has made restitution of the glory which sin ravished from Him, and that, by the sacrifice He made of His own will and of Himself, He has given Him more glory than ever the sacrifices of the Old Law could give—an infinite glory, which He had never before received from man.

Manual for the Total Consecration to Mary

Fifth Day _____

Daily Prayers during the Third Week: *Litany of the Holy Ghost* on page 160, the *Ave Maris Stella* on page 156, the *Litany of the Holy Name of Jesus* or *Litany of the Sacred Heart,* on pages 163 or 165, respectively. Saint Louis De Montfort's *Prayer to Jesus* page 158, *O Jesus Living in Mary* on page 159, and the *Prayer of Saint Augustine* on page 158.

Gospel according to Saint John 19

Then therefore, Pilate took Jesus and scourged Him.

2. And the soldiers platting a crown of thorns, put it upon His head; and they put on Him a purple garment.

3. And they came to Him, and said: Hail, king of the Jews; and they gave Him blows.

4. Pilate therefore went forth again, and said to them: Behold, I bring Him forth unto you, that you may know that I find no cause in Him.

5. (Jesus therefore came forth, bearing the crown of thorns and the purple garment.) And he said to them: Behold the Man.

6. When the chief priests, therefore, and the servants, had seen Him, they cried out, saying: Crucify Him, crucify Him. Pilate said to them: Take Him you, and crucify Him: for I find no cause in Him.

7. The Jews answered him: We have a law; and according to the law He ought to die, because He made Himself the Son of God.

8. When Pilate therefore had heard this saying, he feared the more.

9. And he entered into the hall again, and he said to Jesus: Whence art Thou? But Jesus gave him no answer.

10. Pilate therefore said to Him : Speak Thou not to me? Know Thou not that I have power to crucify Thee, and I have power to release Thee?

11. Jesus answered: Thou should not have any power against Me, unless it were given thee from above. Therefore, he that has delivered Me to thee, has the greater sin.

12. And from henceforth Pilate sought to release Him. But the Jews cried out saying: If thou release this man, thou art not Caesar's friend. For whosoever makes himself a king, speaks against Caesar.

13. Now when Pilate had heard these words, he brought Jesus forth, and sat down in the judgment seat, in the place that is called *Lithostrotos*, and in Hebrew *Gabbatha.*

14. And it was the parasceve of the pasch, about the sixth hour, and he said to the Jews: Behold your king.

15. But they cried out: Away with Him; away with Him; crucify Him. Pilate said to them: Shall I crucify your king? The chief priests answered: We have no king but Caesar.

16. Then therefore he delivered Him to them to be crucified. And they took Jesus, and led Him forth.

17. And bearing His own cross, He went forth to that place which is called

Mancipia Publications

Calvary, but in Hebrew *Golgotha.*

18. Where they crucified Him, and with Him two others, one on each side, and Jesus in the midst.

19. And Pilate wrote a title also, and he put it upon the cross. And the writing was: *Jesus of Nazareth, the King of the Jews.*

20. This title therefore many of the Jews did read: because the place where Jesus was crucified was nigh to the city: and it, was written in Hebrew, in Greek, and in Latin.

21. Then the chief priests of the Jews said to Pilate: Write not, the King of the Jews; but that He said, I am the King of the Jews.

22. Pilate answered: What I have written, I have written.

23. The soldiers therefore, when they had crucified Him, took His garments, (and they made four parts, to every soldier a part) and also His coat. Now the coat was without seam, woven from the top throughout.

24. They said then one to another: Let us not cut it, but let us cast lots for it, whose it shall be; that the scripture might be fulfilled, saying: They have parted my garments among them, and upon my vesture they have cast lots. And the soldiers indeed did these things.

25. Now there stood by the cross of Jesus, His mother, and His mother's sister, Mary of Cleophas, and Mary Magdalen.

26. When Jesus therefore had seen His mother and the disciple standing whom He loved, He said to His mother: Woman, behold thy Son.

27. After that, He said to the disciple: Behold thy mother. And from that hour, the disciple took her to his own.

28. Afterwards, Jesus knowing that all things were now accomplished, that the scripture might be fulfilled, said: I thirst.

29. Now there was a vessel set there full of vinegar. And they, putting a sponge full of vinegar about hyssop, put it to His mouth.

30. Jesus therefore, when He had taken the vinegar, said: It is consummated. And bowing His head, He gave up the ghost.

31. Then the Jews, (because it was the parasceve) that the bodies might not remain upon the cross on the sabbath day, (for that was a great sabbath day) besought Pilate that their legs might be broken, and that they might be taken away.

32. The soldiers therefore came; and they broke the legs of the first, and of the other that was crucified with Him.

33. But after they were come to Jesus, when they saw that He was already dead, they did not break His legs.

34. But one of the soldiers with a spear opened His side, and immediately there came out blood and water.

35. And he that saw it, has given testimony; and his testimony is true. And he knows that it is true; that you also may believe.

36. For these things were done, that the scripture might be fulfilled: "You shall not break a bone of Him."

37. And again another scripture said: They shall look on Him Whom they pierced.

38. And after these things, Joseph of Arimathea (because he was a disciple of Jesus, but secretly for fear of the Jews) besought Pilate that he might take away the body of Jesus. And Pilate gave leave. He came therefore, and took away the body of Jesus.

39. And Nicodemus also came, (he who at the first came to Jesus by night,) bringing a mixture of myrrh and aloes, about a hundred pound weight.

40. They took therefore the body of Jesus, and bound it in linen cloths, with the spices, as the manner of the Jews is to bury.

41. Now there was in the place where He was crucified, a garden; and in the garden a new sepulcher, wherein no man yet had been laid.

42. There, therefore, because of the parasceve of the Jews, they laid Jesus, because the sepulcher was nigh at hand.

Gospel according to Saint Matthew 27, 1-22

And, when morning was come, all the chief priests and ancients of the people took counsel against Jesus, that they might put Him to death.

2. And they brought Him bound, and delivered Him to Pontius Pilate the governor.

3. Then Judas, who betrayed Him, seeing that He was condemned, repenting himself, brought back the thirty pieces of silver to the chief priests and ancients,

4. Saying: I have sinned in betraying innocent blood. But they said: What is that to us? Look to it yourself.

5. And casting down the pieces of silver in the temple, he departed and went and hanged himself with a halter.

6. But the chief priests having taken the pieces of silver, said: It is not lawful to put them into the corbona, because it is the price of blood.

7. And after they had consulted together, they bought with them the potter's field, to be a burying place for strangers.

8. For this cause that field was called *Haceldama*, that is, the field of blood, even to this day.

9. Then was fulfilled that which was spoken by Jeremias the prophet, saying: "And they took the thirty pieces of silver, the price of Him that was prized, whom they prized of the children of Israel."

10. And they gave them unto the potter's field, as the Lord appointed to me.

11. And Jesus stood before the governor, and the governor asked Him, saying: Are you the king of the Jews? Jesus said to him: You have said *it*.

12. And when He was accused by the chief priests and ancients, He answered nothing.

13. Then Pilate said to Him: Do Thou not hear how great testimonies they allege against Thee?

14. And He answered him never a word; so that the governor wondered exceedingly.

15. Now upon the solemn day the governor was accustomed to release to

Mancipia Publications

the people one prisoner, whom they would.

16. And he had a notorious prisoner, that was called Barabbas.

17. They, therefore, being gathered together, Pilate said: Whom will you that I release to you, Barabbas, or Jesus that is called Christ?

18. For he knew that for envy they had delivered Him.

19. And as he was sitting in the place of judgment, his wife sent to him, saying: Have nothing to do with that Just Man; for I have suffered many things this day in a dream because of Him.

20. But the chief priests and ancients persuaded the people, that they should ask Barabbas, and make Jesus away.

21. And the governor answering, said to them: Whether will you of the two to be released unto you? But they said, Barabbas.

22. Pilate said to them: What shall I do then with Jesus that is called Christ? They say all: Let Him be crucified.

Imitation of Christ Book 4, Chapter 1:1-6
With How Great Reverence Christ Is To Be Received

Come to me, all you that labor and are burdened, and I will refresh you. (Matt. 11:28)
DISCIPLE

These are Thy words, O Christ, the eternal truth, though not all delivered at one time, nor written in one place.

Since, therefore, they are Thy words, and true, they are all to be received by me with thanks and with faith.

They are Thine, and Thou has spoken them; and they are also mine because Thou has delivered them for my salvation.

I willingly received them from Thy mouth, that they may be more inseparably engrafted in my heart.

These words of such great tenderness, full of sweetness and love, encourage me; but my sins terrify me, and my unclean conscience keeps me back from approaching such great mysteries.

The sweetness of Thy words invites me, but the multitude of my offenses weighs me down.

2. Thou command me to approach to Thee with confidence if I would have part with Thee; and to receive the food of immortality if I desire to obtain life and glory everlasting.

"Come," Thou sayest to me, "all you that labor and are burdened, and I will refresh you." (Matt. 11:28)

O sweet and amiable word in the ear of a sinner, that Thou, O Lord my God, should invite the poor and needy to the Communion of Thy most sacred Body!

But who am I, O Lord, that I should presume to come to Thee?

Behold, the Heaven of heavens cannot contain Thee and Thou say, "Come you all to Me."

3. What means this most loving condescension, and so friendly invitation?

How shall I dare to approach, who am conscious to myself of no good on which I can presume?

How shall I introduce Thee into my house, who have oftentimes provoked Thine indignation?

The angels and the archangels stand with a reverential awe; the saints and the just are afraid and Thou say, "Come you all to Me." Unless Thou, O Lord, did say it, who could believe it to be true?

And unless Thou did command it, who would dare attempt to approach?

4. Behold Noe, a just man, labored a hundred years in building the ark, that he with a few might be preserved; and how shall I be able in the space of one hour to prepare myself to receive with reverence the Maker of the world?

Moses Thy servant, Thy great and special friend, made an ark of incorruptible wood, which he also covered with the most pure gold, that he might deposit therein the tables of the law; and shall I, a rotten creature, presume so easily to receive Thee, the Maker of the law, and the Giver of life?

Solomon, the wisest of the kings of Israel, employed seven years in building a magnificent temple for the praise of Thy name:

And for eight days together celebrated the feast of dedication thereof; he offered a thousand victims as peace offerings, and brought the Ark of the Covenant in a solemn manner into the place prepared for it, with sound of trumpet and jubilee.

And I, a wretch, and the vilest of men, how shall I bring Thee into my house, who can hardly spend one half hour devoutly? And would I had even once spent one half hour itself as I ought!

5. O my God, how much did they endeavor to do to please Thee!

Alas! how little is what I do! How short a time do I spend when I prepare myself to communicate, being seldom wholly recollected, very seldom free from all distraction!

And yet, surely in the life-giving presence of Thy Deity, no unbecoming thought should occur, nor anything created take up my mind; for it is not an angel, but the Lord of angels that I am to entertain.

6. And yet there is a very great difference between the Ark of the Covenant with its relics, and Thy most pure Body, with its unspeakable virtues; between those sacrifices of the law, which were figures of things to come, and the true sacrifice of Thy Body, which is the accomplishing of all those ancient sacrifices.

True Devotion #249-256
V. Devotion to the Hail Mary and to the Rosary

Those who adopt this slavery ought also to have a great devotion to saying the *Hail Mary* (the Angelical Salutation). Few Christians, however enlightened, know the real value, merit, excellence, and necessity of the *Hail Mary*. It was necessary for the Blessed Virgin to appear several times to great and enlightened saints to show them the merit of it. She did so to Saint Dominic, Saint John Capistran and Blessed Alan de la Roche. They have composed entire works on the wonders and efficacy of that prayer for converting souls. They

Mancipia Publications

have loudly proclaimed and openly preached that, salvation having begun with the *Hail Mary*, the salvation of each one of us in particular is attached to that prayer. They tell us that it is that prayer which made the dry and barren earth bring forth the fruit of life; and that it is that prayer well said which makes the word of God germinate in our souls, and bring forth Jesus Christ, the Fruit of Life. They tell us that the *Hail Mary* is a heavenly dew for watering the earth, which is the soul, to make it bring forth its fruit in season; and that a soul which is not watered by that prayer bears no fruit, and brings forth only thorns and brambles, and is ready to be cursed.

Listen to what Our Lady revealed to Blessed Alan de la Roche, as he has recorded in his book on the dignity of the Rosary: "Know, my son, and make all others know, that it is a probable and proximate sign of eternal damnation to have an aversion, a lukewarmness, or a negligence in saying the Angelical Salutation, which has repaired the whole world." These words are at once terrible and consoling, and we should find it hard to believe them if we had not that holy man for a guarantee, and Saint Dominic before him, and many great men since. But we have also the experience of several ages; for it has always been remarked that those who wear the outward sign of reprobation, like all impious heretics and proud worldlings, hate or despise the *Hail Mary* and the Rosary. Heretics still learn and say the *Our Father*, but not the *Hail Mary* nor the Rosary. They abhor it; they would rather wear a serpent than a Rosary. The proud also, although Catholics, have the same inclinations as their father Lucifer; and so have only contempt or indifference for the *Hail Mary*, and look at the Rosary as at a devotion which is good only for the ignorant and for those who cannot read. On the contrary, it is an equally universal experience that those who have otherwise great marks of predestination about them love and relish the *Hail Mary*, and delight in saying it. We always see that the more a man is for God, the more he likes that prayer. This is what Our Lady also said to Blessed Alan, after the words which I have just quoted.

I do not know how it is, nor why, but nevertheless I know well that it is true; nor have I any better secret of knowing whether a person is for God than to examine if he likes to say the *Hail Mary* and the Rosary. I say, if he likes; for it may happen that a person may be under some natural inability to say it, or even a supernatural one; yet, nevertheless, he likes it always, and always inspires the same liking in others.

O predestinate souls, slaves of Jesus in Mary, learn that the *Hail Mary* is the most beautiful of all prayers after the *Our Father*. It is the most perfect compliment which you can give to Mary, because it is the compliment which the Most High sent her by an archangel, in order to win her heart; and it was so powerful over her heart by the secret charms of which it is so full, that in spite of her profound humility she gave her consent to the Incarnation of the Word. It is by this compliment also that you will infallibly win her heart, if you say it as you ought.

The *Hail Mary* well said—that is, with attention, devotion, and modesty— is, according to the saints, the enemy of the Devil which puts him to flight, and the hammer which crushes him. It is the sanctification of the soul, the joy of the angels, the melody of the predestinate, the canticle of the New Testament, the pleasure of Mary, and the glory of the most Holy Trinity. The *Hail Mary* is a heavenly dew which fertilizes the soul. It is the chaste and loving kiss which we give to Mary. It is a vermilion rose which we present to her; a precious pearl we offer her; a chalice of divine ambrosial nectar which we proffer to her. All these are comparisons of the saints.

I pray you urgently, by the love I bear you in Jesus and Mary, not to content yourselves with saying the *Little Crown of the Blessed Virgin*, but to say five decades, or even, if you have time, fifteen decades of the Rosary every day. At the moment of your death you will bless the day and the hour in which you followed my advice. Having thus sown in the blessings of Jesus and Mary, you will reap eternal blessings in Heaven. "He who soweth in blessings, shall also reap blessings."

VI. Devotion to the Magnificat

To thank God for the graces He has given to Our Lady, those who adopt this devotion will often say the *Magnificat*, as Blessed Mary d'Oignies did, and many other saints. It is the only prayer, the only work, which the holy Virgin composed, or rather, which Jesus composed in her; for He spoke by her mouth. It is the greatest sacrifice of praise which God ever received from a pure creature in the law of grace. It is, on the one hand, the most humble and grateful, and on the other hand, the most sublime and exalted, of all canticles. There are in that canticle mysteries so great and hidden that the angels do not know them. The pious and erudite Gerson employed a great part of his life in composing works upon the most difficult subjects; and yet it was only at the close of his career, and even with trembling, that he undertook to comment on the Magnificat, so as to crown all his other works. He wrote a folio volume on it, bringing forward many admirable things about that beautiful and divine canticle. Among other things, he says that Our Lady often repeated it herself, and especially for thanksgiving after Communion. The learned Benzonius [Rutilio], in explaining the *Magnificat*, relates many miracles wrought by virtue of it, and says that the devils tremble and fly when they hear these words: "He hath showed might in His arm; He hath scattered the proud in the conceit of their heart."

VII. Contempt of and Flight from the World

Those faithful servants of Mary who adopt this devotion ought always greatly to despise, to hate and to eschew the corrupted world, and to make use of those practices of contempt of the world which we have given in the first part of this treatise.

Mancipia Publications

Sixth Day ──────────

Daily Prayers during the Third Week: Litany of the Holy Ghost on page 160, the *Ave Maris Stella* on page 156, the *Litany of the Holy Name of Jesus* or *Litany of the Sacred Heart,* on pages 163 or 165, respectively. Saint Louis De Montfort's *Prayer to Jesus* page 158, *O Jesus Living in Mary* on page 159, and the *Prayer of Saint Augustine* on page 158.

Gospel according to Saint John 20

And on the first day of the week, Mary Magdalen came early, when it was yet dark, unto the sepulcher; and she saw the stone taken away from the sepulcher.

2. She ran, therefore, and came to Simon Peter, and to the other disciple whom Jesus loved, and said to them: They have taken away the Lord out of the sepulcher, and we know not where they have laid Him.

3. Peter therefore went out, and that other disciple, and they came to the sepulcher.

4. And they both ran together, and that other disciple did outrun Peter, and came first to the sepulcher.

5. And when he stooped down, he saw the linen cloths lying; but yet he went not in.

6. Then came Simon Peter, following him, and went into the sepulcher, and saw the linen cloths lying,

7. And the napkin that had been about His head, not lying with the linen cloths, but apart, wrapped up into one place.

8. Then that other disciple also went in, who came first to the sepulcher: and he saw, and believed.

9. For as yet they knew not the scripture, that He must rise again from the dead.

10. The disciples therefore departed again to their home.

11. But Mary stood at the sepulcher without, weeping. Now as she was weeping, she stooped down, and looked into the sepulcher,

12. And she saw two angels in white, sitting, one at the head, and one at the feet, where the body of Jesus had been laid.

13. They say to her: Woman, why weep thou? She said to them: Because they have taken away my Lord; and I know not where they have laid Him.

14. When she had thus said, she turned herself back, and saw Jesus standing; and she knew not that it was Jesus.

15. Jesus said to her: Woman, why weep thou? Whom seek thou? She, thinking that it was the gardener, said to Him: Sir, if thou has taken Him hence, tell me where thou has laid Him, and I will take Him away.

16. Jesus said to her: Mary. She turning, said to Him: Rabboni (which is to say, Master).

17. Jesus said to her: Do not touch Me, for I am not yet ascended to My Father. But go to My brethren, and say to them: I ascend to My Father and to

your Father, to My God and your God.

18. Mary Magdalen came, and told the disciples: I have seen the Lord, and these things He said to me.

19. Now when it was late that same day, the first of the week, and the doors were shut, where the disciples were gathered together, for fear of the Jews, Jesus came and stood in the midst, and said to them: Peace be to you.

20. And when He had said this, He showed them His hands and His side. The disciples therefore were glad, when they saw the Lord.

21. He said therefore to them again: Peace be to you. As the Father has sent Me, I also send you.

22. When He had said this, He breathed on them; and He said to them: Receive ye the Holy Ghost.

23. Whose sins you shall forgive, they are forgiven them; and whose sins you shall retain, they are retained.

24. Now Thomas, one of the twelve, who is called Didymus, was not with them when Jesus came.

25. The other disciples therefore said to him: We have seen the Lord. But he said to them: Except I shall see in His hands the print of the nails, and put my finger into the place of the nails, and put my hand into His side, I will not believe.

26. And after eight days again His disciples were within, and Thomas with them. Jesus came, the doors being shut, and stood in the midst, and said: Peace be to you.

27. Then He said to Thomas: Put in thy finger hither, and see My hands; and bring hither thy hand, and put it into My side; and be not faithless, but believing.

28. Thomas answered, and said to Him: My Lord, and my God.

29. Jesus said to Him: Because thou has seen Me, Thomas, thou has believed: blessed are they that have not seen, and have believed.

30. Many other signs also did Jesus in the sight of His disciples, which are not written in this book.

31. But these are written, that you may believe that Jesus is the Christ, the Son of God: and that believing, you may have life in His name.

Continuation of the holy Gospel according to Saint Matthew 27, 23-44

The governor said to them: Why, what evil has He done? But they cried out the more, saying: Let Him be crucified.

24. And Pilate seeing that he prevailed nothing, but that rather a tumult was made; taking water washed his hands before the people, saying: I am innocent of the blood of this Just Man; look you to it.

25. And the whole people answering, said: His blood be upon us and upon our children.

26. Then he released to them Barabbas, and having scourged Jesus, delivered Him unto them to be crucified.

Mancipia Publications

27. Then the soldiers of the governor taking Jesus into the hall, gathered together unto Him the whole band;

28. And stripping Him, they put a scarlet cloak about Him.

29. And platting a crown of thorns, they put it upon His head, and a reed in His right hand. And bowing the knee before Him, they mocked Him, saying: Hail, King of the Jews.

30. And spitting upon Him, they took the reed, and struck His head.

31. And after they had mocked Him, they took off the cloak from Him, and put on Him His own garments, and led Him away to crucify Him.

32. And going out, they found a man of Cyrene, named Simon: him they forced to take up His cross.

33. And they came to the place that is called Golgotha, which is the place of Calvary.

34. And they gave Him wine to drink mingled with gall. And when He had tasted, He would not drink.

35. And after they had crucified Him, they divided His garments, casting lots; that it might be fulfilled which was spoken by the prophet, saying: "They divided My garments among them; and upon My vesture they cast lots."

36. And they sat and watched Him.

37. And they put over His head His cause written: This is Jesus, the King of the Jews.

38. Then were crucified with Him two thieves: one on the right hand, and one on the left.

39. And they that passed by, blasphemed Him, wagging their heads.

40. And saying: Vah, Thou that destroys the temple of God, and in three days rebuilds it: save Thy own self if you are the Son of God, come down from the cross.

41. In like manner also the chief priests, with the scribes and ancients, mocking, said:

42. He saved others; Himself He cannot save. If He be the king of Israel, let Him now come down from the cross, and we will believe Him.

43. He trusted in God; let Him now deliver Him if He will have Him; for He said: I am the Son of God.

44. And the selfsame thing the thieves also, that were crucified with Him, reproached Him with.

Imitation of Christ Book 4, Chapter 1:7-12

Why then am I not more inflamed, considering Thy venerable presence?

Why do I not prepare myself with greater care to receive Thy sacred gifts, seeing that these ancient holy patriarchs and prophets, yea kings also and princes, with the whole people, have shown so great an affection of devotion towards Thy divine worship?

8. The most devout King David danced before the ark of God with all his might, commemorating the benefits bestowed in times past on the fathers. He

made musical instruments of sundry kinds; he published psalms, and appointed them to be sung with joy; he himself likewise often sang them, playing upon his harp, inspired with the grace of the Holy Ghost. He taught the people of Israel to praise God with their whole heart, and to join their voices in blessing and magnifying Him every day.

If such great devotion was then used, and such remembrance of the praise of God before the Ark of the Covenant, how great ought to be the reverence and devotion which I and all Christian people should have in the presence of this Sacrament, and in receiving the most excellent Body of Christ!

9. Many run to sundry places to visit the relics of the saints, and are astonished to hear their wonderful works; they behold the noble church buildings and kiss their sacred bones, wrapped up in silk and gold.

And behold I have Thee here present on the altar, my God, the Saint of saints, the Creator of men, and the Lord of angels.

Oftentimes in seeing these things men are moved with curiosity, and the novelty of the sight, and but little fruit of amendment is reaped thereby; especially when persons lightly run hither and thither, without true contrition for their sins.

But here, in the Sacrament of the Altar, Thou art wholly present, my God, the man Christ Jesus; where also the fruit of eternal salvation is plentifully reaped, as often as Thou art worthily and devoutly received.

And to this we are not drawn by any levity, curiosity, or sensuality; but by a firm faith, a devout hope, and sincere charity.

10. O God, the invisible Maker of the world, how wonderfully do Thou deal with us! How sweetly and graciously do Thou order all things in favor of Thine elect, to whom Thou offer Thyself to be received in this Sacrament!

For this exceeds all understanding of man; this in a particular manner engages the hearts of the devout, and enkindles their love.

For Thy true faithful, who dispose their whole life to amendment, by this most worthy Sacrament, frequently receive a great grace of devotion and love of virtue.

11. Oh, the wonderful and hidden grace of this Sacrament, which only the faithful of Christ know; but unbelievers and such as are slaves to sin cannot experience.

In this Sacrament is conferred spiritual grace; lost virtue is repaired in the soul; and beauty disfigured by sin returns again.

And so great sometimes is this grace that from the abundance of the devotion that is bestowed, not only the mind, but the frail body also feels a great increase of strength.

12. Yet it is much to be lamented and pitied that we should be so lukewarm and negligent as not to be drawn with greater affection to the receiving of Christ, in whom consists all the hope and merit of those that shall be saved.

For He is our sanctification and our redemption; He is our comfort in our pilgrimage, and the eternal beatitude of the saints.

It is therefore much to be lamented that many esteem so lightly this saving

144

mystery which rejoices Heaven and preserves the whole world.

Oh, the blindness and hardness of the heart of man that does not more highly prize so unspeakable a gift; and from daily use falls into a disregard of it.

13. For if this most holy Sacrament were only celebrated in one place, and consecrated by only one priest in the world, how great a desire would men have to go to that place, and to such a priest of God; that they might see the divine mysteries celebrated?

But now there are made many priests, and Christ is offered up in many places, that the grace and love of God to man may appear the greater, the more this sacred Communion is spread throughout the world.

Thanks be to Thee, O good Jesus, our eternal Shepherd, Who has vouchsafed to feed us poor exiles with Thy precious Body and Blood, and to invite us to the receiving of these mysteries with the very words of Thine Own mouth, saying, "Come to Me all you that labor and are burdened, and I will refresh you." (Matt. 11:28)

True Devotion #257-265

Besides the external practices of the devotion which we have been describing so far, and which we must not omit through negligence or contempt, so far as the state and condition of each one will allow him to observe them, there are some very sanctifying interior practices for those whom the Holy Ghost calls to high perfection.

These may be expressed in four words: to do all our actions *by* Mary, *with* Mary, *in* Mary and *for* Mary; so that we may do them all the more perfectly *by* Jesus, *with* Jesus, *in* Jesus and *for* Jesus.

I. All by Mary

We must do all our actions by Mary; that is to say, we must obey her in all things, and in all things conduct ourselves by her spirit, which is the Holy Spirit of God. "Those who are led by the Spirit of God are the children of God." (Rom. 8:14) Those who are led by the spirit of Mary are the children of Mary, and consequently the children of God, as we have shown; and among so many clients of the Blessed Virgin, none are true or faithful but those who are led by her spirit. I have said that the spirit of Mary was the Spirit of God, because she was never led by her own spirit, but always by the Spirit of God, Who has rendered Himself so completely master of her that He has become her own spirit.

It is on this account that Saint Ambrose says: "Let the soul of Mary be in each of us to magnify the Lord, and the spirit of Mary be in each of us to rejoice in God." A soul is happy indeed when, like the good Jesuit lay-brother, Alphonse Rodriguez, who died in the odor of sanctity, it is all possessed and overruled by the spirit of Mary, a spirit meek and strong, zealous and prudent, humble and courageous, pure and fruitful.

In order that the soul may let itself be led by Mary's spirit, it must first of all renounce its own spirit and its own lights and wills before it does anything. For example: It should do so before prayers, before saying or hearing Mass and before communicating; because the darkness of our own spirit, and the malice of our own will and operation, if we follow them, however good they may appear to us, will be an obstacle to the spirit of Mary. Secondly, we must deliver ourselves to the spirit of Mary to be moved and influenced by it in the manner she chooses. We must put ourselves and leave ourselves in her virginal hands, like a tool in the grasp of a workman, like a lute in the hands of a skillful player. We must lose ourselves and abandon ourselves to her, like a stone one throws into the sea. This can be done simply, and in an instant, by one glance of the mind, by one little movement of the will, or even verbally, in saying, for example, "I renounce myself, I give myself to thee, my dear Mother." We may not, perhaps, feel any sensible sweetness in this act of union, but it is not on that account the less real. It is just as if we were to say with equal sincerity, though without any sensible change in ourselves, what—may it please God— we never shall say: "I give myself to the Devil;" we should not the less truly belong to the Devil because we did not feel we belonged to him. Thirdly, we must, from time to time, both during and after the action, renew the same act of offering and of union. The more often we do so, the sooner we shall be sanctified, and attain to union with Jesus Christ, which always follows necessarily on our union with Mary, because the spirit of Mary is the spirit of Jesus.

II. All with Mary

We must do all our actions *with* Mary; that is to say, we must in all our actions regard Mary as an accomplished model of every virtue and perfection which the Holy Ghost has formed in a pure creature for us to imitate according to our little measure. We must therefore in every action consider how Mary has done it, or how she would have done it, had she been in our place. For that end we must examine and meditate on the great virtues which she practiced during her life, and particularly, first of all, her lively faith, by which she believed without hesitation the angel's word, and believed faithfully and constantly up to the foot of the cross; secondly, her profound humility, which made her hide herself, hold her peace, submit to everything, and put herself the last of all; and, thirdly, her altogether divine purity, which never has had, and never can have, its equal under Heaven; and so on with all of her other virtues.

Let us remember, I repeat, that Mary is the great and exclusive mold of God, proper to making living images of God at small cost and in a little time; and that a soul which has found that mold, and has lost itself in it, is presently changed into Jesus Christ, Whom that mold represents to the life.

III. All in Mary

We must do our actions *in* Mary. Thoroughly to understand this practice, we must first know that our Blessed Lady is the true terrestrial paradise of the New Adam, and that the ancient paradise was but a figure of her. There are,

Mancipia Publications

then, in this earthly paradise, riches, beauties, rarities and inexplicable sweetnesses, which Jesus Christ, the New Adam, has left there; it was in this paradise that He took His complacence for nine months, worked His wonders and displayed His riches with the magnificence of a God. This most holy place is composed only of a virginal and immaculate earth, of which the New Adam was formed, and on which He was nourished, without any spot or stain, by the operation of the Holy Ghost, who dwelt there. It is in this earthly paradise that there is the true tree of life, which has borne Jesus Christ, the Fruit of Life, and the tree of the knowledge of good and evil, which has given light unto the world. There are in this divine place trees planted by the hand of God, and watered by His divine unction, which have borne and daily bear fruits of a divine taste. There are flowerbeds adorned with beautiful and varied blossoms of virtues, diffusing odors which delight the very angels. There are meadows green with hope, impregnable towers of strength, and the most charming houses of confidence. It is only the Holy Ghost who can make us know the hidden truth of these figures of material things. There is in this place an air of perfect purity; a fair sun, without shadow, of the Divinity; a fair day, without night, of the Sacred Humanity; a continual burning furnace of love, where all the iron that is cast into it is changed, by excessive heat, to gold. There is a river of humility which springs from the earth, and which, dividing itself into four branches, waters all that enchanted place; and these are the four cardinal virtues.

The Holy Ghost, by the mouth of the Fathers, also styles the Blessed Virgin the Eastern Gate, by which the High Priest, Jesus Christ, enters the world and leaves it. By it He came the first time, and by it He will come the second. The sanctuary of the Divinity, the repose of the Most Holy Trinity, the throne of God, the city of God, the altar of God, the temple of God, the world of God—all these different epithets and encomiums are most substantially true with reference to the different marvels and graces which the Most High has wrought in Mary. Oh, what riches! What glory! What pleasure! What happiness, to be able to enter into and dwell in Mary, where the Most High has set up the throne of His supreme glory!

But how difficult it is for sinners like ourselves to have the permission, the capacity and the light to enter into a place so high and so holy, which is guarded, not by one of the Cherubim like the old earthly paradise, but by the Holy Ghost Himself, Who is its absolute Master. He Himself has said of it: "My sister, My spouse, is a garden enclosed, a garden enclosed, a fountain sealed up." (Cant. 4:12) Mary is shut, Mary is sealed. The miserable children of Adam and Eve, driven from the earthly paradise, cannot enter into this one except by a particular grace of the Holy Ghost, which they must merit.

After we have obtained this illustrious grace by our fidelity, we must remain in the fair interior of Mary with complacency, repose there in peace, lean our weight there in confidence, hide ourselves there with assurance, and lose ourselves there without reserve. Thus, in that virginal bosom, (1) the soul shall be nourished with the milk of grace and maternal mercy; (2) it shall be delivered from its troubles, fears and scruples; and (3) it shall be in safety against all its enemies—the world, the Devil and sin—who never have entrance there. It is on this account that Mary says that they who work in her shall not sin; that is to say, those who dwell in Mary in spirit shall fall into no considerable fault. Lastly, (4) the soul shall be formed in Jesus Christ and Jesus Christ in it, because her bosom is, as the holy Fathers say, the chamber of the divine sacraments, where Jesus Christ and all the elect have been formed. "This man and that man is born in her."

IV. All for Mary

Finally we must do all our actions *for* Mary. As we have given ourselves up entirely to her service, it is but just to do everything for her as servants and slaves. It is not that we take her for the last end of our services, for that is Jesus Christ alone; but we take her for our proximate end, our mysterious means and our easy way to go to Him. Like good servants and slaves, we must not remain idle, but, supported by her protection, we must undertake and achieve great things for this august sovereign. We must defend her privileges when they are disputed; we must stand up for her glory when it is attacked; we must draw all the world, if we can, to her service, and to this true and solid devotion; we must speak and cry out against those who abuse her devotion to outrage her Son, and we must at the same time establish this veritable devotion; we must pretend to no recompense for our little services, except the honor of belonging to so sweet a Queen, and the happiness of being united through her to Jesus her Son by an indissoluble tie, in time and in eternity.

Glory to Jesus in Mary!
Glory to Mary in Jesus!
Glory to God alone!

If, there had been anything better and more beneficial to man's salvation than suffering, Christ certainly would have showed it by word and example.

Mancipia Publications

Seventh Day ───────────

Daily Prayers during the Third Week: Litany of the Holy Ghost on page 160, the *Ave Maris Stella* on page 156, the *Litany of the Holy Name of Jesus* or *Litany of the Sacred Heart,* on pages 163 or 165, respectively. Saint Louis De Montfort's *Prayer to Jesus* page 158, *O Jesus Living in Mary* on page 159, and the *Prayer of Saint Augustine* on page 158.

Gospel according to Saint John 21

After this, Jesus showed Himself again to the disciples at the sea of Tiberias. And He showed Himself after this manner.

2. There were together Simon Peter, and Thomas, who is called Didymus, and Nathanael, who was of Cana of Galilee, and the sons of Zebedee, and two others of His disciples.

3. Simon Peter said to them: I go a fishing. They say to him: We also come with thee. And they went forth, and entered into the ship: and that night they caught nothing.

4. But when the morning was come, Jesus stood on the shore: yet the disciples knew not that it was Jesus.

5. Jesus therefore said to them: Children, have you any meat? They answered Him: No.

6. He said to them: Cast the net on the right side of the ship, and you shall find. They cast therefore; and now they were not able to draw it, for the multitude of fishes.

7. That disciple therefore whom Jesus loved, said to Peter: It is the Lord. Simon Peter, when he heard that it was the Lord, girt his coat about him, (for he was naked,) and cast himself into the sea.

8. But the other disciples came in the ship, (for they were not far from the land, but as it were two hundred cubits,) dragging the net with fishes.

9. As soon then as they came to land, they saw hot coals lying, and a fish laid thereon, and bread.

10. Jesus said to them: Bring hither of the fishes which you have now caught.

11. Simon Peter went up, and drew the net to land, full of great fishes, one hundred and fifty-three. And although there were so many, the net was not broken.

12. Jesus said to them: Come, and dine. And none of them who were at meat, dare ask Him: Who art Thou? knowing that it was the Lord.

13. And Jesus came and took bread, and gave them, and fish in like manner.

14. This is now the third time that Jesus was manifested to His disciples, after He was risen from the dead.

15. When therefore they had dined, Jesus said to Simon Peter: Simon, son of John, love thou Me more than these? He said to Him: Yea, Lord, Thou know

that I love Thee. He said to him: Feed My lambs.

16. He said to him again: Simon, son of John, love thou Me? He said to Him: Yea, Lord, Thou know that I love Thee. He said to him: Feed my lambs.

17. He said to him the third time: Simon, son of John, love thou Me? Peter was grieved, because He had said to him the third time: Love thou Me? And he said to Him: Lord, Thou know all things: Thou know that I love Thee. He said to him: Feed My sheep.

18. Amen, amen I say to thee, when thou was younger, thou did gird thyself, and did walk where thou would. But when thou shall be old, thou shall stretch forth thy hands, and another shall gird thee, and lead thee whither thou would not.

19. And this He said, signifying by what death he should glorify God. And when He had said this, He said to him: Follow Me.

20. Peter turning about, saw that disciple whom Jesus loved following, who also leaned on His breast at supper, and said: Lord, who is he that shall betray Thee?

21. Him therefore when Peter had seen, he said to Jesus: Lord, and what shall this man do?

22. Jesus said to him: So I will have him to remain till I come, what is it to thee? Follow thou Me.

23. This saying therefore went abroad among the brethren, that that disciple should not die. And Jesus did not say to him: He should not die; but, So I will have him to remain till I come, what is it to thee?

24. This is that disciple who gives testimony of these things, and has written these things; and we know that his testimony is true.

25. But there are also many other things which Jesus did; which, if they were written every one, the world itself, I think, would not be able to contain the books that should be written.

Continuation of the holy Gospel according to Saint Matthew 27, 45-66
Now from the sixth hour there was darkness over the whole earth, until the ninth hour.

46. And about the ninth hour Jesus cried with a loud voice, saying: *Eli, Eli, lamma sabacthani?* That is, My God, My God, why hast Thou forsaken Me?

47. And some that stood there and heard, said: This man called Elias.

48. And immediately one of them running took a sponge, and filled it with vinegar; and put it on a reed, and gave Him to drink.

49. And the others said: Let be, let us see whether Elias will come to deliver Him.

50. And Jesus again crying with a loud voice, yielded up the ghost.

51. And behold the veil of the temple was rent in two from the top even to the bottom, and the earth quaked, and the rocks were rent.

52. And the graves were opened: and many bodies of the saints that had slept arose.

150

53. And coming out of the tombs after His resurrection, they came into the holy city, and appeared to many.

54. Now the centurion and they that were with him watching Jesus, having seen the earthquake, and the things that were done, were sore afraid, saying: Indeed this was the Son of God.

55. And there were there many women afar off, who had followed Jesus from Galilee, ministering unto Him:

56. Among whom was Mary Magdalen, and Mary the mother of James and Joseph, and the mother of the sons of Zebedee.

57. And when it was evening, there came a certain rich man of Arimathea, named Joseph, who also himself was a disciple of Jesus.

58. He went to Pilate, and asked the body of Jesus. Then Pilate commanded that the body should be delivered.

59. And Joseph taking the body, wrapped it up in a clean linen cloth.

60. And laid it in his own new monument, which he had hewed out in a rock. And he rolled a great stone to the door of the monument, and went his way.

61. And there was there Mary Magdalen, and the other Mary sitting over against the sepulcher.

62. And the next day, which followed the day of preparation, the chief priests and the Pharisees came together to Pilate,

63. Saying: Sir, we have remembered, that that seducer said, while He was yet alive: After three days I will rise again.

64. Command therefore the sepulcher to be guarded until the third day: lest perhaps His disciples come and steal Him away, and say to the people: He is risen from the dead; and the last error shall be worse than the first.

65. Pilate said to them: You have a guard. Go, guard it as you know.

66. And they departing, made the sepulcher sure, sealing the stone, and setting guards.

Imitation of Christ Book 4, Chapter 8
Of the Oblation of Christ on the Cross, and of Our Own Resignation
CHRIST

As I willingly offered Myself to God My Father, for thy sins, with My hands stretched out upon the cross, and My body naked, so that nothing remained in Me which was not turned into a sacrifice, to appease the divine wrath:

Even so must thou willingly offer thyself to Me daily in the Mass, for a pure and holy oblation, together with all thy powers and affections, as heartily as thou are able.

What do I require more of thee, than that thou endeavor to resign thyself entirely to Me?

Whatsoever thou give besides thyself I regard not; for I seek not thy gift, but thyself.

2. As it would not suffice thee if thou have all things but Me, so neither can it please Me whatever thou give, as long as thou offer not thyself.

Offer thyself to Me, and give thy whole self for God, and thine offering will be accepted.

Behold, I offered My whole self to the Father for thee, and have given My whole Body and Blood for thy food, that I might be all thine, and Thou might be always Mine.

But if thou will stand upon thine own self, and will not offer thyself freely to My will, thine offering is not perfect, nor will there be an entire union between us.

Therefore, before all thy works, thou must make a free oblation of thyself into the hands of God, if thou desire to obtain liberty and grace.

For the reason why so few become illuminated and internally free is because they do not wholly renounce themselves.

My sentence stands firm: "Unless a man renounce all he cannot be My disciple." If, therefore, thou desire to be My disciple, offer up thyself to Me with all thine affections.

Imitation of Christ Book 4, Chapter 13
That a Devout Soul Ought to Desire, with Her Whole Heart, to be United to Christ in This Sacrament
DISCIPLE

Who will give me, O Lord, that I may find Thee alone, that I may open my whole heart to Thee and enjoy Thee as my soul desires; and that now no man may despise me, nor anything created move me or regard me, but that Thou alone speak to me, and I to Thee; as the beloved is wont to speak to his beloved, and a friend to entertain himself with his friend.

This I pray for, this I desire, that I may be wholly united to Thee, and may withdraw my heart from all created things, and by the Holy Communion, and often celebrating, may more and more learn to relish heavenly and eternal things.

Ah! Lord God, when shall I be wholly united to Thee, and absorbed in Thee, and altogether forgetful of myself.

Thou in me, and I in Thee; and so grant us both to continue in one.

2. Verily Thou are my beloved, the choicest among thousands, in whom my soul is well pleased to dwell all the days of her life.

Verily Thou are my peacemaker, in Whom is sovereign peace and true rest; out of Whom is labor and sorrow and endless misery.

Thou are, in truth, a hidden God, and Thy counsel is not with the wicked; but Thy conversation is with the humble and the simple.

Oh, how sweet is Thy spirit, O Lord, Who, to show Thy sweetness towards Thy children, vouchsafe to feed them with the most delicious bread which comes down from Heaven!

Surely, there is no other nation so great, that has gods so nigh them as

Thou our God are present to all Thy faithful; to whom, for their daily comfort, and for the raising up of their hearts to Heaven, Thou give Thyself to be eaten and enjoyed.

3. For what other nation is there so honored as the Christian people?

Or what creature under Heaven so beloved as a devout soul, into whom God comes, that He may feed her with His glorious Flesh?

O unspeakable grace! O wonderful condescension! O infinite love, singularly bestowed upon man!

But what return shall I make to the Lord for this grace, and for so extraordinary a charity?

There is nothing that I can give Him that will please Him better than if I give up my heart entirely to God, and unite it closely to Him.

Then all that is within me shall rejoice exceedingly when my soul shall be perfectly united to my God; then will He say to me: If thou will be with Me, I will be with thee: and I will answer Him: Vouchsafe, O Lord, to remain with me, and I will willingly be with Thee.

This is my whole desire, that my heart may be united to Thee.

 # *The Consecration*

At the end of the three weeks you should go to confession and Communion, with the intention of giving yourself to Jesus Christ in the quality of a slave of love, by the hands of Mary. After Communion, which should be made according to the method given on page 169, you should recite the formula of you consecration, which you will find on page 167. You ought to write it, or have it written, unless you have a printed copy of it; and you should sign it the same day on which you have made your consecration.

It would be well also that on that day you should pay some tribute to Jesus Christ and our Blessed Lady, either as a penance for your past unfaithfulness to the vows of your Baptism, or as a testimony of your dependence on the dominion of Jesus and Mary. This tribute ought to be according to the devotion and ability of each one, such as a fast, a mortification, an alms or a candle. If you had but a pin to give in homage, and gave it with a good heart, it would be enough for Jesus, who looks only at the good will.

Once a year at least, on the same day, you should renew your consecration, observing the same practices during the three weeks.

You might also, once a month or even once a day, renew all you have done, in these few words: "I am all Thine and all that I have is Thine, O most loving Jesus, through Mary, Thy most holy Mother."

MARIA.

ROSARIO

Prayers

Veni Creator

Come, O Creator Spirit blest!
And in our souls take up Thy rest;
Come with Thy grace and heavenly aid,
To fill the hearts which Thou hast made.

Great Paraclete! To Thee we cry,
O highest gift of God most high!
O font of life! O fire of love!
And sweet anointing from above.

Thou in Thy sevenfold gifts art known,
The finger of God's hand we own;
The promise of the Father, Thou!
Who dost the tongue with power endow.

Kindle our senses from above,
And make our hearts o'erflow with love;
With patience firm and virtue high
The weakness of our flesh supply.

Far from us drive the foe we dread,
And grant us Thy true peace instead;
So shall we not, with Thee for guide,
Turn from the path of life aside.

Oh, may Thy grace on us bestow
The Father and the Son to know,
And Thee, through endless times confessed,
Of both, the eternal Spirit blest.

All glory while the ages run
Be to the Father and the Son
Who rose from death; the same to Thee,
O Holy Ghost, eternally. Amen.

Ave Maris Stella

Hail, bright Star of Ocean,
God's own Mother blest,
Ever sinless Virgin,
Gate of heavenly rest.

Taking that sweet Ave
Which from Gabriel came,
Peace confirm within us,
Changing Eva's name.

Break the captives' fetters,
Light on blindness pour,
All our ills expelling,
Every bliss implore.

Show thyself a Mother;
May the Word Divine,
Born for us thy Infant,
Hear our prayers through thine.

Virgin all excelling,
Mildest of the mild,
Freed from guilt, preserve us,
Pure and undefiled.

Keep our life all spotless,
Make our way secure,
Till we find in Jesus
Joy forevermore.

Through the highest Heaven
To the Almighty Three,
Father, Son and Spirit,
One same glory be. Amen.

Magnificat

My soul doth magnify the Lord. And my spirit hath rejoiced in God my Saviour. Because He hath regarded the humility of His handmaid; for behold, from henceforth all generations shall call me blessed. Because He that is mighty hath done great things to me; and holy is His name. And His mercy is from generation unto generations, on those who fear Him. He hath shown might in His arm; He hath scattered the proud in the conceit of their heart. Put down the mighty from their thrones; and exalted the humble. He hath filled the hungry with good things; and the rich He hath sent empty away. He hath received Israel His servant, being mindful of His mercy. As He spoke to our fathers, to Abraham and to his seed forever. Glory be to the Father and to the Son and to the Holy Ghost as it was in the beginning is now and ever shall be world without end. Amen.

Mancipia Publications

Prayer to Mary

by Saint Louis Marie De Montfort

Hail Mary, beloved Daughter of the Eternal Father! Hail Mary, admirable Mother of the Son! Hail Mary, faithful Spouse of the Holy Ghost! Hail Mary, my dear Mother, my loving Mistress, my powerful Sovereign! Hail my joy, my glory, my heart and my soul! Thou art all mine by mercy, and I am all thine by justice. But I am not yet sufficiently thine. I now give myself wholly to thee without keeping anything back for myself or others. If thou still seest in me anything which does not belong to thee, I beseech thee to take it and to make thyself the absolute Mistress of all that is mine. Destroy in me all that may be displeasing to God, root it up and bring it to nought; place and cultivate in me everything that is pleasing to thee.

May the light of thy faith dispel the darkness of my mind; may thy profound humility take the place of my pride; may thy sublime contemplation check the distractions of my wandering imagination; may thy continous sight of God fill my memory with His presence; may the burning love of thy heart inflame the lukewarmness of mine; may thy virtues take the place of my sins; may thy merits be my only adornment in the sight of God and make up for all that is wanting in me. Finally, dearly beloved Mother, grant, if it be possible, that I may have no other spirit but thine to know Jesus and His divine will; that I may have no other soul but thine to praise and glorify the Lord; that I may have no other heart but thine to love God with a love as pure and ardent as thine. I do not ask thee for visions, revelations, sensible devotion or spiritual pleasures. It is thy privilege to see God clearly; it is thy privilege to enjoy heavenly bliss; it is thy privilege to triumph gloriously in Heaven at the right hand of thy Son and to hold absolute sway over angels, men and demons; it is thy privilege to dispose of all gifts of God, just as thou willest.

Such is, O heavenly Mary, the "best part," which the Lord has given thee and which shall never be taken away from thee,—and this thought fills my heart with joy. As for my part here below, I wish for no other than that which was thine: to believe sincerely without spiritual pleasures; to suffer joyfully without human consolation; to die continually to myself without respite; and to work zealously and unselfishly for thee until death as the humblest of thy servants. The only grace I beg thee to obtain for me is that every day and every moment of my life I may say: Amen, so be it— to all that thou didst do while on earth; Amen, so be it—to all that thou art now doing in Heaven; Amen, so be it—to all that thou art doing in my soul, so that thou alone mayest fully glorify Jesus in me for time and eternity. Amen.

Saint Augustine's Prayer _____

Thou art Christ, my holy Father, my tender God, my great King, my good Shepherd, my one Master, my best Helper, my most Beautiful and my Beloved, my living Bread, my Priest forever, my Leader to my country, my true Light, my holy Sweetness, my straight Way, my excellent Wisdom, my pure Simplicity, my pacific Harmony, my whole Guard, my good Portion, my everlasting Salvation.

Christ Jesus, my sweet Lord, why have I ever loved, why in my whole life have I ever desired anything except Thee, Jesus my God? Where was I when I was not in Thy mind with Thee? Now, from this time forth, do you, all my desires, grow hot, and flow out upon the Lord Jesus; run, you have been tardy thus far; hasten whither you are going; seek Whom you are seeking. O Jesus, may he who loves Thee not, be anathema; may he who loves Thee not, be filled with bitterness!

O sweet Jesus, may every good feeling that is fitted for Thy praise, love Thee, delight in Thee, admire Thee. God of my heart and my Portion, Christ Jesus, may my heart faint away in spirit and mayest Thou be my life within me! May the live coal of Thy love grow hot within my spirit, and break forth into a perfect fire; may it burn incessantly on the altar of my heart; may it glow in my innermost being; may it blaze in hidden recesses of my soul; and in the day of my consummation, may I be found consummated with Thee. Amen.

Prayer to Jesus _____
by Saint Louis Marie De Montfort

O most loving Jesus, deign to let me pour forth my gratitude before Thee, for the grace Thou hast bestowed upon me in giving me to Thy holy Mother through the devotion of Holy Bondage, that she may be my advocate in the presence of Thy majesty and my support in my extreme misery. Alas, O Lord! I am so wretched that without this dear Mother I should be certainly lost. Yes, Mary is necessary for me at Thy side and everywhere: that she may appease Thy just wrath, because I have so often offended Thee; that she may save me from the eternal punishment of Thy justice, which I deserve; that she may contemplate Thee, speak to Thee, pray to Thee, approach Thee and please Thee; that she may help me to save my soul and the souls of others; in short, Mary is necessary for me that I may always do Thy holy will and seek Thy greater glory in all things. Ah, would that I could proclaim throughout the whole world the mercy that Thou hast shown to me! Would that everyone might know I should be already damned, were it not for Mary! Would that I

158   Mancipia Publications

might offer worthy thanksgiving for so great a blessing! Mary is in me. Oh, what a treasure! Oh, what a consolation! And shall I not be entirely hers? Oh, what ingratitude! My dear Saviour, send me death rather than such a calamity, for I would rather die than live without belonging entirely to Mary. With Saint John the Evangelist at the foot of the Cross, I have taken her a thousand times for my own and as many times have given myself to her; but if I have not yet done it as Thou, dear Jesus, dost wish, I now renew this offering as Thou dost desire me to renew it. And if Thou see in my soul or my body anything that does not belong to this august princess, I pray Thee to take it and cast it far from me, for whatever in me does not belong to Mary is unworthy of Thee.

O Holy Spirit, grant me all these graces. Plant in my soul the Tree of true Life, which is Mary; cultivate it and tend it so that it may grow and blossom and bring forth the fruit of life in abundance. O Holy Spirit, give me great devotion to Mary, Thy faithful Spouse; give me great confidence in her maternal heart and an abiding refuge in her mercy, so that by her Thou may truly form in me Jesus Christ, great and mighty, unto the fullness of His perfect age. Amen.

O Jesus Living in Mary

O Jesus living in Mary,
Come and live in Thy servants,
In the spirit of Thy holiness,
In the fullness of Thy might,
In the truth of Thy virtues,
In the perfection of Thy ways,
In the communion of Thy mysteries;
Subdue every hostile power
In Thy spirit, for the glory of the Father. Amen.

Sub Tuum Praesidium

We fly to thy patronage, O holy Mother of God; despise not thou our petitions in our necessities, but deliver us from all dangers, O ever glorious and blessed Virgin.

Litanies

Litany of the Holy Ghost

Lord, have mercy on us.
Christ, have mercy on us.
Lord, have mercy on us.
Father all powerful, *have mercy on us.*
Jesus, Eternal Son of the Father, Redeemer of the world, *save us.*
Spirit of the Father and the Son, boundless life of both, *sanctify us.*
Holy Trinity, *hear us.*

Holy Ghost, Who proceeds from the Father and the Son, *enter our hearts.*
Holy Ghost, Who art equal to the Father and the Son, *enter our hearts.*

Promise of God the Father,
Ray of heavenly light,
Author of all good,
Source of heavenly water,
Consuming fire,
Ardent charity,
Spiritual unction,
Spirit of love and truth,
Spirit of wisdom and understanding,
Spirit of counsel and fortitude,
Spirit of knowledge and piety,
Spirit of the fear of the Lord,
Spirit of grace and prayer,
Spirit of peace and meekness,
Spirit of modesty and innocence,
Holy Ghost, the Comforter,
Holy Ghost, the Sanctifier,
Holy Ghost, Who governs the Church,
Gift of God, the Most High,
Spirit Who fills the universe,
Spirit of the adoption of the children of God,

Have mercy on us.

Holy Ghost, *inspire us with horror of sin.*
Holy Ghost, *come and renew the face of the earth.*
Holy Ghost, *shed Thy light in our souls.*
Holy Ghost, *engrave Thy law in our hearts.*
Holy Ghost, *inflame us with the flame of Thy love.*
Holy Ghost, *open to us the treasures of Thy graces.*

Holy Ghost, *teach us to pray well.*
Holy Ghost, *enlighten us with Thy heavenly inspirations.*
Holy Ghost, *lead us in the way of salvation.*
Holy Ghost, *grant us the only necessary knowledge.*
Holy Ghost, *inspire in us the practice of good.*
Holy Ghost, *grant us the merits of all virtues.*
Holy Ghost, *make us persevere in justice.*
Holy Ghost, *be Thou our everlasting reward.*

Lamb of God, Who takes away the sins of the world, *Send us Thy Holy Ghost.*
Lamb of God, Who takes away the sins of the world, *Pour down into our souls the gifts of the Holy Ghost.*
Lamb of God, Who takes away the sins of the world, *Grant us the Spirit of wisdom and piety.*

    V. Come, Holy Ghost! Fill the hearts of Thy faithful.
    R. And enkindle in them the fire of Thy love.

Let us pray
    Grant, O merciful Father, that Thy Divine Spirit may enlighten, inflame and purify us, that He may penetrate us with His heavenly dew and make us fruitful in good works, through our Lord Jesus Christ, Thy Son, Who with Thee, in the unity of the same Spirit, lives and reigns forever and ever. Amen.

Litany of the Blessed Virgin

Lord, have mercy on us.
  Christ, have mercy on us.
Lord, have mercy on us. Christ, hear us.
  Christ, graciously hear us.

God the Father of Heaven, *have mercy on us.*
God the Son, Redeemer of the world, *have mercy on us.*
God the Holy Ghost, *have mercy on us.*
Holy Trinity, One God, *have mercy on us.*

Holy Mary,
Holy Mother of God,
Holy Virgin of virgins,
Mother of Christ,
Mother of divine grace,
Mother most pure,
Mother most chaste,
Mother inviolate,
Mother undefiled,

Pray for us.

Mother most amiable,
Mother most admirable,
Mother of good counsel,
Mother of our Creator,
Mother of our Saviour,
Mother of the Church,
Virgin most prudent,
Virgin most venerable,
Virgin most renowned,
Virgin most powerful,
Virgin most merciful,
Virgin most faithful,
Mirror of justice,
Seat of wisdom,
Cause of our joy,
Spiritual vessel,
Vessel of honor,
Singular vessel of devotion,
Mystical rose,
Tower of David,
Tower of ivory,
House of gold,
Ark of the covenant,
Gate of Heaven,
Morning star,
Health of the sick,
Refuge of sinners,
Comforter of the afflicted,
Help of Christians,
Queen of angels,
Queen of patriarchs,
Queen of prophets,
Queen of Apostles,
Queen of martyrs,
Queen of confessors,
Queen of virgins,
Queen of all saints,
Queen conceived without Original Sin,
Queen of the most holy Rosary,
Queen of the Family,
Queen assumed into Heaven,
Queen of peace,

Pray for us.

Lamb of God, Who takest away the sins of the world, *Spare us, O Lord.*
Lamb of God, Who takest away the sins of the world, *Graciously hear us, O Lord.*

Mancipia Publications

Lamb of God, Who takest away the sins of the world, *Have mercy on us.*

   V. Pray for us, O holy Mother of God,

   R. That we may be made worthy of the promises of Christ.

Let us pray

   Grant unto us, Thy servants, we beseech Thee, O Lord God, at all times to enjoy health of soul and body, and by the glorious intercession of Blessed Mary, ever virgin, when freed from the sorrows of this present life, to enter into the joy of Thine eternal gladness. Through Christ our Lord. Amen.

Litany of the Holy Name of Jesus

Lord, have mercy on us.
Christ, have mercy on us.
Lord, have mercy on us. Jesus, hear us.
Jesus, graciously hear us.

God the Father of Heaven,
God the Son, Redeemer of the world,
God the Holy Ghost,
Holy Trinity, One God,
Jesus, Son of the living God,
Jesus, splendor of the Father,
Jesus, brightness of eternal light,
Jesus, King of glory,
Jesus, sun of justice,
Jesus, Son of the Virgin Mary,
Jesus, most amiable,
Jesus, most admirable,
Jesus, mighty God,
Jesus, Father of the world to come,
Jesus, angel of great counsel,
Jesus, most powerful,
Jesus, most patient,
Jesus, most obedient,
Jesus, meek and humble of heart,
Jesus, lover of chastity,
Jesus, lover of us,
Jesus, God of peace,
Jesus, author of life,
Jesus, model of virtues,
Jesus, lover of souls,
Jesus, our God,
Jesus, our refuge,

Have mercy on us.

Jesus, Father of the poor,
Jesus, treasure of the faithful,
Jesus, Good Shepherd,
Jesus, true light,
Jesus, eternal wisdom,
Jesus, infinite goodness,
Jesus, our way and our life,
Jesus, joy of angels,
Jesus, King of patriarchs,
Jesus, master of Apostles,
Jesus, teacher of Evangelists,
Jesus, strength of martyrs,
Jesus, light of confessors,
Jesus, purity of virgins,
Jesus, crown of all saints,

Have mercy on us.

Be merciful, *spare us, O Jesus.*
Be merciful, *graciously hear us, O Jesus.*

From all evil,
From all sin,
From Thy wrath,
From the snares of the Devil,
From the spirit of fornication,
From everlasting death,
From the neglect of Thine inspirations,
Through the mystery of Thy holy Incarnation,
Through Thy nativity,
Through Thine infancy,
Through Thy most divine life,
Through Thy labors,
Through Thine agony and Passion,
Through Thy cross and dereliction,
Through Thy sufferings,
Through Thy death and burial,
Through Thy Resurrection,
Through Thine Ascension,
Through Thine institution of the most Holy Eucharist,
Through Thy joys,
Through Thy glory,

Jesus, deliver us.

Lamb of God, Who takest away the sins of the world, *Spare us, O Jesus.*
Lamb of God, Who takest away the sins of the world, *Graciously hear us, O Jesus.*
Lamb of God, Who takest away the sins of the world, *Have mercy on us.*
Jesus, hear us. *Jesus, graciously hear us.*

Mancipia Publications

Let us pray

O Lord Jesus Christ, Who hast said: Ask and you shall receive, seek and you shall find, knock and it shall be opened unto you; grant, we beseech Thee, to us who ask the gift of Thy divine love, that we may ever love Thee with all our hearts, and in all our words and actions, and never cease from praising Thee.

Give us, O Lord, a perpetual fear and love of Thy holy Name; for Thou never failest to govern those whom Thou dost solidly establish in Thy love, Who livest and reignest world without end. Amen.

Litany of the Sacred Heart

Lord, have mercy on us.
Christ, have mercy on us.
Lord, have mercy on us. Christ, hear us.
Christ, graciously hear us.

God the Father of Heaven, *have mercy on us.*
God the Son, Redeemer of the world, *have mercy on us.*
God the Holy Ghost, *have mercy on us.*
Holy Trinity, One God, *have mercy on us.*
Heart of Jesus, Son of the Eternal Father,
Heart of Jesus, formed by the Holy Ghost in the womb
of the Virgin Mother,
Heart of Jesus, substantially united with the Word of God,
Heart of Jesus, of infinite majesty,
Heart of Jesus, holy temple of God,
Heart of Jesus, tabernacle of the Most High,
Heart of Jesus, house of God and gate of Heaven,
Heart of Jesus, burning furnace of charity,
Heart of Jesus, abode of justice and love,
Heart of Jesus, full of goodness and love,
Heart of Jesus, abyss of all virtues,
Heart of Jesus, most worthy of all praise,
Heart of Jesus, King and center of all hearts,
Heart of Jesus, in Whom are all the treasures of wisdom
and knowledge,
Heart of Jesus, in Whom dwells all the fullness of divinity,
Heart of Jesus, in Whom the Father was well pleased,
Heart of Jesus, of Whose fullness we have all received,
Heart of Jesus, desire of the everlasting hills,
Heart of Jesus, patient and most merciful,
Heart of Jesus, enriching all who invoke Thee,

Have mercy on us.

Heart of Jesus, fountain of life and holiness,
Heart of Jesus, propitiation for our sins,
Heart of Jesus, loaded down with opprobrium,
Heart of Jesus, bruised for our offenses,
Heart of Jesus, obedient unto death,
Heart of Jesus, pierced with a lance,
Heart of Jesus, source of all consolation,
Heart of Jesus, our life and resurrection,
Heart of Jesus, our peace and reconciliation,
Heart of Jesus, victim for sin,
Heart of Jesus, salvation of those who trust in Thee,
Heart of Jesus, hope of those who die in Thee,
Heart of Jesus, delight of all the saints,

Have mercy on us.

Lamb of God, Who takest away the sins of the world, *Spare us, O Lord.*
Lamb of God, Who takest away the sins of the world, *Graciously hear us, O Lord.*
Lamb of God, Who takest away the sins of the world, *Have mercy on us.*

V. Jesus, meek and humble of heart,
R. *Make our hearts like unto Thine.*

Let Us Pray

Almighty and everlasting God, graciously regard the Heart of Thy well-beloved Son and the acts of praise and satisfaction which He renders Thee on behalf of sinners; appeased by worthy homage, pardon those who implore Thy mercy, in the name of the same Jesus Christ Thy Son, Who liveth and reigneth with Thee, world without end. Amen.

Renewal of Baptismal Vows

ALMIGHTY and eternal God! Thou knowest all things: Thou seest the very bottom of my heart, and Thou knowest that, however sinful I have hitherto been, I am resolved, by the help of Thy grace, to love and serve Thee for the remainder of my life. And therefore, O my God, kneeling before the throne of Thy mercy, I renew, with all the sincerity of my soul the promises and vows made for me in my baptism.

I renounce Satan with my whole heart, and will henceforth have no connection with him. I renounce all the pomps of Satan, that is, all the vanities of the world, the false treasures of its riches, honors and pleasures, and all its corrupt teachings. I renounce all the works of Satan, that is, all kinds of sins.

To Thee alone, O my God, I desire to cling; Thy word will I hear and obey; for Thee alone I desire to live and to die. Amen.

Mancipia Publications

The Act of
Consecration

The Act of Consecration to Jesus Christ, the Incarnate Wisdom, through the Blessed Virgin Mary

O Eternal and Incarnate Wisdom! O sweetest and most adorable Jesus! True God and true man, only Son of the Eternal Father, and of Mary, always virgin! I adore Thee profoundly in the bosom and splendors of Thy Father during eternity; and I adore Thee also in the virginal bosom of Mary, Thy most worthy Mother, in the time of Thine Incarnation.

I give Thee thanks for that Thou has annihilated Thyself, taking the form of a slave in order to rescue me from the cruel slavery of the Devil. I praise and glorify Thee for that Thou has been pleased to submit Thyself to Mary, Thy holy Mother, in all things, in order to make me Thy faithful slave through her. But, alas! Ungrateful and faithless as I have been, I have not kept the promises which I made so solemnly to Thee in my Baptism; I have not fulfilled my obligations; I do not deserve to be called Thy child, nor yet Thy slave; and as there is nothing in me which does not merit Thine anger and Thy repulse, I dare not come by myself before Thy most holy and august Majesty. It is on this account that I have recourse to the intercession of Thy most holy Mother, whom Thou has given me for a mediatrix with Thee. It is through her that I hope to obtain of Thee contrition, the pardon of my sins, and the acquisition and preservation of wisdom.

Hail, then, O Immaculate Mary, living tabernacle of the Divinity, where the Eternal Wisdom willed to be hidden and to be adored by angels and by men! Hail, O Queen of Heaven and earth, to whose empire everything is subject which is under God. Hail, O sure refuge of sinners, whose mercy fails no one. Hear the desires which I have of the Divine Wisdom; and for that end receive the vows and offerings which in my lowliness I present to thee.

I, (Name), a faithless sinner, renew and ratify today in thy hands the vows of my Baptism; I renounce forever Satan, his pomps and works; and I give myself entirely to Jesus Christ, the Incarnate Wisdom, to carry my cross after Him all the days of my life, and to be more faithful to Him than I have ever been before.

In the presence of all the heavenly court I choose thee this day for my Mother and Mistress. I deliver and consecrate to thee, as thy slave, my body and soul, my goods, both interior and exterior, and even the value of all my good actions, past, present and future; leaving to thee the entire and full right of disposing of me, and all that belongs to me, without exception, according to thy good pleasure, for the greater glory of God, in time and in eternity.

Receive, O benignant Virgin, this little offering of my slavery, in honor of, and in union with, that subjection which the Eternal Wisdom deigned to have to thy maternity, in homage to the power which both of you have over this poor sinner, and in thanksgiving for the privileges with which the Holy Trinity has favored thee. I declare that I wish henceforth, as thy true slave, to seek thy honor and to obey thee in all things.

O admirable Mother, present me to thy dear Son as His eternal slave, so that as He has redeemed me by thee, by thee He may receive me! O Mother of mercy, grant me the grace to obtain the true Wisdom of God; and for that end receive me among those whom thou lovest and teachest, whom thou leadest, nourishest and protectest as thy children and thy slaves.

O faithful Virgin, make me in all things so perfect a disciple, imitator and slave of the Incarnate Wisdom, Jesus Christ thy Son, that I may attain, by thine intercession and by thine example, to the fullness of His age on earth and of His glory in Heaven. Amen.

Mancipia Publications

Practices and Prayers

by Saint Louis Marie De Montfort

A Devout Practice for Receiving Holy Communion

Before Holy Communion

(1) You must humble yourself most profoundly before God. (2) You must renounce your corrupt interior and your dispositions, however good your self-love may make them look. (3) You must renew your consecration by saying: "I am all thine, my dear Mistress, with all that I have." (4) You must implore that good Mother to lend you her heart, that you may receive her Son there with the same dispositions as her own. You will explain to her that it touches her Son's glory to be put into a heart so sullied and so inconstant as yours, which would not fail either to lessen His glory or to destroy it. But if she will come and dwell with you, in order to receive her Son, she can do so by the dominion which she has over all hearts; and her Son will be well received by her, without stain, without danger of being outraged or unnoticed: "God is in the midst thereof, it shall not be moved." (Ps. 45:6) You will tell her confidently that all you have given her of your goods is little enough to honor her; but that by Holy Communion you wish to make her the same present as the Eternal Father gave her, and that you will honor her more by that than if you gave her all the goods in the world; and finally, that Jesus, who loves her in a most special manner, still desires to take His pleasure and repose in her, even in your soul, though it be far filthier and poorer than the stable where He did not hesitate to come, simply because she was there. You will ask her for; her heart, by these tender words: "I take thee for my all. Give me thy heart, O Mary."

At Holy Communion

After the Our Father, just before receiving Jesus Christ, you say three times: "Lord, I am not worthy." Say the first one to the Eternal Father, telling Him you are not worthy, because of your evil thoughts and ingratitude toward so good a Father, to receive His only Son; but that He is to behold Mary, His handmaid— "Behold the handmaid of the Lord" (Lk. 1:38)—who acts for you and who gives you a singular confidence and hope with His Majesty: "For thou singularly has settled me in hope." (Ps. 4:10)

You will say to the Son: "Lord, I am not worthy;" telling Him that you are not worthy to receive Him because of your idle and evil words and your infidelity to His service; but that nevertheless you pray Him to have pity on you, because you are about to bring Him into the house of His own Mother and yours, and that you will not let Him go without His coming to lodge with her: "I held Him; and I will not let Him go, till I bring Him into my Mother's house and into the chamber of her that bore me." (Cant. 3:4) You will pray to Him to rise, and come to the place of His repose and into the ark of His sanctification: "Arise, Lord, into Thy resting place: Thou and the ark which Thou has sanctified." (Ps. 131:8) Tell Him you put no confidence at all in your own merits, your own strength and your own preparations, as Esau did; but that you trust only in Mary, your dear Mother, as the little Jacob did in Rebecca. Tell Him that, sinner and Esau that you are, you dare to approach His sanctity, supported and adorned as you are with the virtues of His holy Mother.

You will say to the Holy Ghost: "Lord, I am not worthy;" telling Him that you are not worthy to receive this masterpiece of His charity, because of the lukewarmness and iniquity of your actions, and because of your resistance to His inspirations; but that all your confidence is in Mary, His faithful spouse. You will say, with St. Bernard: "She is my greatest security; she is the source of all my hope." You can even pray Him to come Himself in Mary, His inseparable Spouse, telling Him that her bosom is as pure and her heart as burning as ever; and that, without His descent into your soul, neither Jesus nor Mary will be formed nor worthily lodged.

After Holy Communion

After Holy Communion, inwardly recollected and holding your eyes shut, you will introduce Jesus into the heart of Mary. You will give Him to His Mother, who will receive Him lovingly, will place Him honorably, will adore Him profoundly, will love Him perfectly, will embrace Him closely, and will render to Him, in spirit and in truth, many homages which are unknown to us in our thick darkness.

Or else you will keep yourself profoundly humbled in your heart, in the presence of Jesus residing in Mary. Or else you will sit like a slave at the gate of the King's palace, where He is speaking with the Queen; and while they talk to each other without need of you, you will go in spirit to Heaven and over all the earth, praying all creatures to thank, adore and love Jesus and Mary in your place: "Come, let us adore." (Ps. 94:6)

Or else you will yourself ask of Jesus, in union with Mary, the coming of His kingdom on earth, through His holy Mother; or you will sue for divine wisdom, or for divine love, or for the pardon of your sins, or for some other grace; but always by Mary and in Mary; saying, while you look aside at

170

yourself: "Lord, look not at my sins;" "but let Your eyes look at nothing in me but the virtues and merits of Mary." And then, remembering your sins, you will add: "It is I who have committed these sins" (Cf. Matt. 13:28); or you will say: "Deliver me from the unjust and deceitful man" (Ps. 42:1); or else: "My Jesus, You must increase in my soul, and I must decrease" (Jn. 3:30); Mary, you must increase within me, and I must be still less than I have been. "O Jesus and Mary, increase in me, and multiply yourselves outside in others also." (Cf. Gen. 1:22 ff.)

There are an infinity of other thoughts which the Holy Ghost furnishes, and will furnish you, if you are thoroughly interior, mortified and faithful to this grand and sublime devotion which I have been teaching you. But always remember that the more you allow Mary to act in your Communion, the more Jesus will be glorified; and you will allow Mary to act for Jesus and Jesus to act in Mary in the measure that you humble yourself and listen to them in peace and in silence, without troubling yourself about seeing, tasting or feeling; for the just man lives throughout on faith, and particularly in Holy Communion, which is an action of faith: "My just man lives by faith." (Heb. 10:38)

The Little Crown of the Blessed Virgin Mary_____

Saint John the Evangelist saw a woman crowned with twelve stars, clothed with the sun, and the moon under her feet. According to the commentators, this woman is the Blessed Virgin Mary, with her virtues and her privileges, especially that of her divine maternity. Thus originated the Little Crown of the Twelve Stars of the Blessed Virgin Mary, which Saint Joseph Calasanctius, Saint John Berchmans and many other saints made it a practice to recite frequently.

In order to make this prayer more attractive, Saint Louis De Montfort added to each Hail Mary one of the praises of the Blessed Virgin, with the invocation, "Rejoice, O Virgin Mary; rejoice a thousand times."

It is this prayer which Saint Louis De Montfort gave to his religious families (the Montfort Fathers and the Daughters of Wisdom) as their morning prayer. He also recommends it to all those who embrace the devotion of the holy and loving slavery of Jesus through Mary.

Little Crown of the Blessed Virgin Mary

I. Crown of Excellence
(To honor the divine maternity of the Blessed Virgin, her ineffable virginity, her purity without stain and her innumerable virtues.)

1. *Our Father.... Hail Mary....*Blessed art thou, O Virgin Mary, who didst bear the Lord, the Creator of the world; thou didst give birth to Him Who made thee, and remainest a virgin forever.
Rejoice, O Virgin Mary; rejoice a thousand times!

2. *Hail Mary....*O holy and immaculate Virgin, I know not with what praise to extol thee, since thou didst bear in thy womb the very One Whom the heavens cannot contain.
Rejoice, O Virgin Mary; rejoice a thousand times!

3. *Hail Mary....*Thou art all fair, O Virgin Mary, and there is no stain in thee.
Rejoice, O Virgin Mary; rejoice a thousand times!

4. *Hail Mary....*Thy virtues, O Virgin, surpass the stars in number.
Rejoice, O Virgin Mary; rejoice a thousand times!
Glory be to the Father.

II. Crown of Power
(To honor the royalty of the Blessed Virgin, her magnificence, her universal mediation and the strength of her rule.)

5. *Our Father.... Hail Mary....*Glory be to thee, O Empress of the world! Bring us with thee to the joys of Heaven.
Rejoice, O Virgin Mary; rejoice a thousand times!

6. *Hail Mary....*Glory be to thee, O treasure house of the Lord's graces! Grant us a share in thy riches.
Rejoice, O Virgin Mary; rejoice a thousand times!

7. *Hail Mary....*Glory be to thee, O Mediatrix between God and man! Through thee may the Almighty be favorable to us.
Rejoice, O Virgin Mary; rejoice a thousand times!

8. *Hail Mary....*Glory be to thee who destroys heresies and crushes demons! Be thou our loving guide.
Rejoice, O Virgin Mary; rejoice a thousand times!
Glory be to the Father....

III. Crown of Goodness
(To honor the mercy of the Blessed Virgin toward sinners, the poor, the just and the dying.)

9. *Our Father.... Hail Mary....*Glory be to thee, O Refuge of sinners! Intercede for us with God.
Rejoice, O Virgin Mary; rejoice a thousand times!

Mancipia Publications

10. *Hail Mary....*Glory be to thee, O Mother of orphans! Render the Almighty favorable to us.
Rejoice, O Virgin Mary; rejoice a thousand times!

11. *Hail Mary....*Glory be to thee, O Joy of the just! Lead us with thee to the joys of Heaven.
Rejoice, O Virgin Mary; rejoice a thousand times!

12. *Hail Mary....*Glory be to thee who art ever ready to assist us in life and in death! Lead us with thee to the kingdom of Heaven!
Rejoice, O Virgin Mary; rejoice a thousand times!
Glory be to the Father....

Let Us Pray

Hail, Mary, Daughter of God the Father; Hail, Mary, Mother of God the Son; Hail, Mary, Spouse of the Holy Ghost; Hail, Mary, Temple of the most Holy Trinity; Hail, Mary, my Mistress, my treasure, my joy, Queen of my heart; my Mother, my life, my sweetness, my dearest hope—yea, my heart and my soul! I am all thine and all that I have is thine, O Virgin blessed above all things! Let thy soul be in me to magnify the Lord; let thy spirit be in me to rejoice in God. Set thyself, O faithful Virgin, as a seal upon my heart, that in thee and through thee I may be found faithful to God. Receive me, O gracious Virgin, among those whom thou lovest and teachest, whom thou leadest, nourishest and protectest as thy children. Grant that for love of thee I may despise all earthly consolations and ever cling to those of Heaven until, through the Holy Ghost, thy faithful Spouse, and through thee, His faithful Spouse, Jesus Christ thy Son be formed in me for the glory of the Father. Amen.

Special Feasts For Consecration

Our Lady of Lourdes, ---------------- February 11, begin January 9.

The Annunciation, -------------------- March 25, begin February 20.

Saint Lôuis Marie De Montfort, ----- April 28, begin March 26.

Our Lady of Fatima, ----------------- May 13, begin April 10.

Queenship of Mary, and

Our Lady, Mediatrix of All Graces, ----- May 31, begin April 28.

Our Lady of Perpetual Help, -------- June 27, begin May 25.

Our Lady of Mount Carmel, --------- July 16, begin June 13.

The Assumption of Our Lady, ------- August 15, begin July 13.

The Immaculate Heart of Mary, ---- August 22, begin July 20.

The Holy Name of Mary, ------------ September 12, begin August 10.

The Seven Sorrows of Our Lady, ---- September 15, begin August 13.

The Most Holy Rosary, -------------- October 7, begin September 4.

Our Lady of the Miraculous Medal, -- November 27, begin October 25.

The Immaculate Conception, -------- December 8, begin November 5.

Our Lady of Guadalupe, ------------- December 12, begin November 9.

Published at the monastery printshop of the
Slaves of the Immaculate Heart of Mary a religious order,
living the life of True Devotion in community.